NEW MILLENNIAL SEXSTYLES

NEW MILLENNIAL SEXSTYLES

CAROL SIEGEL

INDIANA UNIVERSITY PRESS
bloomington and indianapolis

This book is a publication of

Indiana University Press
601 North **Morton** Street
Bloomington, IN 47404-3797 USA

http://www.indiana.edu/~iupress

Telephone orders   800-842-6796
Fax orders   812-855-7931
Orders by e-mail   iuporder@indiana.edu

The paper used in this publication meets the minimum requirements of American National Standard for Information Sciences—Permanence of Paper for Printed Library Materials, ANSI Z39.48-1984.

Manufactured in the **U**nited **S**tates of **A**merica

LIBRARY OF CONGRESS cataloging-**IN-PUB-LICATION DATA**

SIEGEL, CAROL, DATE
NEW MILLENNIAL sexstyles **/ CAROL SIEGEL.**
   P. CM.
INCLUDES BIBLIOGRAPHICAL REFERENCES and index.
ISBN 0-253-33775-5 **(CL : ALK. PAPER)** —
ISBN 0-253-21404-1 **(PA : ALK. PAPER)**
1. sex—**UNITED STATES.** 2. **WOMEN— UNIT-ED STATES—SEXUAL BEHAVIOR.** 3. **FEMINIST THEORY—UNITED STATES.** 4. **HETEROSEXU-ALITY**—united states. 5. **HOMOPHOBIA— UNITED STATES.** 6. **UNITED STATES**—social conditions. **I. TITLE.**

hq 18.u5 s55 2000
306.7'0973—dc21

00-035011

1 2 3 4 5 05 04 03 02 **01 00**

To

GERHARD

CONTENTS

ACKNOWLEDGMENTS

More than anything I have written before, this book reflects my personal experiences in academe. I am, therefore, especially grateful to friends and colleagues who read sections of the book and so provided me with a useful and affirming interpretive community within the larger, more contentious one composed of the disciplines in which I work. Thank you, Virginia Crosswhite Hyde, John Ehrstine, Louise Schleiner, Leland Monk, Ednie Garrison, Ellen E. Berry, Laura Mulvey, Ann Kibbey, Michael Kramp, Crystal Kile, Kelly Mayhew, Thomas Foster, Christopher Toomey, Kelly Cutter-Green, Elizabeth Sargent, Garry Watson, Michelle Kendrick, and Keith Cushman.

For reading the entire manuscript and helping me shape it into a book, I owe a deep debt of gratitude to Bryce Campbell and Denise Garrett, and to Laura Frost, my perceptive reader at Indiana University Press. And, once again, I am very grateful to Robert Sloan, my editor, for all his help and supportiveness. Thanks also to Shoshanna Green for her help with the final preparation of the manuscript.

Many people discussed with me the ideas I present here and made useful suggestions. Particularly deserving of thanks are Noël Sturgeon, Karmen MacKendrick, Diane Gillespie, Joan Burbick, Elizabeth Langland, Tim Hunt, Desiree Hellegers, Wendy Johnson, Valerie Steele, Joanna Frueh, Lillian Taiz, Kristin Kohl, Elisabeth Magnus, Robert Schimelfenig, Jamie O'Toole, Mary Stewart, Toni Town, Emily Pasco, Emily Schleiner, Kampala Taiz, Juanita Smart, and Theresa Thompson.

I could not have completed this project in its present, inclusive form without all the information about music cultures, not to mention tapes, given to me so generously by my graduate students and many of the undergraduates. I will never forget the help I received from the enthusiastic students in my contemporary youth cultures class and the young people who attended my Johns Hopkins Center for Talented Youth Humanities Day presentations on Nine Inch Nails and Marilyn Manson. I thank all of my students also for helping me meet so many other young people who love rock 'n' roll. I am very grateful to those young people, as well, for giving serious, thoughtful answers to my often quite intrusive questions. As I promised I would, I tried to write this book as much for all of you as for myself.

Washington State University provided me with a semester's sabbatical in fall 1997 to allow me time to finish my research and begin serious writing, for which I am thankful.

Part of the introduction's discussion of feminist styles first appeared in my essay "'This thing I like my sister may not do': Shakespearean Erotics and a Clash of Wills in *Middlemarch*" in *Style* 32.1 (1998), and I thank the editor, James M. Mellard, for permission to reprint it here.

An essay I previously published, "Compulsory Heterophobia: The Aesthetics of Seriousness and the Production of Homophobia" in *Genders* 21 (1995), appears in revised form as part of chapter 2. For her permission to reprint that material, I thank the editor, Ann Kibbey.

Material included in chapter 4 also appears in my essay "From Cinderella to Spinderella: New Generation Not Regeneration," included in a collection forthcoming from State University of New York Press, *Wavelengths: Cultural Representations of Contemporary U.S. Feminist Generations,* edited by Ellen E. Berry, Mary Thompson, and Annette Wannamaker, whom I thank for permission to reprint.

I will forever be grateful to all the Portland clubs that provided the musical accompaniment to this research and also provided what I found a very pleasant atmosphere for the study of young people's reception of performances, especially La Luna, Satyricon, EJ's, Roseland, Berbati's Pan, The Crystal Ballroom, Zoot Suite, and the Paris Theater. Thanks, too, to their patrons for never making me feel like some dismal old intruder even when I had thirty years on almost everyone else present.

I could not have become the person who sat on seedy floors throughout California and the Pacific Northwest researching this book in all-ages clubs, dorm rooms, studio apartments, basement music studios, and everywhere else counterculture kids go, or the person who was acceptable to the young rebels I met there, without the influence of my wonderful parents, Dave and Marcella Siegel, who provided me with a model of successful lifelong resistance to the dominant culture. They already know how grateful I am. But most of all I thank Gerhard (Nostalgia is Death!) Magnus for enticing me ever onward, beyond the comfort of countercultures past.

NEW MILLENNIAL SEXSTYLES

INTRODUCTION

MY WAVE

The most cursory examination of popular culture in the United States today suggests that the second wave of feminism was aptly named, in that it swept over America with tsunami force, dislodging social institutions that appeared to be eternal and leaving deposits of new thinking in unexpected places, some of which this book will visit. To extend the metaphor, feminism's vaunted fluidity has manifested itself in the absorption of its central ideas into social trends over the last three decades, even when some of those ideas are so deeply opposed to one another as to constitute separate feminisms. My dual purposes here are first to examine how a multitude of cultural products reveal areas where various feminisms have succeeded in revolutionizing the ways sexuality and gender identity are understood in America, and second to qualify the sense of victory such examination might convey by foregrounding divisions between feminist perspectives that render problematic many of the changes that the varied manifestations of second-wave feminism have wrought. Large numbers of people who support women's rights feel alienated by what might be called the official discourses of feminism, the feminist ideologies promoted within powerful American institutions. I hope to combat that sense of alienation, which I have shared, by explaining my own vision of millennial popular culture's treatment of sexuality, love, gender identification, and feminism, a vision that is informed by second-wave feminism but remains critical of its concessions to conventional morality and its role in the regulation of sexuality. Because I have been deeply involved in late-twentieth-century feminist revolution through all its permutations and also, crucially, because despite my past as a second-wave feminist I find myself more in sympathy with feminisms that have grown out of recent youth cultures, I hope to contribute to the opening up of academic feminism that writers and other activists in the third wave are now bringing about.

Feminism's third wave, by its very existence, attests to the perception among many younger women that the women's rights movement(s) of the 1960s and 1970s have ceased to be directly relevant to current gender politics. The good news is that, after a short period in the late 1980s in which pundits talked about postfeminism, feminism is still alive and generating debate. The bad news is that gender relations are in the midst of such radical change that the majority of feminists who have reached established positions of power, who constitute feminism's only old girls' network, must struggle to rethink the paradigms of gender and sexuality upon which our plans for action have been predicated. So my project here is not only to describe some of the most notable changes but to look into their possible impact on current modes of feminist praxis. It seems to me important to place my own history in relation to the wave sequence I am examining, at the very least to combat the notion that feminism's second wave provided women of my generation with a useful and consistent approach to evaluating our experiences of sexuality and gender identity. We were, after all, the first generation of post-structuralist subjects who knew themselves as such.

After teaching a class on poststructuralist theory with the theme "no more objectivity; no more disembodied voices" to a group of graduate students for whom formalism was so dead they could not imagine reading without taking into account what they knew of the circumstances of a text's production, I decided that I was at last ready to be a situated speaker. My desire to situate my speech is part of my aspiration to become what Foucault describes as a "specific intellectual," that is, one who knowingly and disruptively locates her "authority" within the dynamics of specific, local mechanisms of power and "truth" (*Power/Knowledge* 126, 132–133).

So allow me to introduce myself. Here I am at a characteristic moment of my day, running on a gym treadmill, with my headphones blaring, lip-synching to The Smiths' "You Just Haven't Earned It Yet, Baby," and thinking for the thousandth time that there must be a connection between the rise of fitness culture and the mainstreaming of sadomasochism. Then Morrissey's ironic wail is replaced on my tape with the pounding opening cords of Soundgarden's "My Wave" and I feel the rare delight of absolutely merging with the mood of the song, its disinterested tolerance of differences balanced by hard refusal to enter into the mood of those who see themselves as victims ("cry if you wanna cry / if it clears your eyes . . . just keep it off my wave"). But a few minutes later, coming out of the trance, I have to ask myself, what is my wave?

Running in place like the Red Queen, I wonder, am I still a second-wave feminist? With my frizzy hair, bare face, and chunky body, I resemble a stereotypical one. If I could have only one name for what remains constant as I move between subject positions, I suppose the word would have to be "feminist," yet, as I am often asked, what kind of feminist am I? The research that led to this book came out of various personal and scholarly experiences that made me aware of radical changes in American culture surrounding representations of sexuality, love, and gender. But the book itself has grown out of a life the strangest fact of which may well be that since the mid-1970s, no matter how I have tried to fit myself into any known feminist practice or ideology, and no matter that to this moment I can describe my politics most accurately as "radical feminist," no rhetoric has alienated me as profoundly as that which has come to dominate feminist discourse in the academic world. Lately, among some of the self-described third-wave feminists, I have finally started to feel, once again, at home in feminism. Could feminism's third wave be my wave?

To begin by saying, I am a feminist and I have written yet another book that attempts, among other things, to defend some of the most despised expressions of heterosexuality, feels to me like firing a shot randomly out the window in a war zone. I expect return shots, but I cannot say whence they will come. But to say, I am a feminist and this is a book about love, including the irrational and uncontrolled erotic love that I have sometimes felt for men, seems even more frightening, like declaring myself insane. Loved men beyond reason? Why? In effect I seem to be placing myself beyond self-defense, for how can a madwoman speak on her own behalf? I have already used the personal pronoun here more than I did in twelve years of previous academic publication. Already I want to retreat, to become again "one" or "we," or better to disappear utterly into the passive voice. Yet it seems I must say that this is not only a book about sex and love, how they have been legislated against and vilified, how they have been confined and then have broken through all their boundaries, and about the deliciously beautiful patterns with which their intertwining has decorated the end of the millennium; it is also a book in which my own experiences both as a feminist and as a woman who has profoundly loved men inevitably inform every page. The difference from my other writings is that here I say this openly, admitting that I know what I am, and then proceeding to try to make a style out of it.

In attempting to style myself as a heterosexual feminist critic, I also address the not incidental question of what might be gained by doing so. Style is a term more often associated with homosexuality than heterosexuality. The substitution of the term "alternative lifestyle" for "gay and lesbian" can have the conservative connotation that sexuality could be changed as easily as any other style choice. The term also has the more flattering, and perhaps accurate, implication that homosexual identification can be expressed through being stylish in a certain way. When I, and probably most politically radical Americans, think of gay and lesbian styles, I think first of the wit and charm of homosexuals who achieve parodic distance from the dominant ideology. The sort of radically creative self-cultivation advocated by Foucault also comes to mind. But, alas, the phrase "heterosexual style" conjures up images of unconsciously exaggerated gender role conformity. The implications of this difference for the heterosexual feminist critic attempting to style herself in prose are not promising, and this is important if we allow that the relation between prose style and feminism is significant.

Elizabeth Grosz identifies style as the essential element that can make a text feminist, for the feminist text is one that "render[s] the patriarchal or phallocentric presumptions governing its contexts and commitments visible" in such a way as to question "the power of these presumptions in the production, reception, and assessment of texts" and to "facilitate the production of new and perhaps unknown, unthought discursive spaces" (*Space, Time, and Perversion* 22–23). Style rather than content determines the feminism of a text, because only within a text's style is there "some trace of the process" from which we may read the author's feminism (*Space, Time, and Perversion* 19). Feminist style, then, is a sort of grace under pressure, a way that we speak when we feel that our speech is already forbidden or negated. In fact, a convention of such feminist speech is that we take the risk of being misunderstood or despised so that other feminists may speak; we speak on behalf of all, although no longer *for* all.

Academic feminist styles have evolved away from the convention in early writings of giving just enough autobiography to simulate a specific person's presence in the critical text while still relying on such generalities as "woman's experience." When feminist theory recognized the diversity of its readers in terms of race, homosexual or heterosexual orientation, and class, more distinctive critical personae emerged. Epistemologies were at last anchorable in relation to recognizable speakers with identifiable interests, and ideology did not have to be inferred. But we are still left with the problem of generating a description of sexual and gender relations that do not conform to the acceptable categories of feminist or lesbian theory, a mode of being that seems, thus, to have remained unintelligible.[1]

In feminist theory today there often seem to be only two options allowed as possibilities for heterosexuals. Women can refuse sex except as a component of a committed relationship in which the power balance is very carefully maintained, as is continual movement toward something beneficial to the woman. Or else we can surrender unconditionally to violent, selfish males. This binary disturbingly resembles the ones central to traditional patriarchy, except that feminist theories define what is beneficial to the woman differently. Current feminist narratives of heterosexuality almost never allow that sex can be an area of women's lives in which we experiment fairly freely with various roles, including exercising direct power over males. We need to recognize that some of us not only can but often do use sex in ways traditionally associated with masculine freedom: that is, to feel powerful in relation to another person and as a form of physical recreation through which we experience our bodies and other peoples' as sources of our own pleasure. Because using sex in these ways goes against cultural constructions of femaleness, those women who have such sexual experiences are often much in need of some support and recognition from feminism.

When women withhold this support and recognition from each other, we should probably not attribute their withholding to feminist ideologies, as internal critics of feminism like Camille Paglia and Katie Roiphe have become famous for doing. Instead, we might think of feminisms in a somewhat unaccustomed way, not as a set of ideas external and resistant to mainstream culture, but as a series of movements that have reflected mainstream concerns perhaps as often as they have been conceived in opposition to them. Feminism's second and third waves have been largely determined through dialogue with the ongoing sexual and gender identity revolutions that continue to re-shape American culture in the second half of this century.

As Alice Echols reminds us, "From the beginning, the women's liberation movement was internally fractured" by external political pressures and influences (101). One of the longest lasting and most divisive battles within feminism has been over its relation to sexuality. This battle has never been separate from conflicts over sexual behavior and identity in the rest of society, although feminism's critics have often taken the position that feminists are out of touch with American sexual mores.

While in the 1960s and early 1970s some observers naively conflated feminism with women's pursuit of unrestricted sexual pleasure, by the late 1970s the majority of Americans saw feminism as anti-sexual. The disagreements among feminists over this development in many respects mirrored disagreements in the mainstream over the impact of the new sexual freedom. As America continued to contend with the aftershocks of the 1960s sexual revolution, including the rapid growth of a sex industry that could no longer be forced underground, feminisms were increasingly defined by attitudes about sex: "Women Against Pornography," "Feminists Against Censorship," "Pro-Sex Feminists," and so on. The many fronts on which the 1980s "Sex Wars" were fought suggest how central sexual expression became to second-wave feminist ideology. Topics of debate included not only whether lesbians who practiced sadomasochistic sex could be considered feminist, but whether feminist lesbians should consider orgasm important or whether such an attitude was indicative of a male-identified privileging of goal orientation and genitalia. Heterosexuality was even more vexed by doubts about the feminism of any form of sexual expression, including fantasy, since a sexuality that included the eroticization of contact with men had always been described by some feminists as male-dominated and bordering on the masochistic.[2] In the last two decades of the millennium, the emergence of a still unnamed new wave of feminism gave rise to new gender styles, such as gender-fuck queer, parodic butch/femme, lipstick lesbian, riot grrl, and kinderwhore, which complicated the gendering of sexuality in interesting ways.

For some this very complexity resolved questions surrounding the politics of sexual expression. For instance, the fashion industry's mainstreaming of bondage gear made possible supermodel Naomi Campbell's defense of rubber fetish dresses against charges that they fostered objectification of women. She simply declared, "Grown women can wear whatever they please" (Steele 143). In a more intellectual sphere, Judith Butler's work on gender as performative brought new urgency to academic debate about women's agency in the construction of sexuality and gender. Questions about volition and pleasure have continued to trouble feminist efforts to extend the absolutist pro-choice position from abortion rights to sexual rights. Consequently conflict over sexual expression remains intense within feminism, causing generational and ideological rifts so extreme that the current moment may be the least characterized by shared purpose that feminism has seen.[3]

A 1997 syndicated "women's perspective" column by Maureen Dowd represents the position of a significant number of politically active feminists. Dowd's column laments the appearance of what she calls "courtesan feminism" in women's magazines. She deplores their focus on "enumerating ways to please, and trap, the opposite sex," complaining that "Feminism once held out a promise that there would be some precincts of womanly life that were not about men." The fulfillment of that promise, she believes, would have resulted in "peaceful havens of girl things and boy things," presumably meaning the return of a version of separate spheres. Dowd, like the magazine writers and editors she criticizes, seems to believe that heterosexual pleasure always entails women's striving to please men, "seeing themselves through men's eyes" (10A). This vision of heterosexuality as inescapably male-defined suggests that male sexuality is so powerful that in its presence women have no room for anything but responses.

Such visions of gender relations within heterosexuality are by no means restricted to work produced by women for a female audience. In fact, the limitations of feminist analysis of what is possible within heterosexuality are overdetermined, drawn in response to larger cultural contexts in which feminist ideologies have developed. As much of this book will be devoted to discussing, an enormous influence on both the second and the third waves of feminism has been the gradual pathologizing of erotic love, which has come to be understood as a delusional state about which all intelligent, realistic people must be cynical.

The cartoon cover of the *New Yorker*'s 1997 special Valentine's Day issue, "Love Lessons," exemplifies what has come to be recognizable as the sophisticated view of love. The illustration, by Art Spiegelman, shows a man and woman embracing, with a large arrow passing through both their bodies. The table of contents gives the illustration's title as "Beau and Eros." This, then, is what love is about? Phallic energy as a force that holds a couple together? A force that shoots out of the beau and that he enjoys through his linkage to a female object? Spiegelman's fame for outrageously exposing the disturbing, repressed content of our lives is very much in evidence here. If this is what love lessons teach the educable, then a "new Victorian" rejection of heterosexuality, such as so infuriates self-described postfeminists, does seem the only way to avoid suppression of women's own desires and potential pleasures.

For another vision, I have recourse to my own memories. I never went to kindergarten, so everything I needed to know about the American way of love I learned in the first grade. I entered first grade with a friend named Reed. I habitually summoned him by standing in front of his house and shouting, "Reed—eee!" When his little face appeared at the screen door, I think what I felt was something like love. Later I would learn that, as George Eliot writes, beneath such a "pink-and-white bit of masculinity with [soft] indeterminate features" perfidious Nature "conceals some of her most rigid, inflexible purposes, some of her most unmodifiable characters" (33). But I was not destined to learn this from Reed, because the gender culture of the first grade intervened and spoiled what was for me a perfect love.

The other children viewed our handholding affection with horror. They swarmed around us chanting, "Carol and Reedy sitting in a tree, K—I—S—S—I—N—G, first comes love, and then comes marriage, and then comes Carol with a baby carriage."

That was more than enough for me; I bellowed on the fair boy's lawn no more. That was my first love lesson: affection for the opposite sex infuriates your peers and, if persisted in against all reason, results in domestic entrapment. This lesson was reinforced many times in the years that followed and, modified as part of the curriculum of Girls' Health class, was the only official sex education I would ever receive.

But what if love were something different from an inexorable march toward marital respectability? This was a question to which the sexual revolution tried to be an answer. As the diction of the songs and the slogan "Make Love Not War" told us, "love" and "sex" were two interchangeable names for the same thing. And neither had much to do with marriages and baby carriages. Love/sex was about world peace and harmony, because "love is all you need." I still have no idea what "we" were thinking in those years. Did we think that sexuality freed from all social and cultural constraints would bring with it solicitous caring strong enough to overcome all the world's problems? From the artifacts of my own past that I can unearth, it really does seem that I thought so. And, remembering my adventures in San Francisco's Castro District in the early 1970s, when I felt surrounded by a community of loving brothers who looked out for me just about everywhere the curiosity of my early adulthood took me, I have to say it felt that way to me.[4] As Naomi Wolf writes of her own girlhood in San Francisco, "in the form of the gay liberation movement, we saw love—human, physical, sexual, romantic love—stand as a metaphor for the highest good and animate the idealism of an entire culture" (xxx). But although I strongly disagree with Linda Grant's view that "the sexual-freedom movement of San Francisco" ultimately achieved "[v]ery little" (149), I admit there is a limit to what afterglow and good intentions can do, and by the late 1970s love and sex were clearly separating again in the popular consciousness.

The general movement from increased emphasis on the freedom to have sex to increased emphasis on the right to freedom from unwanted sex seems indicative of what happened when the "love generation" found out that love and sex were not always seamlessly flowing into each other, bringing joy and peace. Feminism was central to many, although not all, of the organized and official movements to protect the vulnerable from sexual predation. American culture fragmented and reformed with new alliances, such as the amazing rapprochement between some branches of feminism and right-wing anti-pornography activists. As commonly accepted definitions of sexual predation and violation expanded to include not only physical assault but coercion and even lustful thoughts (so that a woman might feel violated by her awareness that someone else was reading pornography), conservative moral reformers drew on feminist rhetorics for abstractions more palatable to a secular audience than "sin" and "ungodliness."

Here cultural feminism's interest in the deep causes of women's oppression became useful in ways that few early feminists seem to have anticipated. Ellen Willis argues that feminist "concern about sexual violence and abuse . . . resonates with the present conservative climate, tapping themes in the culture that, far from being feminist, are the very stuff of the patriarchal sexual (and racial) unconscious: the equation of sex with violence with evil, the horror of rape as (black) men's animal nature breaking

CRCC

through the veneer of civilized morality and violating innocent (white) womanhood" ("Villains and Victims" 47). The wide adoption, throughout America, of splinter feminist groups' programs to protect girls and women from sexual activity and experience exemplifies bell hooks's claim, "It is evident that society is more responsive to those 'feminist' demands that are not threatening, that may even help maintain the status quo" (*Feminist Theory* 21).

The damage done to women who could not "get with the program" of the new female purity is incalculable. At the very least they were barred from looking to the law for protection in their early years. Deborah Tolman and Tracy Higgins explain that "the cultural story of male aggression and female responsibility, which is devoid of female desire," results in dangerous misinterpretation of teen girls' sexually aggressive behavior by their feminist would-be advocates. These feminists ask that the girls be legally protected from all sexual activity on the grounds that girls show interest in sex only when they are desperate for nonsexual love and stable relationships (208–209). As Tolman and Higgins point out, this "reinterpretation" of female experience creates a dichotomy in which women either are deemed innocent (and to be protected) or are considered to have consented without reservation to being used by men sexually (and thus have no right to legal protection). The result is our present situation in which "both rape law and statutory rape law reinforce cultural norms of female sexuality by penalizing female sexual desire" (210). In addition, women who persist in understanding themselves as active heterosexual subjects, rather than objects, have become prime candidates for therapy, which is often forced upon them when they are minors.

In harmony with the alliance between the religious right and feminists who theorize pornography and heterosexual promiscuity as oppressive to women, therapy culture has taken a new direction. Correctly identifying experiences with sex and love as the root of much human unhappiness, most therapists try to foster in their clients attitudes toward sex and love conducive to a calm, reasonably contented existence. For many years, various forms of therapy have targeted extreme mood swings as a problem to be eradicated by treatment or drug therapy. For the same reason, therapists began to treat both unsettling romantic attachments and devotion to the pursuit of sexual pleasure as pathologies that interfered with normal, productive life. As I will discuss in the chapters that follow, a major focus of much late-twentieth-century popular culture has been defining the differences between "good" and "bad" erotic love according to this standard.

In her critique of the 1980s "overlap" between "the feminist community" and "the therapy community," Jillian Sandell shows that both "victim" and "power" feminisms share with psychology-based self-help and recovery programs an emphasis on "individual achievement and [financial] success" (24–25). Sandell calls this union of therapy and feminism into question because it undermines feminism's earlier focus on collectivism, it "merely displace[es] dissatisfaction with life onto the realm of individual acts of transformation" (28–29). While this is a valid concern, one might also consider the definitions of individual transformation and success here.

It is tempting to compare the definitions transmitted by the therapy texts Sandell quotes to the conclusion of Walter Pater's *The Renaissance*. Pater advises his reader always to seek intensity in experiences, "to burn with this hard, gemlike flame, to maintain this ecstasy is success in life," for "[n]ot the fruit of experience, but experience itself, is the end" (152). Since Pater deems appreciation of art the highest form of pleasure, this philosophy can—and, in the case of many in the nineteenth-century Aesthetic Movement, did—lead to a valorization of consumerism not utterly unlike Naomi Wolf's recommendations in *Fire with Fire* for feminist fulfillment through purchasing choices, which Sandell deplores (28–29). Interestingly, however, Pater's Neo-Epicurean philosophy lends itself equally well to a doctrine in which the experience of erotic pleasure so strongly signifies success that the would-be successful person must subordinate all lesser goals to the pursuit of intense sexual pleasure. Such a doctrine can only be disruptive of capitalist goals, as all of us know who have ever called in sick one too many times in order to linger in bed with a lover or who have left for a professional meeting without any appropriate attire because we preferred sex to last-minute shopping. The individual transformation that takes place when one decides that material success is a world well lost for love, while not necessarily fostering a turn toward collectivist politics, certainly constitutes a resistance to capitalism that could lead to collectivism, and it is precisely this sort of resistance that 1980s sex therapy attacks.

The late-1980s popularization of the term "sexual addiction," and treatments for the condition, epitomize a change in therapy's focus. On one hand it seems absurd to say that a person whose interest in sex sometimes interferes with her ability to concentrate on her work is the equivalent of, say, a heroin addict. But on the other hand it perfectly fits the ever-increasing popularity, at century's end, of describing as an addiction any condition that interferes with optimum productivity and the meeting of normative standards, for example the tendency of women unhappy with their weight to talk about being "addicted" to sweets. The step from rocking out to Roxy Music's comic bar-cruising anthem "Love Is the Drug" to seriously discussing one's sexual addiction was shorter than we might once have imagined possible.

If we consider the usual effects of the combination of directed physical arousal (sexual attraction) and obsession with one specific person (erotic love), the resultant condition does resemble the ecstatic disorientation that recreational drug use can produce. Viewed in this way, erotic love is a sort of endorphin delivery system that exponentially increases the physical sensations associated with sex. Sexual activity could be roughly equated with soft drug use, as viewed by conservatives, because of its function as a gateway to the more disruptive and dangerous condition of love. As a society, we may fear love because it multiplies the power of sexual desire, making it even more difficult to control than it is ordinarily. Thus love becomes even more dangerous than sex, a sort of terrifying add-on drug like heroin sprinkled over marijuana. Within the therapeutic narrative, as I will discuss later, the notorious "women who love too much" are essentially defined as women who are under the power of erotic feeling.

Of course, love is not to be completely jettisoned. The bumper sticker slogan that rose to prominence in the early 1980s, "Hugs Not Drugs," typifies the rehabilitation that love underwent as the country moved from its flirtation with "free love" as political solution to the (re)pathologizing of promiscuity. While adults were exhorted to give children calm and comforting affection (hugs) lest they become wild thrill-seekers, children were carefully instructed in the difference between "good" and "bad" touching, as if desire could never move like an electrical current through the most apparently innocent gestures. Common to this whole period of redefinition of love and sexuality, whether rooted in conservatism or liberalism, is faith in the possibility of drawing boundaries and setting limits, and finally faith in containment. While it is obviously true that heterosexual desire and love are potentially disruptive of feminist behavior, causing some women to act against their own best interests and, even more typically, against the interests of women as a group, feminists have by no means been alone in their suspicion of and growing hostility toward unrestrained eroticism.

For many feminists the most pertinent question about feminism at the millennium's turn seems to be whether it can or should incorporate the power to say an enthusiastic "yes" to heterosexual relations. This debate, paralleling the nation's continuing fight over legal restrictions on sexual activities, also occurs in relation to a long tradition within feminism. With very few exceptions, feminist theory of sexuality from Adrienne Rich's "Compulsory Heterosexuality and Lesbian Existence" to Judith Butler's *Gender Trouble* relies on an opposition between lesbianism and heterosexuality, always with the assumption that heterosexuality is unavoidably complicitous with the systems of male supremacy that we usually refer to as patriarchy. Traditionally, feminist discourse on heterosexual female desire presupposes either an implicit assent to heteronormativity or a displaced mimicry of homosexuality.

The groundbreaking collections of feminist texts on women's desire, *Powers of Desire* (1983) and *Pleasure and Danger,* which came out of the famous 1982 Barnard Feminist Conference "Towards a Politics of Sexuality," both aimed to complicate this simplistic vision and to fight against morally prescriptive feminism. Still, both books are heavily marked by presumptions about what is possible within heterosexual relations. Essays throughout *Powers of Desire* repeatedly express doubt that any female heterosexuality can escape thorough predetermination by "The Institution of Heterosexuality" (a section title). Most authors in the collection equate heterosexuality with unquestioning absorption of gender ideology. The few departures from this pattern, like Joan Nestle's autobiographical "My Mother Liked to Fuck," provide glimpses of women rebelliously insisting on heterosexual pleasure, but they still rhetorically oppose the figure of the hopeless female romantic to that of the feminist writer, who sees the cultural context of such rebellion as inevitably rendering it tragic.

Because female heterosexual desire is reflexively equated with romance, it is deemed a type of false consciousness. Ann Barr Snitow claims that "While most serious women *novelists* treat romance with irony and cynicism, most women do not" (261; emphasis Snitow's), making startlingly explicit the collection's general implicit opposition between women writers and women. In most of the essays the position of more-than-mere woman is occupied by the feminist theorist, who apparently sees from a vantage point outside the heterosexual institution's confines. Thus E. Ann Kaplan's claim that "sexuality has been constructed in patriarchy to produce pleasure in the domi-

[handwritten marginalia: het desire equated w/ romance]

nance-submission forms," and her conclusion that this construction offers no possibility of control to women, presumably because male pleasure in submission and female pleasure in dominance are both unthinkable ("Is the Gaze Male?" 317). Nestle repeatedly refers to her mother's being beaten and abused in a futile search for love, so that the mother sounds by the end of the account not unlike those benighted teenage girls who submit to loveless sex as a pathetic simulacrum of the affection they crave.

Pleasure and Danger goes further to avoid treating heterosexual women as the objects (or even abjects) of feminism by concentrating on women marginalized by their refusal to be conventional wives. Still, the same structure prevails in most of the essays: the feminist academic investigates the mystifying case of heterosexual women. Female heterosexuals appear most often in the text as heroic sex workers, to be championed, or as masochists, to be lamented. That some women might actually experience sexual interaction with men as fun, not as work or pain, seems just about incomprehensible here.

The only thing about their intercourse with men that heterosexual women are assumed to enjoy is the social advantage it gives them over lesbians. Gayle Rubin's excellent "Thinking Sex" visualizes the cultural hierarchy of sexual values as a "pyramid" in which "most heterosexuals" occupy a higher, more privileged position than the putative perverts below them (279). Overt recognition is lacking that not only do many heterosexuals occupy demonized positions, such as sadomasochism and cross-generational relations, but that many women who indulge such prohibited passions do so in ways that go even further against heteronormativity in that we occupy a position of power. Which is to say that a sexually submissive lesbian with an older, more powerful lover, for example, is more normal in the mainstream culture's terms than a heterosexual female who dominates her sexual interactions with a younger, socially subordinate male lover.

To leap forward in feminist history, lack of sustained attention to the possibility of a disruptive and transgressive female heterosexuality also flaws Lynne Segal's otherwise near-revolutionary 1994 book *Straight Sex*. While she does much to break open the totalization of "heterosexualities" (260), arguing strongly against the female passive/male aggressive binary, she does so primarily through exploration of the pleasure taken by both men and women in "losing control" (41), being penetrated, and submitting sexually. It may be true that "what men want, as often as not, is to be sexually passive" (290), and this knowledge may be comforting for women who feel they are not "good" feminists because they want the same thing. But focus on this issue still avoids confronting another, and perhaps more disruptive, heterosexuality in which women take pleasure in enacting sexual aggression and even dominance.

The invisibility of these desires and activities in almost all feminist writing is surprising, given how visible female sexual dominance of men has become in the actual world. As I have argued extensively in *Male Masochism*, almost the entire 1980s feminist "sex wars" discussion of ritualized sadomasochism ignored the possibility of female dominance of men, although that remains, so far as any sociological research has revealed, the most popular form for such activities among heterosexuals. Cross-generational sex is similarly subsumed academically into discussions of sexual harassment in which the victim is female. When anyone chooses to speak out in defense of these demonized behaviors, she almost invariably legitimates her championing of sexual freedom by arguing for lesbian sexual self-determination. Consequently the image of "woman" as sexual agent in power-imbalanced relations is translated into "lesbian," a stunning return to late-nineteenth-century sexology in which lesbianism was defined "not so much in the object of the woman's desire as in the masculine, aggressive form it took" (Chauncey 119).[5]

Teresa de Lauretis hypothesizes that straight women prefer to imagine active sexuality as lesbian in order to ensure for "women the status of sexed and desiring subjects" (156–157). Again the mere presence of a man in the sexual scenario seems to dictate female objectification. The closest things to different visions of assertive female heterosexuality in academic prose are Eve Sedgwick's claim to experience her sexuality through identification "'as' a gay man" (*Tendencies* 209), and Judith Butler's speculation that "some heterosexual or bisexual women may prefer that their girls be boys," by which she seems to mean we may prefer that our male sex partners enact femininity (*Gender Trouble* 123). I do not mean to reject these alliances through identification between heterosexual feminism and queerness. But I find it equally important to attest to the existence of sexual practices that are both heterosexual and commensurate with feminist goals, practices that entail enacting something understood as femaleness in relation to someone with a male body who enacts something understood by both parties as maleness. I style myself here and now as one who sometimes enjoys these practices, sometimes is tormented by the desire to engage in them, and always finds in them a frame for interpretation.

I have waited most of my professional life for someone else to create a category of feminist authorship that approximates my speaking position closely enough to allow me to follow her in styling my own. There have been moments of tremendous inspiration, for which I am grateful. While several feminist authors have stood between me and despair, the closest to articulating feminisms compatible with my own have been Jane Gallop, in her *Thinking through the Body* and writing from it in ways that resonated for me, and Joanna Frueh writing of the teacher's literal embodiment of knowledge in *Erotic Faculties,* and deploring 1980s academic feminism's "critical and artistic retreat from the body into the theoretical stratosphere from which the artist or critic observes or analyzes but is not the body" (117). But their ways are not exactly my way,[6] and while I waited for another to voice something I could claim as a public feminist identity, I heard countless variations on the same story, of which I will now give an abbreviated and I hope not too parodic-sounding version.

She was a shy child who mostly lived in books and did not date until college. She was attracted to powerful, intellectual men who mentored her. At first she was anxious because she was so different from Molly Bloom and Lady Chatterley. Then she read women authors and developed a feminist consciousness. She learned to accept that women in books by men were only male fantasies, as they were in pornography. She looked for a man who respected her, did not objectify her, and was responsible and kind. Meanwhile she struggled with the academic world, intimidated by sexually harassing male colleagues and administrators, annoyed by a curriculum that stressed texts by men, and depressed by students who rejected feminism. Eventually she triumphed, forcing them to recognize her as a significant scholar, for if she had not done so she would not be able to tell us her tale in print.

Because this is the story of many, it should be kept in mind when we think about women as critics, but it is not the story of every heterosexual feminist woman in academe. Here is mine, which I tell because, as Gallop puts it in a slightly different context, "Experience like mine is currently invisible" (*Feminist Accused* 43). I began dating at thirteen and quickly found out that sexuality was a more reliable form of pleasure than textuality. I was attracted to beautiful, diffident boys who admired my aggressiveness. While they did not always submit to my will, I found the struggle to get my own way mainly entertaining. I discovered pornography when I was fifteen and dreamed of entering that fictional world where there were other women who enjoyed sex and had little interest in monogamy. As an uneducated nineteen-year-old factory worker, I found Molly Bloom so reassuring that I struggled through *Ulysses.* Around the same time I joined a feminist consciousness-raising (c-r) group. I became an activist, but still male writers, my lovers, and my gay male friends often seemed the only ones who could understand a woman like me as anything except some sort of amusing freak. (My two closest longtime women friends were then and remain now exceptions.) I began putting myself through college and read women's literature mostly in an attempt to understand why I felt so alienated from the female norm. My love affairs became increasingly closeted because I could not find the words to explain my attitudes to other feminists. Meanwhile I struggled with the academic world, annoyed by a curriculum that stressed anti-sexual texts and depressed by colleagues who were shocked if I mentioned that a male student was attractive. But no matter how often I published my strange ideas and spoke about them at conferences, they were always received as pertaining to a sensibility that had to be accounted for. The personal question most often asked of me has always been "What do you think makes you this way?"

At this point I want to declare my unwillingness ever to answer that pathologizing question again. Instead, the questions to which I want to say a word in answer are how a pro-sex gender critic, whose vision of heterosexual pleasure does not include female subordination, can style herself as a feminist speaker, and what feminist scholarship might gain by attending to such stylings. To start with the gain, we are currently faced with an unbalanced picture of gender relations whose asymmetricality often either pushes heterosexual women away from feminism, because they feel the only speaking positions it offers them are self-critical or apologetic, or inspires in the less intelligent of them a misplaced resentment of lesbians. Some of the most depressing writing by contemporary female anti-feminists exemplifies both problems. To speak of noncomplicitous heterosexualities can open space for other pleasures to be explored, just as the speaking of one sort of lesbianism within cultural feminism allowed for the articulation of other sorts of lesbian practice. Discussion of noncomplicitous heterosexualities as practices that exist in the world now, rather than as dreams that await a feminist utopia in which they may come into being, may make some women feel deprived, but it may also inspire some heterosexual women to think of feminism not as a series of renunciations but as a practice that can include politically useful sexual expression. And perhaps most importantly, just as critics' and theorists' insistence on lesbian existence has permanently problematized compulsory heterosexuality, calling its assumptions into question, similar expressions of noncomplicitous heterosexuality can further undermine the hegemony of patriarchal ideology.

And how might one style oneself to effect this? Most basically, by coming out. I hope this introductory chapter will stand as a partial answer and suggest that we might begin by speaking about our lives, not necessarily in tedious detail but enough so that we are not, through silence, assumed to be in consent with the norm. To do so, I must forgo the comfort of existing in the texts I produce as just an eye without an I. As David Halperin argues, "If to come out is to release oneself from a state of unfreedom, that is not because coming out constitutes an escape from the reach of power to a place outside power: rather, coming out puts into play a different set of power relations and alters the dynamics of personal and political struggle" (30). Because I believe that it is thus that we might, at last, be ready for a dialogue within feminism about how all of our sexualities can work into feminist praxis, I offer the following vignettes from my life in academic feminism.

"MY BACK PAGES"

First, a short step back to the site of innocent misunderstanding with which I began, elementary school. One of the most disturbing experiences of my childhood was my family's move to a small town in the Southwest where placing people racially seemed to be a major preoccupation of the segments of the population with whom I came in contact. I still have group pictures for three school years in which I am the only dark child, and I remember this as a period of time in which adults would suddenly thrust their faces into mine and inquire in tones that sounded angry to me, "What are you?" My subsequent life as an ordinary, anonymous citizen of San Francisco almost effaced that period of terrified exposure of a difference that was somehow simultaneously immediately evident and uncategorizable. Years later, reading Marjorie Garber's *Vested Interests,* I realized that what I had embodied for the tormentors of my childhood was a category crisis. Without any family money, refinement, or discernible intellectual gifts, I failed to fit their definition of a Jew, but I was too dark to be understood as a white girl. Little did I know, when I entered the academic world, that I would once again gradually come to evoke category crisis, and face the same impossible question and its attendant alienation.

The subject position of academic feminism has, over the last twenty-five years, been constructed in such a way that to position myself as an academic feminist from the working class, who identifies neither as entirely white nor as a woman of color, and who thinks of heterosexuality as a direct source of feelings of power and self-esteem, without feeling in any way complicitous with heterosexism, feels to me a little like putting myself on display as a curiosity. The more I say about my own experience and perspective, the more I am confronted with amazed looks and questions that make me suspect that I am seen as a sort of latter-day Hottentot Venus.[7] Yet, to paraphrase Ntozake Shange's *For Colored Girls,* "Once I was a woman in the world; once I lived in San Francisco." So, to recapture the selves that inhabited that very different, but still academic, feminist history, and to recapture also a bit of the exhilarating (re)visionary moment as the second wave crested, I present the following three "snapshots." Like any memoir, these stories have been extracted from years of retelling and rethinking. I am incapable of removing all the embroidery that the years have left on them, so they must not be taken as accurate records. As Katie King says of her own recollections of this period, "This isn't the 'real' story, it's one story. Origin stories about the women's movement are interested stories, all of them," so all we can do is make clear what our own special interests are (137). Advance apologies to others who were there and saw it differently. Also advance apologies for the extreme feelings and views I once held. Readers might be gracious enough to keep in mind that, as the Bob Dylan song that gives this section its title suggests, in many of our lives political views manifest first in their harshest, least compromising forms. I'm less judgmental than that now.

ACADEMIC FEMINISM I: CITY COLLEGE—THE FIGHT FOR WOMEN'S HISTORY

At the age of twenty-two, "I am born." Tired of factory work and housecleaning, communes and going hungry; still immersed in dizzy love with hitchhiking, local countercultures, and the sweet Nighttown of bars, cafés, and wild streets; spinning slowly outward from spiral-notebook journals and long afternoons of ignorant bliss reading in the downtown library; here I come swaggering in my dirty third-hand Edwardian-cut leather coat and red platform shoes into the community college Ornamental Horticulture Department to study landscape gardening. A year and a half later, after switching to Humanities in preparation for the intimidating move to a B.A. program in English at San Francisco State, I was asked by fellow students to write a feminist manifesto to urge the college to accept Women's History in satisfaction of the requirement in American History for the A.A. degree. The influences on my prose included *The SCUM Manifesto, Sisterhood is Powerful,* and Nikki Giovanni, Judy Grahn, and Marge Piercy, whose poems I read aloud to my friends until they could not take any more.[8] Meeting with others, I helped plan a demonstration.

We had a sort of shared intellectual culture because almost all of our elective credits were spent on classes with "women" in the title. After Anthropology of Women, I began to think of myself as "uncooked." I felt not less of a woman for being uncultured and unsocialized, but more of one. Susan Griffin's *Woman and Nature* and Sherry Ortner's "Is Female to Male as Nature Is to Culture?" gladdened my heart. I was uncivilized and right. My terrifying experiences living on the most precarious edge of poverty culture underwent redefinition as initiation into tribal life. In a savvy double gesture my schoolmates elected me to present to a dean the petition we produced. They were laughingly aware that the reason I wore sheer bright blouses, rhinestones, and platform heels with my jeans was that I did not know any better. I shopped at the cheapest thrift stores in town and the only contact I had with bourgeois style, other than seeing it presented on TV, came from being hired to clean it up. The women students' task force expected an administrative authority figure to read as femininity my garish clothes and head-hanging shyness in the presence of middle-class people. They, however, reassured me that they knew I was not a "nice girl," but a wild animal, and "that's the joke."

What defined academic feminism for me in those days was its capaciousness. It had room for me as no other social structure had ever had. The swaggering toughness that I affected on the street to cover my fear of the more privileged; my frustrated, inarticulate quickness to hit my opponents in arguments; the crude advances that I made to the cute high school boys who skateboarded past the college on Ocean Avenue; my appalling table manners and filthy apartment; all these things were accepted not as signs of a pitiable failure to be womanly but as rebellion and strength. I stood gawky and overawed before the educated older women in my c-r group who first convinced me to go to college. But sometimes I caught on their faces what looked like a surprised admiration. They seemed to see me as being like the famous pro-sex feminist rebels who inspired them, such as Erica Jong and Nancy Friday, and all the better for being cruder, for having never been nice.

At this point, when they asked why I did the things I did, the curiosity seemed mainly friendly. My fellow feminist activists seemed to see my aggressive pleasure in contact with men as in some ways determined by my size and strength. (In the Horticulture program, I chose to concentrate my studies on landscape construction and proudly demonstrated the ease with which I could lift sixty-pound bags of sand in one sweeping motion to my shoulder.) That my politics sometimes, notoriously, resulted in fistfights with men was a point in my favor that overbalanced the neon-blue nail polish criticized by my c-r group.

ACADEMIC FEMINISM II:
STATE UNIVERSITY—RESISTANCE TO "TAKE BACK THE NIGHT"

In the album filled with photos from the celebration of my B.A., one picture shows me with a classmate whose name I have now forgotten. We are freshly attired for the ceremony, both still holding the hangers from which our graduation gowns had dangled on the steel handrail of the M streetcar. I remember her wisecracking, as she gave me the picture, that we looked as if we were graduating from the school of home abortion. The joke fit our Nietzschean image of ourselves ("whatever doesn't kill us . . . "). She was a lesbian, like many of my friends then and now. No definitive lesbian look seems to have emerged among our crowd yet. Our long frizzy hair, hers braided and decorated with flowers, mine hanging loose, and our clean shiny faces look as if we have more in common as counterculture feminists than we have differences between us. We certainly must have felt that way earlier as we planned our counterdemonstration to the Take Back the Night march.

It was at State that I began to feel alienated within feminism, which seemed to me then to be undergoing disorienting changes. Up to my enrollment at State, I had experienced feminism as the woman-oriented side of the Left. On the ordinary Left, as I experienced it, men were revolutionaries and women provided support. A woman who had goals or desires of her own was counterrevolutionary. In our local version of feminism, my friends and I began from the familiar youthful Leftist premises that property was theft, materialism pathetic delusion, and security a word that had meaning only in reference to incarceration, as in "maximum-security prison." It went without saying that "practical career goals" to us just meant "selling out." But unlike the Left as I knew it, the feminism of City College was a place where women's sexual experimentation was not automatically read as decadence or emotional unbalance. Because the feminists of my early acquaintance took it for granted that stable relationships, let alone marriage, were traps in which women were co-opted by "the system" and lost all their power, they were especially leery of recommendations that women link sex and love, or even sex and practicality. Lesbianism still held for us the promise of romance, celibacy was generally considered honorable, but heterosexual promiscuity was an acceptable lifestyle as long as it was purely selfish, using men as a means to pleasure. Pam Kearon of The Feminists called this sort of behavior "Amazon Virginity" (Echols 182).

Prostitutes and strippers, among whose ranks I had many friends, were understood by us to have a realistic view of traditional male-centered gender relations. To them pleasing men through heterosex was *work,* a day job that women held because they could not figure out any less annoying way to meet their basic material needs. We saw it as no more degrading or shameful than any other sort of wage slavery. "After The Revolution," we often told each other, there would be no more prostitution or office jobs. Some women, like me, were too irritable to do such work prior to the revolution, but that was seen as neither a failing nor a virtue.

However, when we said, and we said it frequently, that marriage was legalized prostitution, we meant to be as condemnatory as possible. Prostitutes were outsiders, were against the law that we understood in our own fiercely pre-Lacanian way as the law of the father. We saw economically dependent wives as believing that justice and the law were the same, when to us they were polar opposites. There was no lower state in our ethos. Even women who believed in the corporate world, our own "great Satan," were at least not selling their bodies for nothing but a little sentimentality and an uncertain financial payback.

At City College I gave my first class presentation, on the topic of love and marriage. I began by sketching a cartoon of my own on the blackboard. It showed a huge male figure holding a tiny woman in his palm, his index finger pressing down on her head. Balloons coming out of both their heads contained the words "I love you, let's get married." Next to them, I wrote "equality?!?" My fellow feminists applauded as soon as I finished drawing. The talk was a collection of statistics on such things as lack of equal pay for equal work, second-shift housework, and domestic violence. My thesis was that one could no more expect romantic love to survive such circumstances than one could expect to find it between slave owners and their slaves.

Imagine, then, my growing sense of horror when my c-r group first began to focus on "economic empowerment," which appeared to be an endorsement of capitalism and the American dream: freedom through a high-paying job and the purchase of a car and a house. Next, to my reeling shock, came outreach to "homemakers," not, as previously, in the spirit of missionary work, but to welcome them and legitimate their choice as one that could be considered equally feminist.[9] Next, to add insult to injury, the new recruits to our ranks began, as I then expressed it, "to rag on" prostitutes.[10] This was how I and my closest friends interpreted the purpose of the Take Back the Night march, which was scheduled to go through North Beach, embarrassing patrons away and calling attention to the anger (some) women felt about the ways women were represented in the shows and sex aids for sale there. Chanting about women's volition in matters of dress and sexual behavior seemed to me fine in some contexts, but misdirected here. After all, what man in a neighborhood full of working prostitutes assumes that any provocatively dressed woman he sees is trying to signal her willingness to give him some "free love"?

I felt then (and still feel now) that it would be easier to legally protect prostitutes from rape and beatings than it is to offer the same protection to women on conventional dates, since in the former case expectations and prices are stated up front, while the economic barter involved in the latter arrangements is disavowed. Conventional marriage represented to me the area of women's greatest vulnerability to male exploitation and violence because wives' status in relation to the male so-called partner is so ambiguous. Thus the irony of married women who were financially dependent on their husbands setting out to "free" the prostitutes just about floored me. The final straw was that the plan seemed to be to free the sex workers by scaring away their customers and thus taking away their livelihood.

Picture me and my lesbian friend goggling our eyes at each other in the Women's Center as a number of our fellow feminists, including some women whom we had heard on prior occasions complaining about being compelled to provide sexual service to their disagreeable husbands, discussed shutting down the strip clubs and live sex shows in North Beach. As Jane Gallop writes, about a meeting she attended about twenty years later, "Around the table, we were all women and all feminists. . . . But now we were speaking two different languages" (*Feminist Accused* 61). At this time two of my friends were barkers for these clubs, a third was "an erotic masseuse," another a "nude lady mud wrestler," and a fifth was a pioneering lap dancer at the most notorious sex show in town. A sixth trawled the clubs looking for the elderly tourists that were the only customers she'd accept, for safety reasons. My stomach turned at the thought of these generous women whose children I baby-sat being publicly harassed and embarrassed by some self-righteous women who, if they had their way, would deny them their only chance to make enough money to get out of "the life." (Four of the six were full-time students.) My lesbian friend, who also had friends who depended on the North Beach clubs to get by, decided that we would stage a counterdemonstration, walking alongside the official Take Back the Night marchers, shouting (not very imaginative or pithy) slogans of our own devising like "good for you!" and "sex is a good thing!" "Legalize prostitution!" was our most popular. But no one seemed to know exactly what we were trying to do. The march went down in history; we got hoarse and frustrated and wandered off into oblivion. We were feminists and we were academics, but somehow we seemed to have gotten outside the boundaries of academic feminism.

ACADEMIC FEMINISM III: GRADUATE SCHOOL—THE VOTE AGAINST MEN

The defining moment in my student experience of the institutionalization of feminism came when my first graduate seminar on feminist theory voted on whether men should be admitted into women's studies seminars in the English department. This was an issue because the Ph.D. program was so over-enrolled that professors regularly had to turn away at least half of the students qualified to take their seminars. And nothing was more popular than feminism, which was rumored to be a potential ticket to employment. The whole situation, from the institutionalization of feminism to the power of the women students, was the very opposite of what I had expected.

The day I walked into orientation for my Ph.D. program, I must have looked like a wary animal. In a Virginia Woolf seminar the previous year I had discovered feminist literary criticism and was reading it voraciously. I had just finished Judith Fetterly's *The Resisting Reader* over the summer. My expectation, based on the autobiographical parts of that book, was that there would be almost no women in the program and the men would be mean as junkyard dogs. Upon entering the English lounge, I scanned the room for another woman, and upon finding her, introduced myself with a hearty handshake. As she would later confess, she, too, expected to be an isolated and besieged representative of our sex. In fact, half of the entering class was female.

Still, my unease persisted. Idiotically, I had actually chosen to attend what was then one of the most prestigious English programs in the United States, not because I knew anything at all about its reputation, but solely because it was within commuting distance of my home in San Francisco. I had no idea that the school was a magnet for people whose accounts of their lives sounded to me like something out of *The Great Gatsby*. Prior to this I knew of only three social classes. Poor meant you went hungry a lot and had trouble getting work because of your clothes and the way you talked. Middle-class meant you earned wages sufficient to feed, clothe, and shelter yourself and any dependents. Rich people were mysterious but their distant lives had some recognizable features. They bought everything new and engaged in activities like vegetable gardening, canning, and sewing only for fun. They rented only when young, later owning houses, which included separate bedrooms for any children, even when they had more than two. They seemed to expect to have more than one bathroom. They traveled to foreign countries for vacations. And most notably, the women almost never worked for wages. After a year in the graduate program and careful study of Paul Fussell's *Notes on Class,* which I read like a desperate anthropologist marooned among the members of a particularly alien tribe, I could have written my own book about those my parents had always referred to as "rich people," and the first sentence would have been "Without exception they all think they are middle-class." There were so many middle classes I could not decide whether I was on the border of one or not.

Conversely, racial difference seemed less complex than it was in my regular life in San Francisco, where to my delight, one of my Black friends called me "off-white girl." In graduate school, Jews were considered generic white people, and there was some controversy over whether Asian Americans were to be considered members of minorities. The only other races ever mentioned were Black and Chicano. So, after those concerning social class, the largest number of new differences I had to assimilate surrounded gender issues. The most extreme differences pertained to self-presentation, and resulted in the effacement of the sort of sexual electricity that had previously enlivened most of my college classes.

In a journal for that first year in the Ph.D. program, I wrote a little note to myself: "what you think is ugly, they think is beautiful, try to look as ugly as possible." I then went on to describe the favored style of dress among my fellow female graduate students as loose, earth-toned clothing, straight hair, knee socks, and absolutely flat shoes. The nail that stood up was hammered down. Breasts bigger than cup size B were compressed in "minimizer" bras. No-fat diets produced no-bulge bodies. Women's faces were discreetly made up to have a uniform matte color. I was unaware that this was a standard costume for American female intellectuals, who unlike the French or Eastern Europeans cannot be culturally understood as having brains and bodies both. With their short hair, square-cut sport jackets, and baggy pants, the men were equally subdued, perhaps to escape seeming effeminate because they were intellectual.

Although I realize in retrospect that these people were conditioned to respond to much more subtle forms of attractiveness than I was and so may well have been excited by each other, I perceived the atmosphere as one from which all potential for sexual pleasure had been purged for reasons unknown to me. Gone were the dramatic, self-flaunting students of all sexes who would enter classes tossing back their wild hair, twitching their hips in skintight jeans, smoothing down their short shiny jackets, playing with their sparkling junk jewelry, and laughing with their mouths wide open. And as a consequence, gender relations really seemed, for the first time, as unrelievedly dismal as described in the early 1980s texts in feminist theory that I was then reading. Men and women were just competitors, and although in some future heaven of professorial employment they might become colleagues, they scarcely had the luxury of thinking of themselves in those terms yet. As Naomi Wolf observed of San Francisco in the 1970s and '80s, "the City made us feel that we were not alive if we were not being sexual" (9). Unlike her, I did not consider this a problem until graduate school made me feel that to succeed I must renounce my past and my values and become one of what I saw as the walking dead.

I did form a few alliances with other outsiders (male and female) who, like me, were engaged in negotiating some sort of compromise between submission to standards that made us feel like class traitors and utter hypocrites, and the stubborn adherence to the familiar that made us feel authentic but despised by the more powerful. The homosocial structure of the graduate student culture caused me to spend most of my time with other women, and I was frequently the object of their reform. In graduate school I was repeatedly questioned in a way that made me want to run screaming from academe back into the absolute depths of poverty. Why did I wear such *bright* colors? Weren't such tight clothes uncomfortable? Didn't I brush my hair? Had I been out in the sun? (Why was my face so red and shiny and my hair so bushy?) Did I *really* have sex with men *like that?* What did I get out of it? Didn't I feel degraded? What had my family been like? Was I molested as a child? (How can anyone start having sex in their early teens and claim to enjoy it unless they have been the victim of some horrific form of abuse?)

I would never again feel the easy blending of my academic and other lives that had been such a joy to me at City College. For the first time I experienced multiple iden-tifications as painful and disorienting rather than exciting. While I had been laboriously acquiring some knowledge and a lot more skill through graduate studies, I had run the course of one marriage and begun another—very much to the horror of my radical feminist friends outside academe, some of whom boycotted both weddings for political reasons. In growing distinction from the "official" position I adhered to at school, that men were agents of that undifferentiated mass conspiracy the patriarchy, my "home" view resembled the one about women attributed to conventional men, "can't live with 'em, can't live without 'em."

Unlike Naomi Wolf, who, around the same time in San Francisco, was trauma-tized by receiving "the message that being a monogamous heterosexual was worse than being boring and stupid" from the local cult surrounding *The Rocky Horror Picture Show,* I was not at all appalled to see hipness locally defined by "making fun of the idea of heterosexual marriage" (175). I could easily accept casual sexual experimentation as an ideal and saw it as a weakness in myself that life without at least one permanent lover was unthinkable to me, for very much the same reasons that I imagine it is to conventional men. Casual dates were fine for sex, but, I asked myself, without a loving boyfriend, who would fix me little snacks when I was writing, tidy up my apartment, find my watch and keys, keep my laundry from coming out streaked with pink from the red socks, make me drinkable coffee, type my papers, and otherwise raise the level of my daily life from the chaotic filth it has always descended into whenever I live alone? And more importantly, who would build up my intellectual self-confidence by listening to my ideas and helping me organize the contents of my mind? I was learning from academic feminism that such relationships were regarded by most women as desirable, but almost impossible to achieve with men. Perhaps because of the type of relations I have had with men or the type of men to whom I am attracted, these seemed to me reasonable expectations. In fact, prior to academic feminism, they simply constituted what I would have described as the benefits of living with a man. And in graduate school I was not only leaving one such relationship and settling into another, I was intensely, passionately in love.

I did understand that living with a man could have a negative side; my resentment of anything that could be construed as an attempt to restrict my sexual self-expression was virtually boundless. I wanted to feel both completely nurtured and absolutely free. My complaints about my relationships were unreasonable, as I can now readily admit, but in the terms of the academic feminist discourse of the day they were simply unintelligible, insane. In the criticism and theory we read, it was a given that female sexual pleasure depended on trust and the promise of stability. Women were understood to want freedom from domestic service and from men's sexual demands, but where the man provided domestic service and his sexual attentions were always quite welcome, how could one identify a problem? What did I want to be free to do, for heaven's sake? It was annoying enough to be constantly asked that by my husbands and lovers; to face the same question from my fellow feminists made me feel as if I must be deviant indeed. I had come full circle to represent as much of a category crisis to those around me as I had in the third grade.

There I was, an angry feminist refusing to compromise with the demands of the patriarchal dominant culture. But I was also defying the standards of the feminism dominant in academe by presenting myself as a sexualized body. And the strangeness of this was compounded by my assumption of the role of aggressive sexual subject rather than decorative, responsive object. My opposition to the patriarchy did not restrain my desire to exploit the sexual revolution for all the fun I could possibly get, nor did I see this attitude as capitulation to males. While many other feminists busily elaborated on theories about differences in men's and women's sexualities, I continued to act upon what I had learned as a very young girl: a person who has sexual relations only with people whose company arouses her intensely and who initiates what pleases her is very likely to find satisfactory the sex acts that follow. My anger at men did not include any criticism of their sexuality—in fact, that was the only thing I consistently liked about my lovers. I was confident of my ability to survive economically in the world their group controlled, since after all I had been working for wages since I was thirteen, but I knew I could never nurture or entertain myself as delightfully as they could do those things for me. And I bitterly resented the level of commitment they required in exchange.

When my feminist theory seminar voted not to allow men into women's studies seminars, my hand went up with all the others, and yet what would have been a moment of supreme solidarity six years earlier at City College felt more to me like another instance of my existence in a limbo of feminism, where I did not know what the others were thinking, knew they were in the same situation with respect to me, and had no idea what to do about it. The reason I wanted to exclude men was that I was afraid they would cut me out of a job teaching women's literature, because even male feminists seemed to be perceived by the majority of the women in my program as less confusing and irritating than I was. At least the guys had the sense to say that the sexual revolution had failed women.

"TALKIN' 'BOUT A REVOLUTION"

In the last few years, as so many of my friends have gotten tattoos, I have often been tempted to follow suit and have "Stamp Paid" permanently inscribed, after Toni Morrison's character in *Beloved*. Because, whether I look back in bitterness or with pleasure, I cannot escape the feeling that, as my coevals used to say, I have paid my dues. Of course, my sufferings cannot be compared to those of someone who underwent slavery, but still I have learned, as Stamp tells Paul D., that the only answer to the question of how many insults a person must take before giving up the struggle is "all [s]he can" (235). Much of my bitterness has come from repeated realizations that the therapy culture that seems to provide so much comfort to other Americans can address neither my problems as a lover nor those I face as a fighter.

This section title comes from Tracy Chapman, who also, in "For My Lover," provides one of my favorite condemnations of psychoanalysis's failure to read love in a way satisfactory to sex radicals. The singer comments on the enforced therapy she underwent during a jail term undergone for her lover: "Everyday I'm psychoanalyzed . . . They dope me up and I tell them lies . . . And everybody thinks / That I'm the fool/ But they don't get / Any love from you." The lesson she learns, as expressed on the same album in the song "For You," is that love that exceeds what therapists consider healthy must be concealed, "Safe from the guards / Of intellect and reason." To love like this seems like falling outside of culturally authorized interpretive systems that might allow us to make sense, any sense at all, of our experiences, and thus to feel that our sufferings are not meaningless.

I turned to feminism for help with my intense feelings in a spirit somewhat like what I attribute to Morrison when she embraces identity-based liberational politics, partly in order to place the pains of love within a narrative of meaningful resistance. It is the reconstruction of a history of racial oppression that allows Sethe to love Paul D. without restraint and to understand such love not as self-abnegating surrender but as rebellion against a world that would destroy her. The popular video "Unpretty" by the African American girl group TLC visually dramatizes this type of strategy by alternating depiction of the undermining of one group member's self-confidence by her boyfriend's insistence that she get breast implants with even more disturbing visuals of another group member being assaulted at school by white racists. Sexual pride and physical self-assertion such as have made TLC justly popular appear as the answers to these woes. Just as analysis of racism can explain to a Black woman the seemingly excessive pain she may feel when love hurts her sense of her bodily integrity, and can also help her develop a productive mode of response, so, I thought, academic analysis of gender politics could help me understand why love was sometimes so painful and what I could do to enhance its positive possibilities.

It is odd, then, to reflect that among all the prices I paid for my current position as a feminist professor, including the inexpressible alienation of class jumping, the largest cost was to my satisfaction with the philosophy that had originally motivated me to change my life radically. The ignorant pleasure I took in my early, uneducated feminism is gone now. Academe made it impossible for me to continue thinking of my sex-radicalism as something that fits seamlessly into my feminism. I face conferences on women's issues with a sense of dread not much less sickening than I felt prior to making my first appearance in fourth grade. If misery always loved company, I might find it consoling that disagreements between feminists have reached such an incredible pitch of intensity in the last few years that we can no longer expect to share a view of the most fundamental women's issues, as Camille Paglia's and Katie Roiphe's writings on rape show. Yet my mood as I anticipate the twenty-first century is far from mournful. Instead, this book is intended to open windows onto some of the new worlds that are coming into view as sexuality and gender change, worlds in which aspects of the familiar second-wave feminisms may be losing relevance, but exciting new feminisms are even now taking shape.

There is probably no point in known history at which one could not locate changes in sexuality and gender. Feminist analyses of gender relations almost invariably treat love as a crucial element of women's experience of both sexuality and gender identity, so my discussions are structured around intersections of the three. However, a survey of the entire history of sexuality and gender, even if limited to the aspects of that history that also concern women in love, is beyond the scope of this book. Instead, I will sketch in some of what I consider the most remarkable and extreme changes that are reaching their culmination as the new millennium opens. Within the context provided by these sketches I will focus closely on a few cultural artifacts, such as courtship and marriage manuals, films, and music performances, that seem to me strongly indicative of alterations in concepts of sexuality, gender, and love that can be best explained in reference to chronologically and geographically situated cultural forces and countercultural formations. The reader is invited to see this book as, among other things, the extended and personal answer of a "local intellectual" to a question I was asked, during a major campaign of the Oregon Citizen's Alliance against gay and lesbian rights, by a young heterosexual male San Franciscan friend: "They're against homosexuals—Why?"

"Styling Love," the first section of the book, takes off from Foucault's arguments about the transformation of subjectivity in the nineteenth century, as psychology invented categories of sexual identity and conferred on them the status of core being. It is also heavily indebted to Gilles Deleuze and Félix Guattari's theorization of the antagonism between extreme eroticism and some main goals of capitalism. Deleuze and Guattari's work supplements Foucauldian discourse theory by providing an explanation of how political interests are served by our present taxonomies of desire, which naturalize domesticity and pathologize passion. My purpose in this section is to illustrate how a vantage point within feminist noncomplicitous heterosexuality—or perhaps, in the case of some other critic, a perspective cognizant of the possibility that such a vantage point exists—can result in a different type of reading of mainstream cultural artifacts than feminist criticism most commonly produces. To this end, I look at understandings of sexuality that have slowly developed throughout the twentieth century, resulting in approaches to romantic love that come to dominate both feminist and nonfeminist discourses by the millennium's end.

This section begins with an examination of some ways that past and current didactic writings on courtship and marriage refine and reflect upon a general cultural re-evaluation of the romantic that is always inflected by both feminist and capitalist ideologies, often in strange and unsettling combinations. The second chapter of this section begins by pointing out major changes in anti-gay rhetoric of the 1990s and then focuses on the film *Basic Instinct,* which was protested during its production as misogynist and homophobic. Because I approach the film with assumptions about female sexuality, and consequently about love and gender identity, different from those most often endorsed by academic feminisms, I foreground the radically subversive messages the film conveys about conventions in the representation of romantic love that are now expected to accompany aspirations to be taken seriously within American culture. The chapter then goes on to look at some film conventions in the representation of gender-trouble-in-flight and what has happened to them recently, as Hollywood finally began to assimilate feminist ideas.

Both chapters explore how fear of the disruptive power of erotic feelings between men and women results in a cultural phenomenon I call heterophobia. Heterophobia is not a homosexual devaluation of heterosexuality. Instead, it is almost always accompanied by demonization of homosexual Eros, which has traditionally been considered less amenable to social control and even more likely than outlawed forms of heterosexual passion to disrupt the containment of the erotic within bland domestic consumer units. By demonstrating how widely heterophobia has permeated current mainstream concepts of psychic health and true love, I hope to call attention to the dangers posed by continued transmission both of ideas on gender and sexuality that are central to therapy culture and of the feminisms compatible with it that rather alarmingly inform so much current academic discourse on gender.

cf. "joyful girls" concept of passion in feminist academic writing + other disruptive pleasures

"Millennial Sexstyles," the second section of the book, turns to a more encouraging part of the American sexscape with consideration of revolutionary changes within some youth subcultures that are built around the performance of popular music. Beginning with a chapter analyzing information gathered through my informal interviews of people between the ages of thirteen and twenty-five, I argue that attitudes about sexuality and gender have already altered considerably from those that most feminist theory still takes as intrinsic to our culture, as the inspiring question from my bemused young friend in San Francisco may suggest. Having provided some indication of how a fairly large number of young people respond to the endless flow of official and unofficial information they receive about sex, love, and gender identity, the section goes on in its next two chapters to present close examinations of recent major cultural movements associated with pop music. One chapter looks at rock performers and performance artists who go beyond valorization or resignification of either the feminine or the masculine to create a new, cyborgian image of being that seems to float free of binary difference. The next looks at the music and self-stylings associated with so-called Girl Culture and its centrality to third-wave feminism.

The point of this book, like the point of my life so far, is to find a way to incorporate into feminism some of the intellectual and also the more emotional pleasure I associate with sexual experience, the rush of power, the delirium of letting go the tired old cultural narratives that impose identities, the shock of awareness of the beautiful reality of another being outside the self. Although I take issue with some ideas popularly associated with feminism and go so far as to interrogate the premises that seem to underlie specific academic feminist positions, I write this book as a very politically engaged feminist, whose dearest desire is that feminist identification will be a less confusing and troubling experience for my young friends than it has been for me.

My other primary wish for this book is that it will bring back the good news from the clubs to those of my friends who cannot bear the smoke and sweat, screaming guitars and pounding drums that are like the essence of life to me. Because when I think of all that I have gained from the immersion in youth cultures that my personality demanded of me in these last few years, the wonderful days and nights spent learning to understand subjectivity in the ways so many hip young people do, I am tempted to change that tattoo design to read "Stamp Reimbursed."

I do not make these allusions to *Beloved* lightly. All my life I have wanted no less from feminism than emancipation from forced confinement in gender, and I have often despaired, thinking that freedom would never come. We distinguish between liberal feminism and radical feminism, among other permutations of women's liberation philosophy, but in our actual lived experience of a world where being a woman is still a financial handicap and a threat to physical safety, all feminists are radicals. It can be especially discouraging for radicals to grow older and see our dreams of life after the revolution fade, but it seems to me vital, as we move into the twenty-first century, to recognize that at least as far as sex, love, and gender are concerned, the revolution we waited for is underway.

PART I

STYLING LOVE

FEMINISM, LOVE, AND REALISM

NONSENSE TERMINABLE AND INTERMINABLE

Forever in debt to your priceless advice
—Nirvana, "Heart-Shaped Box"

Among Freud's many interesting remarks in *Civilization and Its Discontents* is that the "sexual life of civilized man" is so "severely impaired" that "it sometimes gives the impression of being in the process of involution as a function, just as our teeth and hair seem to be as organs" (58). This remark is all the more striking, and rather charming, in contradicting the endless chorus of complaints about the overemphasis on sex that characterizes public discourse in the twentieth century. Pronouncements that we are not preoccupied enough with sex are so few and far between that it is entertaining to imagine sex receding like a middle-aged man's hairline as we pass into the new millennium. However, I must agree with the majority that interest in sex does not seem on the wane. What does seem to be changing are the ways in which this interest is expressed and, once expressed, is handled by individuals and by the culture.

We could follow Freud in considering the changes in concepts of sexuality and gender at the end of the twentieth century inevitable, biological evolution, but that will not be my position here. Instead, I will consider some cultural forces that interfere with, and shape, the various ways Americans try to make sense of their sexuality in relation to their gender identifications. I start in agreement with Joanna Frueh that "the erotic is expansive but it has become shrunken due to misunderstandings of it and accommodations to dullness" (114). Culture is not something independent of the subjects it informs; rather it is an ever-changing set of interlocked ideas reflecting the relationships among people within a society and that society's institutions. Culture tells us what we are expected to feel about social structures we have created. Because marriage, generally known as "The Family" in political rhetoric, is a central institution in American social life, I will frame this discussion of changes in concepts of sexuality and gender within an examination of major trends in official stories about marriage, the putatively nonfictional narratives that form what might be called an American marital culture. In examining these narratives, my focus will be on what I refer to, for convenience's sake, as the advice genre, because it is here that all the expansiveness of love seems to be stuffed into the heart-shaped box of domesticity, or, to rephrase in the terms of the advice genre itself, it is here that Americans learn what work is required to achieve and maintain an exemplary marriage.

In listening to Americans talk about their marriages, one might first notice the pervasiveness of the idea that maintaining a good marriage requires continual effort.[1] The nonfiction literature of marriage that our mainstream culture has generated throughout the twentieth century suggests that we all work on our marriages as we do on old houses, always searching for weak spots in the structure, constantly assessing and attempting to repair. If ever an institution merited the descriptor "constructed," surely it is American marriage, which ideally never just happens, but is always built and then periodically renewed or even reformed. Pleasure may certainly be found in this pursuit—consider the popularity of home renovation. But the astonishing proliferation of contemporary writings about making, maintaining, and recovering from marriages suggests that other feelings predominate.

If there is one genre of writing whose very existence attests not just to the constructedness of human interactions but to the uncomfortable feeling of artificiality connected to them, it is the advice genre that deals with social etiquette and romance. I call this *one* genre because the two types of advice generally overlap, centering as both do on the establishment and maintenance of domestic arrangements that ensure one's social status. How to secure the affections of a person with high social status and how to conduct oneself as a person of high social status are not unrelated concerns. Obviously, if one could satisfy society's demands simply by following the dictates of the "conscience," as formed by early moral instruction, one would not need guidance in these matters. The popularity of conduct guides can be seen as an index of the unease or sense of inadequacy a given group feels about their culture's mores, as numerous cultural theorists have shown.

Nancy Armstrong claims conduct books "most often imply a readership who desires self-improvement and for whom the self-improvement promises an elevation of social position." As Armstrong shows, this aspect of the conduct book becomes particularly interesting when, as in the eighteenth- and nineteenth-century texts she discusses, marriage becomes the culturally preferred vehicle for elevating social position, and within literary writings "the sexual contract" functions as a "narrative paradigm" to do "much the same work that Rousseau imagined the social contract would perform" (269, 42). When narratives of social advancement and marriage plots are conflated, choosing the right fork suggests one's ability to choose the right spouse.

Deleuze and Guattari maintain that "[i]t is with one thing, capitalism, that the unavowable begins: there is not a single economic or financial operation that, assuming it is translated in terms of a code, would not lay bare its own unavowable nature, that is, its intrinsic perversion or essential cynicism (the age of bad conscience is also the age of pure cynicism)" (*Anti-Oedipus* 247). Whether one considers the act of marrying for economic reasons a crime to be disavowed depends on what one counts as virtue. As that exemplary Deleuzian Kathy Acker observes, "The poor can reply to the crime of society, to their economic deprivation retardation primitivism lunacy boredom hopelessness, only by collective crime or war. One form collective crime takes is marriage" (7). The overlap of advice on achieving social advancement with advice on achieving a happy love life presents no difficulty, as long as most members of the society agree on two points: 1. That spontaneous behavior is by definition bad (because acting naturally means following animalistic impulses); and 2. That marriage is the appropriate place to attain social status and express erotic love. The increasing emphasis on the last idea, since the rise of "love matches" in the late eighteenth century, may have somewhat strained the ability to assimilate a vision of correct behavior that runs so deeply counter to most people's experience of what gives pleasure. But so long as it is held as given that the most morally meritorious behavior is the least natural feeling, advice to the lovelorn and advice to the socially awkward can be sensibly combined. If one starts from the assumption that any spontaneously felt eroticism is an evil to be avoided, or in the most pernicious cases gotten through as quickly as possible, like a storm that catches one out unprepared, then to the degree that marriage disciplines feeling it can be understood as an ideal locus for the refinement and perfection of eroticism that would otherwise be a destructive force. In this schema marriage becomes a sort of superior windmill for the gales of sexuality.

Nonsense, perhaps, but terminable in that it has limits. Outside the boundary of marital duty, expression of undisciplined passion may find a place, just as other behaviors deemed natural but rude or distasteful may still be indulged at some times, in some places. It is only when we insist that erotic love is both natural and good, and that the healthy person will spontaneously experience it as ideally expressed within marriage, that nonsensical advice spreads unbounded to touch every aspect of sexuality. Thus I will argue that it is not until the late twentieth century that the advice genre reaches its apex of self-contradictory and, worse, self-perpetuating nonsense. And, as in the Nirvana song that I quote for this chapter's epigraph, this genre's "priceless advice" becomes a torment to those who value sexual passion and erotic love.

Since the 1960s, the natural (as Americans construe it) has probably attained its greatest popularity in recorded history.[2] From that time to the present, simply adding the word "natural" to a label has increased the value of the goods to which it is affixed. In defiance of what common sense tells us about foodstuffs, which is that they usually require some processing in the way of cleaning, and often cooking as well, in order to be edible, "natural" and "healthy" have become synonymous, both used to describe food meant to improve one's physical condition. "Natural" behavior is the standard. The idea that illness results from unnatural behavior has been adopted by American society to such an extent that grotesque problems result, ranging from the common belief that repression of emotions causes cancer to the frequent self-poisonings of enthusiasts of herbal remedies. Religious fundamentalists in sects that formerly advocated repressing natural impulses as manifestations of original sin now draw on the rhetoric of the natural and organic to describe AIDS as a punishment for "unnatural" sex acts. The previous tendency of such people to consider many other sex acts, such as rape, both natural *and* evil, because animalistic, might have caused a descriptive quandary, had the advice genre not joined forces with therapeutic discourse to formulate a relatively new way of understanding sexual relations.

Even more astounding was the working agreement, in the 1980s, among extreme religious conservatives, numerous therapists, and a large faction within feminism that pornography, once deemed evidence of humanity's bestial (read "natural") fallen condition, is an unnatural expression of sexuality. But these peculiar alliances could not have occurred without an epistemological crisis stemming from the adoption of naturalness as a universal standard. To trace the emergence of that crisis, let us turn to the lowest rank of therapeutic discourse, the advice genre.

A comic indication of the crisis in the advice genre brought about by the new naturalness's re-evaluation of behavior codes appeared in the many letters featured in Judith Martin's "Miss Manners" etiquette column complaining that the use of the word "Dear" to address letters was insincere unless the writer actually held the addressee dear, and that such closings as "sincerely yours" were unusable because not literally true. To see how thoroughly the idea that every social form must be filled with deeply felt emotion has permeated late-twentieth-century consciousness, one might compare some points in Martin's discussion of conventions in letter writing to Emily Post's 1942 treatment of the same issue.

Post apparently finds it necessary to remind her readers that those who receive their letters may attach some meaning to what the writer felt was only an empty convention. Typical remarks indicative of this concern occur in her cautions about maintaining gender difference in correspondence styles. For example, we are told that "No lady should ever sign a letter 'respectfully,'" because it denotes inferior status (563). In contrast, men are encouraged to adhere to courtly conventions of deference, so "'Faithfully yours' is a very good signature for a man in writing to a woman . . . the President of the United States, a member of the cabinet, an ambassador, a clergyman, etc." (564). She acknowledges a private space where even more intense devotion might be expressed: "The phrases that a man might devise to close a letter to his betrothed or wife are bound only by the limit of his imagination and do not belong in this, or any, book" (565). Here the limits to prescriptivity about gender relations are evident. A private space outside the purview of both society and advice columns is reserved for lovers as well as marital partners. Those who wish to avoid conveying impressions of deference are urged by Post to restrict themselves to "kindest regards" or, for formal notes, "very sincerely yours" (563). But she regrets the passing of an age of more personal and "graceful" closings, "with little flowers of compliment" (563). Here, for both Post and her audience, conventional phrases seem rather like poetry, operating within strict formal boundaries to rework the raw material of feeling into something decoratively stylized. Like writing sonnets, closing letters is a process that often involves exaggeration, but is no less valuable because of it.

Miss Manners's 1980s correspondents could hardly be more different from Post's wartime advisees. They often seem agonized by their search for salutations and closings cold enough to reflect their absence of emotion, and she must remind them that when they devise deliberately insulting phrases of greeting or closing they have departed from etiquette. Apparently exasperated beyond measure by her advisees' horror of insincerity, *Miss Manners' Guide for the Turn-of-the-Millennium* includes a section on "Conventional Phrases: The Meaningless Exchange" in which she tries to explain that a certain amount of "insincere" expression of mild affection or good will toward others is part of the "ritualistic" maintenance of comfort in social interchange (70–71). Still, she acknowledges that the current mood has undermined that comfort: "Conventions work only when people understand their function and repeat the conventional response. All this overinterpreting has confused people" (71).

Martin's placement of the blame for this dismal state of affairs is suggested by her remark that Miss Manners "is just bored to tears by the literary and psychological analysis of simple conventions" (71). Here we may infer annoyance with the union of close reading and psychology that has become so much a part of the way Americans process written and visual information since formalist criticism met the popularization of Freud in the 1950s.[3] Her position seems not unlike the complaint of some anti-psychoanalytic literary critics that this approach reduces all writings to the status of symptoms. But, to treat her own remark as culturally symptomatic, it also suggests the etiology of specific changes in acceptable ways of reading social signs that followed in the wake of the definitional crisis brought on by the rise of the natural. Where once we sought to know the virtuous way to handle social situations and also the most effective way to use those situations as means of advancement, and lived in hopes that a wise advisor could direct us to behavior that would be both, we now add to the already difficult problem of how to simultaneously be good and do well the condition that the behavior must also be perfectly natural. As Martin's comment suggests, our standard resource for help in this endeavor is psychology.

However, the psychological theories we turn to are not those that denaturalize social forms and institutions, such as Freud's many famous writings on the stress caused by culture's demands that we repress our instincts in favor of the interests of the group.[4] Because Freud sees the formation of families and societies as both necessary to individual survival and fundamentally in conflict with innate drives, he insistently qualifies his claims that analysis can help mitigate unhappiness. Unhappiness appears always in his works as the basic human condition. We must bear in mind that Freud defines pleasure as the absence of displeasure. A Freudian analysand traditionally seeks to understand intrapsychic conflicts and conflicts with others in order to manage them better, rather than to do away with them. Others remain in a necessarily hostile relationship with oneself as each inevitably strives to dominate social interactions. In contrast, the advice genre is informed by the more cheerful theory, which pervades popular psychology, that complete truth-telling is in itself both liberatory and healing. When all is known, American therapy culture suggests, all will be understood in beneficial ways.

If this is reminiscent of religious practices in which confession and absolution are always linked, it is not coincidental. Foucault's brilliant tracing of the evolution of the Christian concept of the confessional into psychoanalytic practice elucidates the atmosphere that, after considerable time, gave form to the present therapy culture, and gives insight into the logic that brought ordinary Americans, like Miss Manners's correspondents, to transfer a passion for scrupulous revelation of emotions and motivations from the private space of the religious confessional or the Freudian consultation to their everyday communications. According to Foucault, in the wake of the Counter Reformation "[a]n imperative was established: Not only will you confess to acts contravening the law, but you will seek to transform your desire, your every desire, into discourse." And thus the West entered a regime of confession characterized by "an increasing valorization of the discourse on sex; and . . . this carefully analytical discourse was meant to yield multiple effects of displacement, intensification, reorientation, and modification of desire itself." As psychology developed, "[t]he obtaining of the confession and its effects were recodified as therapeutic operations" (*History of Sexuality I* 21, 23, 67).

In its emphasis on direct expression of all of one's emotions, therapy culture functions as one answer to the unease that questioning social conventions brings about. Although it goes against some of the last two centuries' most revered ideas to do so, marriage can be explained in the same way that Martin describes what she calls "meaningless social gestures," because it is a conventional social form that allows people to interact comfortably as long as all agree to treat the form as if it had a standard, pleasant content. Treating marriage in this way means acting as if we believe that the couple will stay together for the rest of their lives, raising children, protecting goods and property that they hold in common, and generally sharing social and economic interests. The marriage may be as empty of any real emotional content as the "sincerely yours" that one writes at the end of a business letter—and most worldly people realize that a large number of marriages are so empty. Understanding marriage as a permanent arrangement whereby two people are for most purposes one allows marriages to continue to function as "the building blocks of society," as conservatives like to call them. However, as soon as divorce became easily attainable, the fictionality of "till death do us part" became harder to maintain. As marriage was revealed to be a site of conflicting interests for many people, the anxiety that Martin attributes to the questioning of conventional, meaningless forms began to become evident.

A possible answer to the question of what to do when the form seems in blatant contradiction to the content is to change the form. Instead of closing a letter threatening a collection agency with a suit for harassment with the standard polite phrase, we might choose to say, "and to hell with you!" Likewise, custom and law could have adopted new ways of dealing with married people more in line with the obvious fact that they might not be together in the future. Instead, as a culture we cling to marriage, idealizing it all the more as the extent of its fragility comes to light.[5] Serious institutions, such as banks, favor marriage over other living arrangements as if it were the only permanency detectable on earth. And most of the rest of society follows this example, as is apparent in sociological phenomena as humble as the numerous letters in "Dear Abby" and "Ann Landers" columns asking for clarification of the protocols for dealing with divorced or unmarried couples. The tone of these letters is always that of a person faced with an extraordinary situation for which there is no known precedent. More pernicious are the ongoing legal battles to "protect" heterosexual legal marriage by denying homosexual and unmarried heterosexual couples the same benefits extended to the married.

As Nan Hunter explains, much of the opposition to homosexual marriage is founded in the sexism that currently inheres within the legal treatment of marital partners. In late-twentieth-century practice, "Marriage enforces and reinforces the linkage of gender with power by husband/wife categories that are synonymous with the social power imbalance between men and women." Allowing homosexual marriage "has fascinating potential for denaturalizing the gender structure of marriage laws for heterosexual couples" (112). The increasing urgency with which mainstream Americans attempt to bolster the institution of monogamous heterosexual marriage as a stably gendered system fits into a general movement away from the 1960s interest in changing society to the subsequent "self-help" movement in which ameliorating one's personal situation is always translated as a sort of social work. To the myth of marriage's permanence is added the idea that within the marital domestic space the current and future quality of the society is determined. Unhappily married women are urged to change because marriage cannot.

The public discussions surrounding the new drug Viagra in the late 1990s provided one arena for the display of Americans' determination to preserve traditional marriage as a form and to fill it with content deemed appropriate. In the initial discussions of the drug, most pundits and publicists insisted that it did not cause arousal, but only compensated for physiological dysfunction so that a man who was aroused but could not achieve or maintain an erection would be able to function as he desired. It seemed that Viagra worked for men as vaginal lubricants can for women who are aroused but, for physiological reasons, cannot lubricate sufficiently to make intercourse comfortable. Later information revealed that a substantial number of men could take Viagra in circumstances where they were not aroused and subsequently experience both erection and a powerful feeling of sexual excitement. In the case of men, most seemed to consider this simply an interesting oddity, but as this news came out, married women began to ask the relationship pundits if Viagra could help women desire sex and enjoy it. In no discussion of which I am aware was any question raised about why a woman who is not sexually aroused would want to excite herself by ingesting a chemical. Such intentions were not publicly considered unnatural. Nor was it discussed as problematic that apparently a large number of women regularly engage in sex acts that they wish aroused them, but that do not. Consequently it seems that to many Americans a woman's inability to feel sexual excitement when engaging in intercourse with a socially appropriate partner is now considered a failure of her natural sexual responsivity, to be addressed by some sort of individual treatment, therapy or medication. This attitude has been some time in the making.

As Todd Gitlin observes, blockage of "collective expression" in American politics was followed by belief that "the self could still be transformed at will" and that such transformation would make one's life "whole" (426). Wendy Simonds historicizes Gitlin's perspective, arguing that since "the 1960s, self-help books [have] revitalized the age-old American notions that material attainment and personal well-being are the results of properly focused desire. Individual destiny is seen as unfolding in accordance with hard work—but a new kind of hard work in which people turn their efforts inward," or no further outward than toward an unsatisfactory "partner" (144). The refocusing of energy from the group or culture to the self or the marital pair seems selfish. However, this is not how those central to the self-help movement would define their focus. They frequently evoke or allude to spiritual traditions that value work on the self equally with or more than work in the world. Probably the most potent of these for the average American is the Protestant version of the confessional, the private journal of spiritual development, informed by Biblical study and structured by group devotional practices. The keeping of such a journal bears a striking resemblance to the use of the self-help book, with its characteristic checklists and spaces for diary entries and its supporting therapeutic value system. Among Simonds's findings is that self-help books are far from constituting "a secular genre." In the place of psychology's traditional Freudian concept of religion as illusion, Simonds finds in these texts a mystical American "therapeutic worldview" which "seriously limits the social consciousness of its adherents" because of its insistence that changing one's consciousness is synonymous with changing the world (50).

The pertinence of this problem to feminism can hardly be overestimated, in that "American women have long used religion as a means of reassurance that a better world existed, creating woman-centered, comforting, and empowering religious communities" (Simonds 55). Spiritualized therapy culture diverts attention from feminist political action, compounding the problem by co-opting many of the fundamental ideas and approaches of feminist consciousness-raising (c-r), such as the famous concept of the personal as political. Where feminist c-r was originally meant to complement political activism, in its self-help form consciousness-raising becomes the political activity itself. To those like Gitlin and Simonds (and myself), who remain convinced that social problems cannot be changed through individual changes of attitude alone, this new focus appears as denial of the realities of the current situation of marriage in America. We need to deny realities about domestic violence and economic competition between wives and husbands that are daily brought before us by news media in order to think of marriage as a space typically defined by the work of two loving partners always moving toward permanence and perfection. We must also deny that our society is economically structured in such a way that the majority of married people must risk falling into a lower social rank if they divorce. The popular-psychology version of therapy offered by self-help books attempts to ease the enormous anxiety that inevitably accompanies such profound denial.

Therapy culture, as promulgated by the self-help book, steps in to preserve both the traditional form of marriage and the sense that it must have meaningful emotional content, by analyzing the feelings of the parties involved and, most crucially, comparing them to a standard that pathologizes any deviations. The situation that results is every bit as strange as if one were to say that when a letter writer's emotions fail to match the standard forms of greeting and closure, she must work to make them do so. Because therapies vary widely, it is on one level absurdly reductive to speak of all the advice from self-proclaimed relationship experts that barrages the late-twentieth-century American as if it were part of a univocal "therapy culture." Still, certain similarities are evident in virtually every advice text, and it is on those similarities that I will concentrate as I draw samples from the huge number of texts available.

To begin, let us turn to an acknowledged expert, Paul Pearsall, who, we are told by the cover of his book *The Ten Laws of Lasting Love,* is also the "founder and former director of the Problems of Daily Living Clinic, Sinai Hospital, Detroit." Pearsall's ideas are important to understanding what has happened to the official story of sex and love at the end of the millennium because, as Simonds points out, he is "the only sex-manual author of the past five years to gain best seller status," for his earlier book *Super Marital Sex* (171). For readers like those Simonds describes, who believe a book is "authoritative if its author demonstrates credentialed expertise" (Simonds 27–28), one like Pearsall can be invested with the wisdom of the religious figure who judges and comforts as well as with the sort of power Lacan believes patients wish to attribute to the analyst, "the subject who is supposed to know" (*Four Fundamental Concepts* 232–233). Lacan cautions analysts that this relation with patients is perilous because it always results in transference and the attribution of "infallibility," even when the therapist does not mean his statements or gestures to be taken as authoritative (234), but Pearsall is not so wary of assuming the mantle of the sage.

Pearsall divides marriages into two groups, called Low and High Monogamy to designate each group's prospects for staying strictly monogamous. He laments that Low Monogamy marriages are typical of our times, a situation supported by "psychology, psychiatry, economics, sociology, and biology," because the abandonment of "Lasting Love," indicated by lapses from monogamy, reveals an individualistic attitude (24). A few interesting assumptions are packed into this diagnosis. The least surprising are that individualistic behavior has no place in marriage and that any departure from monogamy means that the partners no longer love each other. This is standard American ideology of love and marriage; however, Pearsall claims to stand alone in valorizing permanence and fidelity in marriage. We shall see about that in a moment, but first a look at his recommendations for beating the odds and filling marriage with such appropriate emotional content that monogamy becomes the only natural outcome.

Throughout the book Pearsall places strong emphasis on the work entailed in marriage and defines that work as intellectual. While partners in the Low Monogamy marriage believe that "love is an irresistible and profound feeling that overcomes and involuntarily overwhelms you," High Monogamists know that "loving is a way of thinking, not a way of feeling." He goes on to explain: "Love is a choice of a point of view regarding another person and a decision about how to relate with someone you elect to invest your life in. It is volitional, not emotional." The partners in successfully monogamous marriages "don't 'fall' in love—they think themselves through it" (34). In taking this position, Pearsall is not as isolated as he thinks. His prescription bears close similarity to the recommendations made by many less highly credentialed or currently less prestigious advisors over the last century.

For example, in his 1948 *Guide to Confident Living,* Norman Vincent Peale favors the same sort of logical approach, beginning a chapter called "How to Attain Married Happiness" with the blunt statement that "happy married life is possible to those who will apply to themselves a few simple, common sense principles" (186). After dismissing as foolishly complicating a straightforward matter "the custom of this day to rationalize most marriage failures on the basis that the partners were not by Nature adjustable to each other," Peale tells his readers to maintain religious practice, show appreciation for each other, and be honest (187). The result can be nothing else but "enjoyment of married happiness" (210). Like Pearsall, Peale refuses to consider the obvious fact that large numbers of people are unhappy in their marriages because they want to experience an exciting emotional connection with their spouse, not simply the sort of trust and respect that one feels for a family member who cheerfully fulfills obligations.

Much more recent books coming out of the recovery movement characteristically agree that marriage is about thought and work, more than it is about passion and intense emotions. Typical are *Perfectionism: What's Bad about Being Too Good,* by Miriam Adderholdt-Elliott, and *Little Miss Perfect,* a book for "adult children of alcoholism," by Megan LeBoutillier. Adderholdt-Elliott tells us that permanently satisfying marriages reward those who remember that "relationships take work, and some of it isn't fun. We have to be honest with others, and we have to be willing to listen when they're honest with us, even when that hurts" (47). Likewise, LeBoutillier puts "Honesty, telling the truth, being able/willing to hear the truth" and "Direct expression" first in her list of "Intimacy Skills" (66–67). These books at least have the virtue, common in the recovery movement, of a sort of neo-Freudian skepticism about how much bliss is possible to humans not under the influence of mind-altering substances. As their book titles suggest, these authors, like Emily Post writing about what conventional forms can and cannot express, fear that their readers will want to put too much into a container not meant to hold it, will want perfectibility where it is impossible. Thus Adderholdt-Elliott warns that it is "unrealistic to expect another person to meet all your emotional needs" (47), a refrain voiced by others too numerous to mention. But this admonition raises the question of why we would have such unrealistic expectations. After all, few people expect one friend to provide all the companionship they will ever need. That question returns us to the idea that not only strict monogamy but the desire to maintain it are the measure of a good marriage. Because, if we are to be scrupulously honest, must we not admit that heterosexual monogamous unions cannot satisfy everyone's emotional needs? And so, back to Pearsall.

Stress lines begin to show in Pearsall's argument when he addresses what is natural in love. Under the heading "Why Most Marriages Are Heterosexual," he explains that "the two genders are halves of nature's whole" so that while "it is possible" that homosexual marriages could meet the requirements of High Monogamy, "it is less likely that [the partners] are naturally opposite enough to make a sufficiently enduring and dynamic whole" (194). A certain contradictoriness seems to enter here. If High Monogamy pits intellect against "biology," how can the putatively innate complementarity of the sexes and the concept of biologically determined wholeness be brought in to naturalize social biases against homosexual union?

Pearsall's reasoning here is illustrative of a trend that appears throughout the American marital/sexual advice genre. He not only insists that marital happiness must be based on the renunciation of desires that conflict with monogamy, but naturalizes this renunciation by claiming that there are two sorts of erotic love. Sexual desire belongs to an ephemeral, immature, and possibly delusional state. Monogamy helps people realize their true and natural desire for closeness without sex.

So we learn that "sex can be a risk to intimacy" (33). Homosexuals are deluded people in that they believe, as do all Low Monogamists, that love depends in some way upon the sexualized qualities possessed by the other person, for instance his or her gender. High Monogamists know better. Pearsall goes so far as to say that marriage is what you make it, no matter what the other person is like (34). One might pause for another moment to consider what can be made of marriage to a mentally disturbed and violently abusive person, to bring up an extreme example of how ridiculous this sort of advice is. Pearsall, however, is concerned here not about a spouse who constitutes a threat to the other's life, but rather about the spouse who is perceived as disappointing for less dramatic reasons. In his view, we are always in danger of being led astray by sexual and romantic feelings that cause us to believe the beloved is unique and meant for us. Such feelings are the basis of later disappointment when the beloved proves to be more ordinary and less stimulating than anticipated. Luckily, even when we are fool enough to marry because of passionate attachment, all is not lost, because "Marriage is designed so that we fall out of romantic love and into loving reality. . . . The natural decline from romantic high and passionate longing is a sign of maturing love, not a failing marriage" (41).

In *Super Marital Sex* (1987), Pearsall promises his readers that in return for fidelity and commitment they will achieve a sex life within their marriages that constitutes "the most erotic, intense, fulfilling experience any human being can have" (170), but just six years later, in *The Ten Laws of Lasting Love* (1993), he shows a real hostility toward his advisees' interest in sexual activity, telling them repeatedly that "good or frequent sex really has little to do with a good marriage" (82). How can we account for such an amazing turn? We might begin by considering market forces. Like the readers of self-help books, the editors of this genre value "authoritative" authors, but the editors' criteria for awarding authority depends on the "timeliness" of the author's pronouncements (Simonds 102). They want to see the writer affirm a belief that is both perceptibly new and yet attaining cultural currency. Placing Pearsall's work in the context of a changing therapy culture illuminates why, in order to preserve his authority, it may have been necessary for him to abandon in the 1990s the views he had expressed in the 1980s.

While commitment both to naturalizing monogamy and to privileging the mind over the feelings remains fairly constant in the advice genre, concepts of the place of sexuality in the happy marriage do not. One can see a slow transformation here that suddenly accelerates as we near century's end. Alexander Geppert's essay on the best-seller status of Marie Stopes's 1918 *Married Love*, "Divine Sex, Happy Marriage, Re-generated Nation," neatly sums up in its title what seems to have been the prevailing view, on both sides of the Atlantic, of the ideal function of sexuality. As he shows, Stopes's version of "liberating women sexually, that is enabling them to control their own fertility and experience sex as pleasure," was rigidly constrained by her equal investment in a eugenics dependent on monogamous, reproductive heterosexual marriage, with all other forms of female pleasure dismissed as "inadequate, aberrant, or detrimental" to both the woman and society (431). In an even more moralistic vein, Boudinot Seeley's 1919 *Christian Social Hygiene* provides a particularly condensed treatment of these issues by beginning, "Marriage is the normal relationship for mature people." Seeley quickly proceeds to recommend marriage as a "cure for all the evils of sex," while stressing that "for its right conduct it, too, requires rigid self-discipline" (77). On this issue most advice writers can agree: while it is the most normal and natural of relations, marriage paradoxically entails discipline and regulation, and nowhere more than in sexual matters.

This remains a large part of American ideology of marriage into the next generation. Among the twenty-six essays and extracts collected in the 1931 Modern Library anthology *The Sex Problem in Modern Society,* there are none that seriously question either the naturalness of monogamous, male-dominant marriage or the necessity of maintaining it through hard work. Will Durant sums up the general attitude reflected in the essays: "The last word, however, must be for monogamy. The lifelong union remains the loftiest conception of human marriage. . . . There is something cowardly in divorce, like flight from the field of war" (166). He promises "reward" in the form of "steady affection" that comes, after years of struggle, to supplant "the transitory ardor of physical desire" (166–167).

Elinor Glyn gives the same message a more ecstatic twist in her 1923 *The Philosophy of Love,* telling her readers "it should be realized that monogamous marriage is an *ideal* state, not a *natural* state, and it must be admitted to be such and lived up to as an ideal" (21; emphasis Glyn's); however, this ideal state can be attained on earth, resulting in a love that "rises so high that it is beyond the reach of change" (14). All it takes is "understanding of Life, and understanding of Nature instincts and sex instincts" (46). Although we are urged to realize that "love depends, not upon the will of the individual, but upon what attracting power is in the other person," this realization does not result in a feeling of helpless fatedness. Instead, when the involuntary quality of attraction is "clearly understood, intelligence can suggest the most suitable methods to use to accomplish the desired end, namely, the retaining of the power to draw love mutually" (187).

A variant on the theme of love and sexuality as work is provided by The Voice of Experience, a popular radio advisor of the 1920s and early '30s whose advice was collected and published in 1932. The Voice differentiates in great detail between passion (sexual feeling) and love (a harder-to-define mixture of conventional virtues) and stresses that "For a marriage to be mutually happy and permanent, love must reign supreme and passion remain its obedient servant" (77). But although he does at one point say that readers must "Marry for Love" rather than for "convenience, preferment, for titles, for wealth, for fame," he sternly admonishes them not to marry "because of physical attraction" (188, 144). The predominant message of the book is not to marry because of "'falling in love,'" because marriage is not about pleasure; "it is a job" (173). This task must be undertaken because "man was made for woman and woman was made for man" (157). In each of these texts, and many others, because heterosexuality is taken to be a part of natural human life, some pleasurable sexual activity is assumed as a side effect of doing one's marital work. A combination of quiet familial love and the sufficient sexual gratification that will "naturally" result are expected to produce a marriage that eventually gives both partners profound contentment.

A rebelliously Freudian counterpoint to the promises of the early years of sex advice is provided by André Tridon's 1922 *Psychoanalysis and Love*, which attempts to counsel the marital pair while teaching them basic psychoanalytic concepts. He begins with an unqualified statement: "Love, like hunger, is an absolutely involuntary craving" (1). He informs us that we cannot hope to control our erotic feelings, because sexuality is never "a matter of free choice" but either "an organic compulsion" or "an unconscious mental compunction" (158). In contrast to Pearsall, this sophisticated Freudian believes "lasting love is a matter of fixation and fetishism" (87). Consequently, a couple can only hope to preserve monogamy if each tries to retain the qualities originally fetishized by the other (317). But Tridon tempers even this faint hope with his "pessimistic belief that there is no permanent solution for any human problems" (96). Married people can adjust to each other and their state with some degree of success, but only, in Tridon's view, if there is "democracy in the home" (325). He concludes the book by stating that without full economic independence for both partners there is no real partnership at all, only an endless angry battle for control. One might fantasize about what political changes might have ensued had official American marital advice followed this course. Unfortunately, the genre has much more typically offered us fantasies of a very different nature.[6]

Meryl Altman describes the sexual advice books of the late 1960s and 1970s as promoting the compensatory fantasy through which a conservative American culture more disturbed than dismantled by "the first stirrings of a desire for genuine sexual liberation and openness, conditioned by the beginnings of the second wave of feminism and of gay liberation," dealt with its "tremendous anxiety" through creation, and consumption, of "a new genre that could rechannel these energies into the mainstream

—the middle-class family—hiding its representation of contradictory possibilities behind the rhetoric of emancipation" (127). This new genre is a form of marriage manual that partially disguises its focus on marriage by codifying anything that might make marriage impossible as a sexual dysfunction that "must be eliminated or silenced in order to make the happy ending possible" (124–126). As Altman shows, some of the most famous sex guides and "studies" of the period, such as David Reuben's *Everything You Always Wanted to Know about Sex* (1969) and *Any Woman Can* (1971), Masters and Johnson's *The Pleasure Bond* (1970), the anonymously published *The Sensuous Woman* (1969) and *The Sensuous Man* (1971), and Alex Comfort's *The Joy of Sex* (1972) and *More Joy of Sex* (1972), have in common a "preoccupation with getting rid of 'problems' which can get in the way of 'normal' sexuality, always ultimately described as fairly traditional marital relations" (124). She claims that "the appearance of romantic love in these books . . . covers over the struggle of the narrative to reconcile the 'opening' of discourses about sex with a cultural ideology that focuses on normality and reproduction" (126). While I agree with Altman that the books do attempt to use references to romantic love in this way, the type of love they actually describe bears little resemblance to that emotion at its most intense and disorienting. Instead, love in the advice books of this genre, like sexual physiology in the earlier books, is reassuringly simplistic and easily controlled. It is summoned with a modicum of well-placed effort, in just the place where one wants and expects it, the marriage bed. Just like the male erection in the books of the earlier part of the century, which rises at a touch, the idea that love occurs when needed is naturalized so that it hardly seems possible that a couple who touched each other's bodies in the prescribed manner could not enjoy it.

That many readers recognize as a consoling fantasy the picture of marriage presented by self-help books does not stop readers from enjoying the books (Simonds 62). Instead, as Simonds suggests, the books have several features in common with the romance genre fiction that many women read compulsively. Altman notes that, like "mass market formula romances such as Harlequin and Silhouette," *The Sensuous Woman* and Helen Gurley Brown's *Sex and the Single Girl* depict a young woman whose "social manipulation" is rewarded by marriage (121). The books begin with a situation in which an insecure but basically superior woman (a stand-in for the reader) meets a difficult, selfish, and hard-to-understand man and becomes fascinated with him. Both romance and advice genres develop narratives of romantic interaction in which the woman is always well-meaning, although she makes many interesting mistakes, and the man is always elusive and deceptive. Often a contrastive male figure comes on the scene. The woman makes the right choice and lives happily ever after. As Simonds notes, readers of the marital self-help books receive a sense of "emotional release or compensation" analogous to that received by romance readers (46–48). Both genres valorize marriage as closure and as remedy for women's life problems, beginning from the premise that there is no real alternative.

They are marketed to women who either are in marriages that they do not want to end or are unmarried but unable to imagine a happy future not based on marriage. To the woman who lives in terror of her abusive husband or, less dramatically, the wife whose days are filled with boredom and disappointment, the advice genre offers the fantasy of transforming herself in such a way that her husband and marriage will be renewed. With their many recommendations that the reader think rather than feel or act, the books foster a dreamy quietism that occupies itself in making lists, concentrating on the positive, waiting and hoping. The books are, thus, not really about change in the ways they claim, but about adaptation to a situation that can be nearly unbearable for reasons not within the woman's control. This actual situation must be masked in order for the book to attain commercial success.

Theodore H. Van de Velde's *Ideal Marriage: Its Physiology and Technique* (1926), described by Altman as "the quintessential 'marriage manual'" (115), illustrates what Americans have preferred, through numerous reprintings, over the gloomy acceptance of an imperfect reality advocated by Freud and his popularizers like Tridon. Van de Velde begins, "I show you the way to Ideal Marriage." He acknowledges that "the honeymoon of rapture" is "all too short, and soon you decline into that morass of disillusion and depression," but do not despair because this is not how it was meant to be. "The bridal honeymoon should blossom into the perfect flower of ideal marriage" (3). This is fortunate because there is no alternative to marriage. "It offers the only—even though relative—security to the woman's love of love, and of *giving* in love," and to men "the best background for useful and efficient work" (3–4).

Unlike the advice texts of the 1990s, Van de Velde's book lists "a vigorous and harmonious sex life" as one of the "four cornerstones of the temple of love and happiness in marriage" (4). His conservatism causes him to consider the husband "the active partner and initiator" (100). This sex role bias makes him place almost all responsibility for female orgasms on the male. It is best, he decides, after brief consideration of other possibilities, that the wife move only slightly in "appreciation" during "coital friction" (160). During foreplay women may do a bit more, but not much. Men are directed to caress their wives' erogenous zones and to be gentle. The wife may touch the husband if she likes, to good effect. We are told that, if she is aroused, she will "invariably, almost automatically" try to touch his penis, and "he will be, by that time, in full erection, or if not, will become so, at her touch" (151). Van de Velde seems always supremely confident that with a bit of initial work to learn the body parts and their functions one can reasonably expect a natural progression to great pleasure. The connection between this confidence and the book's popularity is obvious. But the paradox of why what is so natural as to be "automatic" would have to be learned at all is not addressed.

In "The Sexual Relationship in Marriage" (1948; originally published in 1937), Frederick Harris sets out to explain this strange situation. Beginning with the claim that "what we receive from nature is a powerful and imperious organic impulse," Harris expresses perfect faith in "sex education" to integrate "this disturbing drive" harmoniously into "true partnership," so that "perfect mutuality shall be established" (97). Throughout the first three decades of the twentieth century, marital advice has consistently applauded itself for providing the basis of a discipline that leads to perfection. As always, honesty is part of the discipline. The couple must be "utterly frank with each other" (98). Nature, however, begins to be de-emphasized in the 1930s and, in secular as well as religious writings, more stress, in both senses of the word, falls on the exercise of strong mental control. Harris is leery of letting "nature show the way," pointing out that "the sexual behavior of the lower animals and of undeveloped races is more or less casual, largely self-centered, and quite probably violent." In contrast, civilized human couples treat sexual intercourse as "an artistic achievement and artistic achievements do not just happen" (99). There will be obstacles to perfect union, but they "are nearly all surmountable by patience and skill," and can be "readily removed by intelligence" (100). Like other art forms, sexual activity within marriage can be usefully inspired by Nature, but Nature unaided is more likely to cause problems than to resolve them. Only the mind can create marital sexual pleasure.

At this point one may be developing, as I did while researching this chapter, a profound sympathy with D. H. Lawrence's railings against "sex in the head" and willed attempts to love and desire in ways society judges appropriate. But the worst is still to come. Edward Parrish's *Sex and Love Problems* (1935) is a prototypical marital self-help book before its time in its firm reliance on the power of a specific combination of thought and Nature to overcome all sexual problems. Sensibly enough, considering his goal of making marriage a purely rational matter, Parrish begins by dismissing "romantic attachment" as a basis for marital choice (29). Readers are urged to base their choice on the other's dependability and suitability for a future role as a parent. That any couple who followed Parrish's advice would not be romantically in love, having married only for practical reasons, is not seen by him as likely to cause sexual problems. Instead sex inevitably becomes problematic because "a woman's nature is quite different from a man's."[7] A partial cure to women's usual sexual frustration is provided "when they become pregnant and the sex instinct, by Nature's magic, is transformed into feelings and thoughts of motherhood alone" (32). But that solution leaves the husband jealous of his own children. The only real answer, Parrish argues, is to turn from Nature to the library and attain "knowledge of the intricate organs of procreation, and with understanding of the psychology of sex, the marriage is likely to be a success, and the children which result from it healthy, happy citizens of the world" (33).

Parrish proceeds to offer a simple cure for a great number of sexual problems that have perplexed lesser minds. (My favorite is a regimen of hot and cold sitz baths for impotence.) Like Van de Velde, he raises the specters of sexual dysfunction and lack of affection between the married pair only to assert over and over that these problems can be easily overcome by common sense. Education and mental activity must lead one to Nature's proper way, as opposed to Nature's deceptive way. For example, through private meetings with two unhappy patients, he discovers that their tragic "infertility" is caused by the wife's refusal to have sex. The case is closed when he persuades the woman that "she had refused a natural condition" and that "marriage was in reality the legitimization of sexual relations, which when understood and practiced as Nature intended, could be beautiful and entirely above reproach" (77–78).

Parrish seems deeply troubled by homosexuality, calling it "the most threatening and prevalent general condition which holds forth in the by-ways of sex, but which also has possibilities for prevention and cure" (109–110). He finds hope in the idea that homosexuality is unlikely to be a person's natural condition, but is instead imposed by the behavior of others. In what may be the most curious sentence in the English language, he seeks to explain the circumstances that can make a homosexual out of a potentially "normal" but "gentle" youth: "In boyhood, perhaps in early manhood, and rarely in later life, he may turn to the society of persons who are actually addicted to homosexual traits and where secondary sex characteristics, such as gait or voice or dress, color the picture they present to the critical or the morbidly suspicious" (112). Such youths must be reminded that they "should never . . . turn their backs upon the natural habits of their sex" (112). And that should be enough. Parrish warns against belaboring the point. Obviously, we are in a world of what should be, where wishing, thinking, and believing make it so. But keep in mind those disruptive "persons who are actually addicted" to forms of sexuality and romance not consonant with the "art" of marriage, as they will return to trouble the dream of marital perfection in which Nature, under the control of reason, becomes handmaiden to practicality in order to decisively banish any possibility of sexual incompatibility.

Even this short examination of the advice on marriage produced in the early part of the twentieth century reveals some consistent trends. Monogamous marriage is always treated as a necessity to be preserved at all cost. This creates a background against which both love and Nature must be split. Nature appears in its beneficial manifestation when it urges us to marry. Those who do not feel inclined to marry—for example, homosexuals—can be shown that those all around them do feel this "natural" inclination and so, it is hoped, be persuaded to follow the same path. Nature's less socially beneficial aspect is shown in the desire to marry a person one finds attractive, and, in the worst cases, to keep sexual excitement alive by any means, including having sexual relations at will with that person or even with others. Now love must be split, as well, into good and bad. Good love can most concisely be defined as love that one finds it possible to discipline, control, and direct toward the goal of a happy (and socially advantageous) marriage. Bad love is anything that interferes with a happy marriage, including the impulse to marry physically attractive people who are not likely to be useful for anything but generating sexual excitement in the home. Since Nature is not yet all good, one can struggle with bad natural feelings and thus attain good love. Faith in the power of sex education and "frankness" to solve all problems of sexual incompatibility accompanies this neat division of Nature and the erotic.

Not one advice text I saw entertains the idea that communication about sex could ever *cause* problems. Starting from the assumption that husbands expect little but compliance and that wives are ignorant and fearful, the experts conclude that even slightly decreasing the husband's roughness and the wife's inhibitions will make both partners extremely, almost boundlessly happy. H. W. Long's *Sane Sex Life and Sane Sex Living* (1919) is typical of the genre in telling us that on occasions when for some reason a woman cannot allow her husband to have intercourse with her, "it would help the situation wonderfully if *she* would take his penis in *her* hand and 'play with it' till he spent. He would love her for it, kiss her for it, give her his soul for it!" (125; emphasis Long's).

By mid-century, it seems to have become impossible for writers to sustain this sort of optimism. Relatively uninhibited discussions of sexual experience, within marriage at least, featured prominently in popular publications. A sadder but wiser note began to sound fairly regularly in the advice genre. Such statements as these, from Joan Malleson's *Any Wife or Any Husband* (1951), are typical: "Readers who have themselves encountered sexual disappointments will realize that, although their own problems may not prove fully soluble, they have the opportunity to do better in handling and bringing up children" (11) and "orgasm is by no means possible for all women" (133). Here new fantasies take the place of the old. This is evident in Malleson's discussion of female orgasm, which briskly dismisses its importance to intimacy, love, or marital happiness. Bodies and psyches are vexing things, Malleson suggests, and we must make the best we can of our lives without too much unrealistic expectation. If we stop worrying about orgasm, we will find that we soon forget about it. Such books are consoling in a different way than are those that offer nothing but fantasies of lasting ecstasy and perfection easily attained, but they are likely to be less marketable. Other market forces than those governing book sales, however, are also at work.

As I began this chapter by pointing out, in America, as in all cultures with private property, marriage is traditionally expected to maintain, remediate, or increase the partners' social position and financial standing. It is a financial transaction. Consequently, advice on love may be as bracingly realistic as David Burns's textual shout, "There is a difference between wanting and needing something. Oxygen is a *need,* but love is a *want.* I repeat: LOVE IS NOT AN ADULT HUMAN NEED!" (284). But his patients may not be as wrong as he thinks to feel depressed by their position as solitary women. These particular women can "cope" independently, but as the credit card people remind us, Americans want more economically than mere survival.

Ironically, when birth control was so unreliable and employment and wage inequities between men and women so great that almost any woman who wanted to have a sex life had to marry in order to survive, marital advice texts had little to say about the need to make a financially advantageous match. A few cautions about not marrying "socially unsuitable" people suffice. One may assume that the near silence on this issue in early texts reflects the unquestioned ideological belief that men must support their wives and wives must care for their husband's goods, and that only one in a state of love-induced folly beyond the help of written advice would need to be told so.

Cultural changes in the middle of the twentieth century, including marked improvement in birth control technologies and the opening of numerous professions to women, meant that marriage was no longer an economic necessity—or NOT A NECESSITY! as Burns might remind his patients. The question was then raised, not only for the exasperated therapist to the "love-addicted," but for the general population, why marry? Once again we have recourse to Nature, because it certainly sounds better to say that one wants to marry because it is natural to do so than to say that one wants to marry so that one can get cheaper health care and afford a mortgage. Still, the question remains, what exactly is the place in marriage of Nature, transformed in the 1960s from a troublesome many-faced temptress to the only manifestation of absolute good on earth? How can we bring to our marriages the purity that is post-sixties Nature?

The answer is, of course, through naturalizing capitalist concerns. Because female readers will no longer begin with the assumption that they are faced with a choice between celibacy and marriage, sexuality must be reconceptualized. In the earlier splitting of love, "good" love could retain some of its erotic charge, although in a diminished, manageable form. This is also generally true in the advice genre through the mid-1980s. But as we move closer to the millennium, a change occurs throughout the genre. The move from the image of marital sex as an arena of communication so electrified with meaning that one genital caress can fix the most pernicious dysfunction to the view that sex has no real bearing on happiness is so great that we can expect it to be overdetermined. It is beyond the scope of this chapter, or this book, to account for every reason that sex came to be devalued as a part of marriage, at least in advice texts. However, one important explanation seems to be that when what was natural could no longer ever be understood as bad, sexual feelings had to be reimagined as unnatural within the context of marriage. Thus we return to Pearsall's (and many other authors') odd pronouncements about the fortuitousness of the ebbing of desire experienced by most married couples. When the troublesome, hard-to-manage desire for sex diminishes, the reasoning goes, one can better see what really matters: security and permanence. And, as the advice books of the late 1980s and the 1990s insistently remind us, these terms pertain to money.

In analyzing the 1960s and '70s sex manuals inspired by Masters and Johnson, Simonds observes that they are deeply entrenched in capitalist ideology in that they "draw on the concurrent popular psychology: sex is an exchange, in which man and woman attempt to have their respective 'needs met'" (157).[8] This observation is particularly provocative when compared with her insight that feminism has been fundamental to the development of the contemporary self-help genre, to the extent that Betty Friedan's The Feminine Mystique can be analyzed as the first of "the recent spate of self-help books for women" (181). Feminism's exposure of the marital exchange between man and woman as a mask for a system in which men maintained patriarchal power through exchange of women has had and continues to have repercussions among socially conservative women, as well as among avowed feminists. It is the norm for women of all political persuasions writing in the late twentieth century on sex and love to claim that without male recognition of our subjectivity, sexual pleasure is impossible for women. Sexual objectification is considered insulting by almost all women writing in any genre, with the exception of a few sex radicals.

In an essay on the Canadian legal system's persecution of homosexuals, one such radical, Shannon Bell, characterizes as "liberal fascism" the movement by "'helping' professionals" to protect certain populations, like women and teenage boys, from their own putative "false consciousness," which leads them to think that they enjoy amorous encounters that involve a power imbalance and do not enhance their social status (302–305). While one need not go so far as to deem "fascist" theories that begin from the premise that erotic feeling must have a specific bourgeois use value in order to deserve recognition as authentic love, it is worth pointing out that, like the liberal fascism that discounts socially designated victims' accounts of their own experience, current discourses of love are, in Bell's words, "univocal reflections of a moral economy of equivalence" within which dissent cannot be heard as such (304). Moreover, they partake, although usually in a more genuinely sympathetic mode, in the continuation of that nineteenth-century project identified by Foucault as "the inter-weaving, the intrication of two great technologies of power: one which fabricated sexuality and the other which segregated madness" (*Power/Knowledge* 185). It is easy to see in these discourses a long-deferred heritage of the Enlightenment: Do we persist in loving without reason? Outside of reason? Then truly we must need help, for we are mad.

While feminists dissatisfied with heterosex and unafraid of being seen as mad-women may choose radical lifestyle changes, such as lesbian separatism, in response to discovering that where they expected to find a mutual exchange of pleasures they are simply being used as if they were objects, women without any commitment to political change may decide to make the best of their situation as objects and embrace commodification. Despairing of gratification of their sexual needs, these women become determined to get financial benefits out of intercourse with men. The marital advice genre tells women that the desire to profit from exchanges with others is perfectly natural. Only a woman with no self-esteem, we are repeatedly told, would give without wanting to receive in return. The books set out to help women understand how to remake themselves not into objects that will be used and discarded but rather into rare commodities to be treasured and paid for. Among Simonds's most disturbing conclusions, all the more so because it is so well justified, is: "Self-help teaches women marketing strategies to use on ourselves" (223).

Connell Cowan and Melvyn Kinder's *Smart Women/Foolish Choices: Finding the Right Men and Avoiding the Wrong Ones* (1985) is a transitional text that exemplifies the hardheaded approach that will come to dominate marriage and courtship advice as the century wanes. It is in some ways reminiscent of *Moll Flanders,* although by no means as entertaining. Like Defoe's novel it presents us with a bizarre combination of feminist, or at least pro-woman, statements and a doctrine of accommodation to a world in which males have all the economic advantages and real power. Cowan and Kinder use Carol Gilligan's *In a Different Voice* as a basis for their theory that "most women, despite dramatic contemporary changes in conscious attitudes and behaviors, continue to view independence as uncomfortable and anxiety producing." Cowan and Kinder credit second-wave feminism with giving women "a sense of options and a clearer vision of their worth and potential" and "believe that a new era is now emerging for both men and women" as a result. But this new era is not one in which independence will be among the smart woman's options, since she will realize that autonomy "too frequently pays off in loneliness, economic woes, and regret" (17). "Career," we are told, is not enough for "self-realization" (18). At least, *one* career is not.[9]

As in *Moll Flanders,* the ambitious wench encounters an annoying shortage of men. Cowan and Kinder estimate that "80 per cent of the single women are interested in 20 per cent of the available men," a problem caused by women's focus on "men who are both materially successful and have attractive personalities" (146). "Most women want a man whose earning power is greater than theirs" (148), and naturally enough, since men are supposedly easily reduced to "the new impotency" by women who threaten them by being too aggressive or too financially successful (70–82). Cowan and Kinder warn that although some couples may believe that they prefer a female-dominant relationship, men can only (unconsciously) understand this as a return to childhood, and "boys resent their mothers" (82), so such relations will always fail. In contrast, "ordinarily, there exists a natural healthy affinity between girls and their fathers," so this is clearly the relationship to replicate in later life (19). As a result of their need for men who can play the role of good, financially supportive fathers, "smart women need to become more realistic in their expectations if they want to form close long-term relationships with men" (146–147).

Realism here is defined just as it is by Moll. A checklist for assessing potential mates at the back of the book lists three choices under "Income": "a. Under $30,000; b. $30,000 to $60,000; c. Over $60,000." Throughout the checklist choices listed under "a" seem patently undesirable. Given that $30,000 was a substantial middle-class family income in 1985, the list suggests that unless men are more affluent than the economic norm, they are not serious objects of romantic attachment, not even, apparently, for a woman who makes the minimum wage.

If women are to be so uncompromising about income, where are they to make realistic compromises? As might have been expected, women must school themselves to respond to men they consider "boring," an adjective repeated frequently in the text to designate the "smart" choice. In a chapter called "How Exciting Men Can Make Women Miserable," Cowan and Kinder warn women not to "lose interest if there is no dynamic tension, no excitement or mystery" (87). We must not "expect to feel intense and wonderful emotions" or to experience "a sense of aliveness that is totally different from our usual state of mind" (98). Cowan and Kinder define "genuine love" as devoid of excitement and longing; rather, it is characterized by feelings of both boredom and security (102). Case histories "prove" that women who choose economically successful but dull men are the winners (208–218). Not surprisingly, the book says almost nothing about sex or sexual pleasure, except to caution readers against "love addiction." This condition is defined as a failure to enjoy "the simple elements relationships can realistically provide" and, instead, a longing for "romantic encounters" (169). "Love addiction differs from normal, healthy desire when the accompanying feelings are greatly exaggerated, distorted, and fleeting" (170).

And so the need to affirm the natural and healthy life, according to the new valuation of Nature, brings us to a tautology in which genuine love is lasting love, and lasting love is recognizable because it lasts. If a feeling diminishes, it was not real in the first place, and since all emotion is transient, it seems best to feel nothing at all. The sophistication that causes Millamant in Congreve's *The Way of the World* to include in her verbal prenuptial contract with Mirable a proviso for the time when their passion would diminish is exposed as the pseudo-sophistication of a young girl. If she had really understood love, as do Cowan and Kinder, she would have known that "genuine love" is a state always indistinguishable from indifference. Because it is experienced as ennui from the beginning, it has nowhere to go. In the last decade of the twentieth century this peculiar ethos dominates the advice genre, with "love addiction" playing an increasingly important role as the repository of feelings that cannot otherwise be integrated into the scheme (Simonds 117–118, 208–211).

Denis Boyles's jocular book, *The Modern Man's Guide to Modern Women* (1993), adopts the hearty, no-nonsense tone of the older brother trying to awaken a foolishly fond boy to reality. Love is repeatedly described in terms like "your inebriated, druglike state" (36), presumably in an attempt to win the confidence of a youth who "knows better" but cannot help being swept away by the strength of his feelings. He must be brought into a state of cynical awareness because "women are Darwinists: they *despise* weakness in men. Women want you to be strong like Dad" (44). Men are warned also that this translates into an expectation of financial success. In an era when most families require two incomes to sustain the standard of living usually called middle-class, Boyles tells us that "A man's job is often the most attractive thing about him" (49), and "Some things will never change, and this is one: A man's job is to earn his own keep and provide for those he loves. If he fails at this he succeeds at nothing" (43). And least of all marriage, because "*the best women aren't terribly sentimental about this marriage business* (109; emphasis Boyles's). Permanent marriages begin when a woman "browses for a husband with all the wild abandon of a spinster buying sensible shoes made to last" (109). Beyond the addictive state that characterizes immature relations with women is the safe harbor of parenthood attainable after a man grows up and realizes that his first priority should be to "marry a woman who wants to be a good mother" (96).

The shadow narrative here seems to be the much told story of American soft drug use.[10] Judging by our national attitudes about the exposure of soft drug "experimentation" by public officials in their youth, it seems that these substances are generally understood to be played with by people in their late teens or early twenties at parties and on dates. We expect virtuous people to outgrow such behavior when they get serious about their careers and relationships, and in no cases are we so unforgiving as when the drug user has children. Twelve-step program tests for substance addiction usually include questions about the impact of the substance's use on work and family. In the popular media, people are considered addicted to substances that are considered safe in moderate doses (like alcohol) not so much when they begin to consume much larger quantities, but when they can no longer play their social roles as expected. Similarly, sexual excitement and the soaring emotions accompanying romantic love are acceptable in the young as an interim phase on the way to mature enactment of prescribed roles.[11] Here we can also see the return of those "persons who are actually addicted to homosexual traits," in whose society the young may pass some entertaining hours before the intervention of "the critical or the morbidly suspicious" brings them to their senses. But to their senses they must come.

Narratives of addiction spill over into narratives of madness, just as all rejections of what is deemed the correct role within capitalism are automatically coded as outside sanity. In *Beyond Cinderella: How to Find and Marry the Man You Want*, Nita Tucker confirms Boyles's view of women by comparing a woman's search for a mate to shopping for a house or car. Tucker claims it is a practical project that should be approached in a rational, systematic way. In this book, as in *Glengarry Glen Ross,* one must "always be closing." Emotions that do not lead to closing the deal, the only action with reality status in this system, are unreal, hence "One of the things that throws many women off is 'chemistry'" (57). Tucker admits that this sort of physical response to men "has its place in life" as an inspiration for songs and a marketing device for perfume, but she insistently reminds us that it is neither practical nor reasonable. Two of the other mistakes one might make are "expect[ing] the relationship to turn you on, to provide the excitement that's missing in your life" (99) and putting the beloved "on a pedestal and get[ing] obsessed with [him] (104). Here, as Foucault could have pointed out, Tucker's thought could hardly be more traditional, for in his view passion has been considered since the eighteenth century not "simply one of the causes—however powerful—of madness [but] rather . . . the basis for its very possibility" (*Madness and Civilization* 88). One of the signal characteristics of madness, thus understood, is the refusal to understand an image, such as the loveliness of the other, as something to be judged, measured, and ultimately transcended; instead, one "surrenders to its immediacy" (94). To lose oneself in the other becomes a sign of having lost connection to the dyad of society and sanity.

Because erotic feeling is unpredictable and extremely disruptive, the best way to manage it is scrupulously to avoid any opportunity for its arousal. The advice books of the 1990s treat passion the way drug prevention programs treat crack cocaine. They constantly warn their readers not to try even the tiniest taste, lest they become hopelessly addicted. "America's Premier Matchmakers" (self-described) John and Julie Wingo, in *At Long Last Love: How to Find the Best Relationship of Your Life* (1994), initially seem less terrified of erotic excitement than most. They claim that although "the 'high' of romance doesn't last," one can regard this as "an opportunity—because it's *after* romance that two people really start learning how to help and support each other" (8). But how much better, they soon suggest, never to experience that delusional state. To that end, women are told to get over "our cultural focus on appearances" and stop "Looking for Mr. Goodlooks" (25). Although the advice that "people reorder their priorities and learn to look for what counts over the long term" is initially presented as gender-neutral, the Wingos find themselves "often in the unpleasant position of telling women who are in the upper reaches of their medically approved weight range that they're probably a little too heavy to be attractive to most men" (26). While men can have "a little paunch," women "need to be on the thin side" (56). If marriage is a buyer's market, we can see who the buyers are. This makes sense when one considers that "Most women want a man who has enough on the ball to be fiscally responsible and on his way to making something of himself"; "there's nothing wrong with expecting a mature man to have a reasonable degree of financial security and responsibility" (71). In fact, because it is "natural" for women to want children and a "nice" home, the primary aim of women's lives is likely to be finding a mate with whom they can "build a solid financial foundation together" (172). The Wingos have almost nothing to say about sex except to recommend waiting at least "a couple of months" before the first encounter (156).

Here, as throughout millennial writings on sex and love, the concept of love addiction helps to differentiate between good and bad love. In good love we emulate the approved roles in a consumer culture. We remake ourselves as desirable products; we secure the job of marriage, and go cheerfully and sensibly to work. Bad love is uncontrolled consumption. Whereas in the early part of the century advice writers warned the highly sexed not to overwhelm their partners with bestial behavior, in the age of Nature's perfection we are forced to consider a high sex drive unnatural, like drug addiction and not unlike runaway consumerism. As Simonds says, "Addiction presents a convincing image of our problems because it recognizes the salience of disguised yet uncontrollable consumption in American culture" (225). Plump women figure, in every sense, this out-of-control consumption, as well as the nightmare reversal in which the object-to-be-consumed takes on the agency of the consumer. Therefore, even in books like Boyles's that recognize the interest most men continue to show in curvy bodies, or, as he puts it, in "giant breasts" (49) and "puffy, rounded edges," men are sternly told to seek "lithe, sleek" women who will wear well (96).

Simonds sadly summarizes her findings: "Self-help books tell us about relationships based on commerce. Underneath, though, is this thing called love that we pretend (and self-help helps us to continue to pretend) can be unaffected by a culture based on consumerism" (226). Perhaps the mournfulness of her tone would have deepened had Simonds known what was coming when the pretense fell away, as it does in the advice genre around 1995. Two books from that year, one a huge success and the other a rather obscure self-published venture, illustrate just how commercial an arrangement advice writers and their audiences are willing to deem marriage.

To start with the most obvious, Alan Schlossberg's *Marriage: This Time Will Be Perfect!* begins with an appeal to the dual American dreams of perfectibility and permanence, not just in the title, but in the first lines: "YES, IT'S POSSIBLE! YOU CAN ENJOY A PERFECT—OR NEARLY PERFECT—MARRIAGE WITH ONE PERSON. FOREVER!" (1). Schlossberg believes his credentials "as an MBA . . . and as a business student and analyst" make him the ideal marital advisor because, as he tells us in boldface print: "many ingredients that make a solid business merger also make a strong marriage" (4). His book reads like a two-hundred-and-twenty-page prenuptial contract in that it consists mainly of a series of questions to ask prospective spouses. Beginning with questions about preferred room temperatures, his book would be perfect, indeed, for choosing a roommate, and it seems predicated on the idea that his readers find spouses necessary for the same reason that people generally seek a roommate: because they cannot make it alone financially.

In answer to the question he imagines coming from his readers, "Isn't marriage supposed to be based on LOVE?" he responds, "money—or the potential to earn it—is extremely important for the growth and development of a successful marriage." His explanation is worth quoting in full. "Many women, and men too, may use the words 'security,' 'support,' or 'being taken care of' as phrases describing the ideal marriage relationship. They're not talking only about mental and emotional support; the word 'security' in English also means money" (35). A visual aid fills the next page, images of a hundred-, a fifty-, and a twenty-dollar bill. A quotation from Dr. Joyce Brothers on the book's front cover sums up his view: "This is what dating is about."

Some chapters of the book group two issues together. One can see how far the advice genre has come, from the naturalization of (hetero)sex to the naturalization of capitalism, when we note that "Money and Health" are grouped together. Although we are warned that "An unfulfilled sex life can cause serious problems, eventually leading to a bitter separation or divorce," sex is relegated to sharing a chapter with "children" and receives much less detailed attention than money (23). Readers are only told that they may want to ask a potential partner about masturbation and oral sex, as "these items are important to between thirty and fifty percent of married and single people" (24).

Nor, despite its rosebuds-and-ribbons romantic pink cover, is love as the poets have described it particularly relevant to the definitive dating manual of the 1990s, *The Rules,* by Ellen Fein and Sherrie Schneider. This book purports to be a remedy for the overly practical approach to courtship and marriage that the authors, correctly, find typical of our times. At the onset, "real lasting marriage" is distinguished from "loveless mergers" and readers are reassured that "*The Rules* are not about getting just any man to adore you and propose; they're about getting the man of your dreams to marry you" (3, 8–9). Soon, however, readers are being cautioned that "for long-lasting results we believe in treating dating like a job" (55) and being asked to seriously consider whether they can settle for "someone who doesn't live up to his earning potential" (92). By the end of the book, it develops that "the kind of men who once nauseated you . . . you now find attractive and desirable," and where once you felt boredom, you now feel love, because "you love with your head, not just your heart" (160–161). Once love was about sex and excitement; now it is about sexual "self-restraint" (81): "rules girls . . . don't initiate sex" (84); "You have high self-esteem because you are not sleeping around" (160). Because the "rules girl" has learned that "in a relationship, the man must take charge" (9) and that her only power is attained through flirtatious evasion of a man's "biologically" determined pursuit (127), she comes to understand that love is only meaningful when it is the road to marriage, and satisfying marriage means both financial security and the confidence that comes from being the object of someone else's obsession. Under the benefits conferred by following "The Rules" the authors list: "He gets angry when you don't pay attention to him. He wants your constant attention and companionship. . . . He's always walking into whatever room you're in" (157). The "rules girl" is not simply an object, she is a "product," as chapter 4 begins by reminding the reader (115). To be desired and purchased, to be owned and jealously guarded, these are the pleasures marriage offers women. The authors tell discontented wives, "Practice being happy with what you get instead of expecting him to fulfill your every romantic fantasy" (165). Natural, healthy, sane, and sensible love doth so!

The subtitle of the book, *Time-Tested Secrets,* and the constant references to the problems "feminists," "modern women," and "educated girls" may have following "The Rules" frame this advice as a corrective to contemporary views by returning to a fantasy collapsed past, a fusion of the Victorian era and the 1950s, in which women were able to act "serene and unselfish" because men took responsibility for everything (164). But like most of the ideas in this book, its self-presentation as a return to traditional values is slightly skewed. *The Rules'* biologizing and naturalizing of deliberately manipulative behavior in romantic matters reverses the trend since the nineteenth century toward an ethos of authenticity in love. This book is a good index of the extent of the change that the elevation of the natural wrought in the confessional aspect of the disciplining of love and sexuality. Because of *The Rules'* insistence that man is inherently the sexual hunter and woman the natural object of his hunt, and its added, but crucial, argument that as a consequence it is natural for woman to manipulate and deceive men who approach her, the text exposes the growing rift between openness and Nature. The importance of being earnest, mocked as empty ideology by Oscar Wilde at the end of the nineteenth century, seems retired as a component of virtue, perhaps worn out by the 1960s. At long last artifice and Nature blend, as it becomes most natural to be unnatural.

An interesting comparison between twentieth-century trends in the advice genre and in art products is suggested by Stephen Kern's *The Culture of Love.* Kern both exemplifies and analyzes a contemporary valorization of twentieth-century literature and visual arts above those of the Victorian period. He considers the former "more authentic" in their representations of love. He even goes so far as to claim that "between the Victorian and the modern period love became more authentic as men and women came to reflect more profoundly on what it means *to be in love*" (1; emphasis Kern's). Some affinity between these views and those in the marital advice of the first half of the century is apparent, even though Kern observes that "in comparison with Victorian novelists, Modernists reflect more on the deficiencies of marriage as an institution" (354). Many of the earlier advice writers might agree with Kern that "Modernists were scornful of the ritualized institution of marriage they inherited from the Victorians. Ritual is inauthentic because it determines courses of action, even ways of feeling, without requiring the personal reflection about meaning essential for authentic loving" (371). Although the Modernist novels Kern praises often depict marriage in ways more bleak than the early-twentieth-century advice writers do, surely most of these writers would like his emphasis on the necessity of thinking about one's feelings and also his demand that authenticity fill the conventional forms, or rituals, with appropriate, matching meaning. Like Kern's book, and like most of the Modernist works he describes, the advice genre expresses faith both that we can know what is natural, or authentic, and that this knowledge will improve our lives.

Kern's attitude, along with those of most of the twentieth-century authors and artists he discusses, departs from that generally espoused by the advice writers in two ways: first, in considering expression of sexual feeling more meritorious as well as more natural than repressive self-discipline, and second, in considering marriage as a situation that one need not always attempt to preserve. *The Culture of Love* presents a picture of what changed and why in American views of marriage[12] that might be summed up thus: if we insist that unfettered sexual and amorous expression is natural and that what is natural is good, then we must allow that many marriages, or monogamy within them, should be considered temporary arrangements. That Kern finds the pervasive acceptance of impermanence in love one of the most laudable qualities of Modernist art illustrates this point. Because the advice genre cannot celebrate marital impermanence, the realities of sexual liberation, in the forms of the possibility of safer sex outside marriage and also of heteronormativity and much easier access to divorce, necessitated a radical revision in the traditional equation of authenticity and the natural.

Still, a whole subgenre of relationship advice does take into account that some relationships fail. *Coming Apart: Why Relationships End and How to Live through the Ending of Yours* by Daphne Rose Kingma explains how to reject the unreasonable and unnatural impulses that may arise in such situations. Step away from that ledge; there is no need for despair as long as you realize you can do better next time simply by facing truth. One must begin by "Exploding the Love Myths" to discover "Why Are We Really in Relationships." The most pernicious myth, we are immediately told, is that love "will conquer all," when in reality love is not an end in itself (17). On the contrary, "The reason we fall in love is to help us accomplish our external and internal developmental tasks" (18). At those times when we feel, like Heathcliff bereft of Cathy, that "the entire world is a dreadful collection of memoranda that she did exist, and that I have lost her!" (Brontë 255), we must remind ourselves that, as Kingma says, "the reason [relationships'] endings are so important is not just that when they are over we miss the company: it is because through them we undertake the process of bringing ourselves into being" (36). The reward for recognizing that the pernicious attachment that made his name the most magical word in the world to you is simply a means for accomplishing developmental tasks is that then "you can choose someone who is a more appropriate partner for you, both in terms of your emotional preference, goals and values, and your growing edge as a person" (162–163). These values persist not only in the advice genre texts but, in an often only slightly different form, within the descriptions of love generated by feminist theory.

What is perhaps more surprising than the dismissal of romantic heterosexual love as a sort of false consciousness by lesbian and heterosexual theorists alike is the continual recourse to an underlying standard of reciprocity as the test of love's truth. This is exemplified by Teresa de Lauretis's discussion, in *The Practice of Love,* of lesbianism's fantasy function for all women as a place where they can desire as subjects and consider satisfaction possible, as opposed to being "confined in the patriarchal frame of 'a heterosexual love story'" (156–157). De Lauretis's overview of the role that "lesbianism performs, within feminist theory and vis-à-vis the question of female subjectivity and desire" (156), suggests that women's objectification within culture automatically means to many feminists that women cannot conceive of themselves as lovers except of other women. A corollary idea implicit here is that in the absence of full reciprocation love cannot be experienced. Although far less crudely than in most of the popular relationship advice genre, here too love becomes a matter of exchange.

Object relations theories within feminism, no matter how sophisticated otherwise, are also in accord with advice columns in stressing that reciprocity is the measure of "real" love, as is evidenced by Jessica Benjamin's argument throughout *The Bonds of*

Love that idealization of the other, often taking the form of a belief that the other can make or unmake our happiness, is mere "fantasy" standing in the way of the realistic and sober "mutual recognition" that is everyone's true desire (224). In another analytic vein, Julia Kristeva's *Tales of Love* focuses on Romeo and Juliet as the exemplary couple and, coming close to Friar Laurence's exhortation to "love moderately" (2.6.14), not only concludes that the unreasonable intensity of their passion marks their love as ephemeral, but also claims that in such situations "analysis sets out to be the lucid wakening of lovers" (233). The very structure of the book, with its alarming case histories interwoven into theorizing about passion, suggests that love is a form of dementia from which we must be rescued to survive. And Kristeva's conclusion, although beautifully phrased, rather distressingly echoes that of Kingma's book in that it asserts the value of love as "a true process of self-organization" (381).

Once we get ourselves organized, it is to be hoped that there will be no more of this nonsense about the irreplaceability of some mere man. This confidence in the mind's ability to consciously reorient physical desire is echoed in writings by a large number of feminist theorists. Katie King points out that Alix Dobkin's claim, on her album *Lavender Jane Loves Women,* that "'any woman can be a lesbian' . . . is an important assumption in the women's movement" (134). King argues that the availability of this option to all women enables a new kind of radicalism (134–135). Here political radicalism itself depends on one's belief in both the possibility and the desirability of thinking oneself into a new sexual orientation. Yet this stance seems to deny the motivations of millions of women who have defied all dangers to come out as lesbians, not because it was a politically useful move, but because they were swayed by passions they experienced as irrepressible. Once again Eros becomes something to control, lest it control you.

Most of my readers are probably well aware that since the 1960s another strand of sexual advice has become available outside of the pornographic underground. The radical sex counterculture has produced a vast array of books that do not urge their readers to work on marriage or to avoid passion but that concentrate instead on instructions for attaining the most intense sexual pleasure possible. Some writers in this genre, such as Nancy Friday and Susie Bright, alternate writing erotica and advice, or combine the two in the same collections. Others, such as Cynthia Heimel, parody the relationship advice genre while still offering tips apparently intended to comfort and even help the lovelorn. Advice seekers who care more about pleasure than productivity and status can also consult hip columns written by "sexperts" from Pat Califia, the originator of the term, to Dan Savage. However, because this particular millennial trend has taken form in reaction to much, although not all, of the reasoning governing the mainstream American marital advice genre discussed in this chapter, it has more relevance to the new concepts of sexuality and gender emerging in youth cultures, which I will address in the second section of the book.

Because the traditional good/bad dichotomy in romantic matters has opposed sexual and loving feeling, the increasing hostility toward love in the American advice genre may seem rather strange. Clearly, unrestrained sexual feeling can disrupt monogamy, but one might wonder why these late-twentieth-century authors do not stress more heavily, as nineteenth-century writers tend to do, the saving grace that powerful feelings of attachment can provide to men or women who feel tempted to stray from their mates. Advice such as is given in *The Rules* or *The Ten Laws of Lasting Love* to will one's self to care for an appropriate person in a specific way, or at least to act as if one felt that way, in faith that loving feelings will come eventually, seems substantially different than the traditional call to follow one's heart, as opposed to one's genitalia, in romantic matters. As I hope my sketch of the advice genre in this chapter has demonstrated, mainstream love has become a cold business, with the emphasis on business. Is this simply because the advice texts I have considered here usually conflate desire and attachment to create a picture of love as a kind of addictive, obsessional madness? Or is love in any form now considered essentially incompatible with the aim of making the most of marriage socially and financially?

While some of the twentieth-century advice genre authors I have discussed here might admit to a certain practicality that could be interpreted as coldness, it seems obvious that all would indignantly reject my description of their work as illogical. All the texts discussed insist upon their own rationality, and even take pride in their advocacy of reason. It is within a specific construction of rationality, which emerges in these texts, that the most conservative advice writers and many feminist critics seem to find some common ground. In the next chapter, by examining both some representations of transgressive love and forbidden gender identifications in late-twentieth-century films and the politics of critical reception of these representations, I will look for answers to the question of how changes in perceptions of the erotic in twentieth-century culture may affect my generation's ability to read narratives of love that do not valorize its translation into practical domesticity and that, consequently, do not affirm our own anxiously and tenuously held values, whether we construe these values as "family" or "feminist."

HORIZON VISIONS AND UNCHAINED MELODIES

In the previous chapter, through consideration of the love advice Americans have been receiving over the last century, I tried to suggest why generalizations about erotic experience still remain areas of intense anxiety within feminism as well as within the culture as a whole, even while they often appear to be accepted as truth by all but the most radical. By discussing how artifice was rewritten as naturalness, how love came to mean exchange, and how passion came to signify the absence of love, I have tried to unmask some of the dangerous nonsense that is now generally read as common sense. Here I take my cue from Emily Dickinson's "Much Madness is Divinest Sense," with its central claim that what "the Majority" consider "the starkest Madness" can appear otherwise to "a discerning Eye," and try to look oppositely at films taken by the general public, and by many feminists, to be dangerous nonsense, but which, as I will attempt to illustrate, might illuminatingly be read as "divinest sense."

Dickinson's poem resonates with contemporary theory in complex ways. In the glory days of second-wave feminism, English studies often seemed exhilaratingly "Girls Against Boys," as a male Punk band sarcastically styles itself. A generation of feminist readers schooled by Gilbert and Gubar's *The Madwoman in the Attic* to look for truths told slant in women's writings read the poem as describing minoritized female authorship pitted against hegemonic patriarchy. Gilbert and Gubar end their study of female traditions with Dickinson, their discussion of this poem coming in the penultimate paragraph (648). Her "life a loaded gun," all right, and we knew at which 49 percent of the population it was pointed.[1]

In fact, during my last two years of graduate school I lived in El Cerrito, California, near a gun shop that had an enormous model pistol on its roof. My visitors often cracked jokes about Dickinson's poem, typically involving the concept of gender war. Now things have changed, in part because, as Jane Gallop ruefully notes in *Feminist Accused of Sexual Harassment,* feminists often target as their enemy the expression of sexuality (11–12). In the atmosphere from which Gilbert and Gubar's first collaborative book emerged, woman seemed clearly placed by culture on the side of madness, and man on the side of crushingly mundane sanity.[2] In the current atmosphere, where not only sexuality but also passionate erotic love can scarcely be conceptualized except as deviant to the point of criminal insanity, it is harder to tease a feminist political stance out of the poem.

One might begin such a project by comparing Dickinson's rather explicit warning against attempting to express the "divinest sense" of madness to Foucault's discussion of the function of art as a medium for just this sort of expression. As he points out, the science of the mind has failed in its project of reading unreason. He claims, "psychoanalysis has not been able, will not be able, to hear the voices of unreason, nor to decipher in themselves the signs of the madman" (*Madness and Civilization* 278). Managing instead only to overwrite the voices of unreason with another discourse, psychoanalysis "remains a stranger to the sovereign enterprise of unreason. It can neither liberate nor transcribe, nor most certainly explain, what is essential in this enterprise." In contrast, art has a more literally productive relation to madness. "Madness is the absolute break with the work of art; it forms the constitutive moment of abolition, which dissolves in time the truth of the work of art; it draws the exterior edge, the line of dissolution, the contour against the void" (*Madness and Civilization* 287). Thus:

> through madness, a work that seems to drown in the world, to reveal there its nonsense, and to transfigure itself with the features of pathology alone, actually engages within itself the world's time, masters it, and leads it; by the madness that interrupts it, a work of art opens a void, a moment of silence, a question without answer, provokes a breach without reconciliation where the world is forced to question itself. (288)

Dickinson's poem opens precisely such a void. In cautioning readers that any dizzying flight from the world's standards of sense will cause them to be "handled with a Chain," she forces the world to question itself. Because the poem does not speak what is forbidden, because the divinest sense of the unconventional mind remains unspoken, we are left with a silence that communicates resistance. If we still imagine the status quo to be disadvantageous to women, and it seems to me that even the most extreme post- and anti-feminists do not go so far as to say that we are currently inhabiting the best of all possible worlds for women, then calling the social order of things into question can be considered a feminist act in itself. At the very least, to ask why the majority are allowed to render the minority silenced and enslaved still opens a space for women to speak in our own interests.

In this chapter, I am moving toward a description of the ineffable sweetness of some of youth cultures' still unheard melodies (unheard, at least, in the mainstream of academe), through looking first at the moment when revolutionary questions are raised, if not answered, in film. I turn to film because the performative blending of visual and aural media, which the last section of the book focuses on, creates conditions in which third-wave feminism's resistance to binary gender difference may be most fully realized. The central question in this chapter is, how does gender difference actually appear at the horizon, where we see a blending of what is usually defined through contrast (earth and sky, figure and ground) and understood as easily perceptually separable? What happens to gender difference where the shapes and perspectives customarily imposed by our culture are all falling away? And why does this falling away of binary difference seem so difficult for critics to recognize?

Cultures provide what I am calling horizon visions in places where it becomes nearly impossible to distinguish between things usually conceptualized as binary opposites: where, for instance, as in the cases of a number of recent films, some critics see especially vicious sexism in the same places others see sites of feminist pleasure. Some critics see homoeroticism where others see homophobia. If some sort of madness is contained, enchained, in these images and through the narratives in which they are embedded, what else slips the chain?

Preliminary to attempting to describe what escapes, it is necessary to look at the chain itself and at society's mechanisms for desire's enchainment. Following Foucault's genealogical method, we must determine what is bound up into systems of meaning, for it has much to tell us about what remains under the label of unreason, unexplained and thus unbound. Because of the academic world's increasingly tight enmeshment of feminist interests with gay and lesbian interests, I will begin by looking at an end-of-the-twentieth-century development in homophobia that attempts much more ambitiously and pervasively than the medico-juridical discourses at the end of the last century to put the resistant "unreason" of homosexuality into a discourse that is logical, as defined by the logic of managed sexuality and domesticated love.

On Valentine's Day, 1999, I received a telephone call from a distraught friend in San Francisco. He had just been asked by his two-year-old son, "Daddy, why is Tinky Winky bad?" I flicked on the television to hear a CNN discussion of Jerry Falwell's alleged condemnation of the Teletubby. Like most parents of my acquaintance, my friend had hoped to wait until his son was quite a bit older to explain sex to him. For the entire preceding year televised debates over the details of the President's consensual affair with another adult had forced American parents to explain the difference between oral and vaginal sex to their children. Now a religious group's anxiety about the sexual orientation of a fantasy character on a program aimed at toddlers forced my friend to discuss homosexuality with a two-year-old. How did we get here? Why does conservatism now increasingly mean introducing small children to graphic details of sexuality?

The previous chapter considered not only changes in American concepts of love, but also a late-twentieth-century response to social and cultural structuring of the erotic that I call heterophobia. Heterophobia is an understanding of erotic love that leads either to a binary opposition between "good" familial feeling and "bad" lust, or, in more sophisticated minds, to a binarity in which the feelings compatible with domestic life are associated with reason while to the extent to which passion and romance move to realization outside domestic enclosure, they are associated with madness and disavowal of reality. Once such a system of analysis has been established, not only will types of heterosexuality be placed in a hierarchy, but inevitably heterosexuality and homosexuality will also be ranked according to how amenable they are to discipline. Within this system homosexuality will almost always be ranked below heterosexuality as less easily disciplined, more resistant to the logic that transmutes emotion and sensation into reason. Thus the dyad heterophobia/homophobia calls into question the commonplace that hostility toward homosexuality is the natural result of an excess of heterosexual feeling, and also the corollary idea that distaste for heterosexual passion reveals a closeted inclination toward homosexuality. It would seem that, instead, those who find the wilder manifestations of heterosexuality disturbing are often even more unsettled by homosexuality.

The early years of the century's last decade featured what one might call the return of the repulsive on a number of fronts in the ongoing battle against homophobia. 1992 was a year of organized political backlashes against gay and lesbian rights legislation. No sooner was one anti-gay ballot measure defeated than several more popped up to take its place. In many parts of the United States reactionary political groups won serious victories against the extension of constitutional protection from discrimination to homosexuals. The Oregon Citizens Alliance (OCA) worked steadily in Oregon, Idaho, and Washington to pass legislation with aims similar to those expressed in the infamous Measure 9, which was defeated in Oregon in 1992, and their efforts met with success in some small cities, suburbs, and rural counties.[3] Living in one of the storm centers, Portland, Oregon, I was unable to avoid hearing from homophobes about their concerns and hopes.

One of the most surprising things I learned is that members of the homophobic extreme right wing no longer want to pretend in front of the children that homosexuals do not exist. Instead, our antagonists seem preoccupied with institutionalizing a pernicious variety of education about differences in sexual preference. Measure 9 offered the OCA version of sex education. The paragraph of the measure that provoked the most ridicule from educators states:

> The amendment would require state, regional, and local governments and their subdivisions, including specifically the State Department of Education and the public schools, to assist in setting a standard for Oregon youth that recognizes homosexuality, pedophilia, sadism and masochism as abnormal, wrong, unnatural, and perverse. In addition, the standard would recognize that homosexuality, pedophilia, sadism, and masochism are to be discouraged and avoided. (*Official 1992 General Election Voter's Pamphlet* 93)

Months of public debate (and merriment) followed over exactly what the OCA wanted every teacher in our schools to tell children. What is most interesting (as opposed to most darkly amusing) about this proposal is how far it goes beyond the usual conservative efforts to remove certain books from school libraries and to keep homosexuals from teaching in public schools, and why the proposal takes the direction it does.

Measure 9 shifts the emphasis in legislating "morality" from the usual endorsement of censorship to a plan for dissemination of what must be called misinformation, even according to the conservative terms of the American Psychiatric Association's definition of perversity, which leaves out mention of homosexuality while still stigmatizing other less popular consensual sexual preferences. Note that in the text of Measure 9 recognition of homosexuality is mandated as strongly as condemnation of it. OCA leaders explain that the young should be taught about specific sexual practices and then taught to avoid them. Homosexuality is apparently such an attractive nuisance that it cannot be effectively opposed by privileging the dominant culture's values and sexual practices or even by silencing dissenting voices.

One might compare the emphases here to those of the "Sex Respect" abstinence education program developed by Phyllis Schafly's Committee on the Status of Women in 1985. While not as strongly focused on homosexuality, this program, which was used in one out of eight of America's school districts in 1997, contains grotesque misinformation about condom use and flatly states that all sexual activity outside marriage harms "someone" (Fuentes 17). "Abstinence Only" education, as described by the Heritage Foundation, which promotes it, "teaches the importance of attaining self-sufficiency before engaging in sexual activity" (Fuentes 18). This importance is not taught through silence about the alternatives to waiting for sex until one can afford a bourgeois home, but through verbose, negative, and dishonest descriptions of nonreproductive sexual activities. Within this context, the OCA represents an extreme but logical extension of the new compulsion to engage in detailed discussion of sexual practices with the young.

While in years past it apparently seemed to conservatives that most teenagers would develop an interest in heterosexual activity without any prompting, clearly the framers of Measure 9 believe that unless schoolchildren are indoctrinated into normative heterosexuality by adults in authority, large numbers of the children will become homosexuals. Two letters in support of Ballot Measure 13, the Oregon successor to the defeated Measure 9, make an especially strong case for this view. Lon Mabon, chairman of the OCA, attributed the 1994 passage of anti-gay ballot measures in Albany, Junction City, Marion County, and Turner, Oregon to "more moderate language" in these measures, which were limited to banning "specific civil rights protection for homosexuals" and prohibiting spending public revenues "to promote or express approval of homosexuality" (Rubenstein A14).

But, in the *Official 1994 Oregon General Election Voter's Pamphlet,* his supporters' "arguments in favor" tell a different story. Frantic appeals to "common sense" and "logic" abound in the "arguments in favor" section, with the plea of "A Liberal Democrat" standing as typical in its insistence that removing "books about homosexual lifestyle issues" from schools is a "rational, wise, and fair" measure necessary to "save our children and society" (76). However, this "don't ask, don't tell" policy is atypical in its reliance on censorship alone. Another voter, who calls himself "The Voice They Want Silenced," speaks for what has been so far the OCA's main agenda. This man complains that he was "recruited" into homosexuality in his youth, but is now "a normal heterosexual man." His position is that "MANY homosexual men try to recruit young boys and often succeed," because, tragically, these wayward teens "believe they are old enough to decide for themselves." Only authoritative voices speaking against "the pro-gay bias of the media" can keep young people from being "drawn into homosexuality" (77).

Fascinated by this turn in homophobia, I sought out everyone I could find who supported the legislation and asked them why. Variations on one statement recurred regularly in each one of these conversations: "if we don't tell kids how bad homosexuality is, what will keep them from taking the easy way out?" Despite having been socialized in San Francisco, I have long been aware of manifestations of homophobia like gay-bashing and have always thought of the choice to act on homosexual feelings as a courageous move outside of society's usual protections. One could think of homosexuality as opting out of struggle only if one also sees heterosexuality as the quintessential human battle, one so fraught with perils that any other is rendered a mere avoidance. That the ballot measure's supporters consider it necessary to reify compulsory heterosexuality in law suggests that in times and places where homosexuality is not criminalized our previous understanding of how and why heterosexuality is compelled may have become inadequate.

Adrienne Rich introduced the idea of "compulsory heterosexuality" into feminist studies to explain the difficulty of moving outside the concept of sexuality as a contact between oppositely gendered beings, and thus the difficulty of moving beyond our culture's pervasive misogyny and homophobia. The difficulty derived, in her view, from cultural naturalization and idealization of heterosexuality, which, as she shows, was maintained in much of the psychologically oriented feminist theory written in the mid- to late 1970s. Both prior to and after the publication of Rich's essay, feminist theorists extensively investigated the effects of heterosexuality's privileged status as the paradigm for intercourse of all types. However, as numerous theorists, including Rich, have pointed out, a great deal of feminist theory has also been marked by an apparently inadvertent privileging of the heterosexual model of difference, so that what is meant to be a critique of traditional gender norms often ends by reinscribing and essentializing them.

For many feminist critics, the 1980s' constructionist critiques of essentialism provided a much needed escape from entrapment in the tropes belonging to a heterosexist perspective. We believed that, while attaining a vantage point beyond gender difference might be impossible, we could at least attain an outside perspective on essentialism in order to subvert the authority of its narratives and the power of its binaries by consciously manipulating the signs of gender. Nonetheless, deliberate manipulations of the signs of gender have not been universally popular among feminists. Heated arguments over the political value of "gender-fuck" performances such as parodic transvestitism and exaggerated sex-role playing have continued to divide gay, lesbian, and other feminist communities since the 1970s. The sort of performances least likely to be seen as furthering feminist and gay liberation agendas generally seem to be male-authored stagings of men's gynophobia.

Through a psychoanalytically based logic of reversal, accounts of men's fear of heterosexual contact are usually read as allegories in which the real terror is of the unfixing of gender hierarchy. This reading practice has two major political advantages. First, it exposes the misogyny that often lies at the bottom of what might otherwise be disarming confessions of male weakness in relation to women. Second, it empowers feminist critics to read the repressed, rescuing the texts' unconscious content and so putting what many describe as "the feminine" back into circulation. But there is also a problem with the practice of reading all accounts of male fear of heterosexual contact as misogynist. Such a reading practice erases all possibility that a male-authored text can deliberately oppose gender categories instead of always opposing women. If our methodology erases that possibility, then male and female authors are rewritten as absolute, essential enemies.[4]

Under this interpretive system, the indisputably different male is marked as feminine, so that radical diversity within the two officially recognized genders—which should explode them as categories—is recontained into the binary of masculine and feminine. Should the feminist critic claim for herself the role previously reserved for the psychiatrist as decoder supreme, always revealing the hidden, disruptive feminine voice that constitutes the unconscious of the masculine text and bestowing authority on that voice? A certain satisfaction can accompany this sort of role reversal. However, it reinscribes gender difference and thus calls into question the possibility of conscious, meaningful resistance to heterosexism, let alone heterophobia.

Can a male-authored tale of fear of heterosexuality be about something other than unconscious fear of gender instability? Rather than coercively idealizing heterosexual relations, as the theory of compulsory heterosexuality claims the dominant culture does (Rich 183–184), while disclosing a troubled (textual) unconscious hatred of women and thus providing us with material ripe for deconstruction, some male-authored representations of gynophobia flaunt their consistency with a tradition of ridiculing and denying heterosexual love. I will turn now to the controversial film *Basic Instinct* (directed by Paul Verhoeven) because it is a case in point.

"ONE LITTLE ROOM AN EVERYWHERE"

Films and texts like *Basic Instinct* provide a horizon vision by illuminating the space between the reflexive patriarchal misogyny that attempts to resolve the woman question through repression and a gynophobia that is an open admission of male defeat. In this space we can see how homophobia arises from sources other than devaluation of the feminine. *Basic Instinct* not only presents the war between the sexes in a wildly extreme fashion, it also, through this exaggerated performance of gender difference, provides an exterior perspective on the legacy of textual and cinematic construction of gender norms. And in addition, a close look at the film and its reception illuminates much about how heterosexuality is both compelled and embattled wherever homosexuality is legal.

To many, the film itself and its enthusiastic popular reception, including the many low-budget imitations and parodies of it, constitute a particularly obnoxious example of the new homophobia. Picketed for its depiction of lesbians by Queer Nation and the Gay and Lesbian Alliance Against Defamation during its production in San Francisco in 1991 and again after its distribution, *Basic Instinct* was also excoriated as revoltingly misogynist by many critics shortly after its release. Rebecka Wright's verdict, delivered in *Gauntlet*, is typical: "*Basic Instinct*, as the title itself suggests, is about as far from elevated consciousness as it gets" (120). If the film questions the naturalization of gender difference, one must address why it has been considered anti-feminist and homophobic by so many people.[5]

Basic Instinct's commentaries on gender are inextricable from its narrative structure. Unlike easily recognizably feminist films from the same period that focus on women's empowerment through control of narrative, such as *Strangers in Good Company* (1991) and *Fried Green Tomatoes* (1991), *Basic Instinct* has no pretensions to being a woman's guide to life. Nor is it presented as if from a woman's perspective, although it does include a woman's narrative, in the form of a story being written throughout the film by the mystery writer, Catherine Tramell (Sharon Stone). The woman's narrative is peripheral in the sense that it is almost never heard. Yet the female narrative's power emanates from the margin it inhabits, informing the film's "own" narrative or major narrative, which could be understood both as a counterstory and as one struggling to contain all that the female protagonist writes.

The film's main method of diegesis might most accurately be described as the would-be dominant narrative, but for brevity's sake I will call it the major narrative. This narrative is strongly identified with the male protagonist, Nick Curran (Michael Douglas), because it comes to us almost entirely through point-of-view shots and shots in which he is the focus character. On the rare occasions when he is absent, as in the sequence that takes place under the opening credits, what we see is out of focus or shot from a confusingly oblique angle, as if his presence were essential to clarity of vision. But despite the camera's endorsement of his vision, the major narrative fails to account adequately for what the audience sees. Catherine's narrative rivals the major narrative and challenges it in ways that Nick's point of view cannot seem to fully incorporate into the story we see.

The major narrative's double failure, both to pull all the plot details into coherence and to contain the woman's narrative, is crucial to the film's many plot twists. Like the noir classics it imitates, *Basic Instinct* tells us its story deceptively, almost always as if from within the defective viewpoint of its male protagonist, a stereotypically paranoid, macho, rebellious police detective with the requisite substance abuse problems and haunted past conventional to contemporary police stories. But a technical difference from classic film noir works against narrative coherence. Voiceover is conspicuously absent, leaving the story without an enunciated moral center.[6] The film breaks most decisively from noir conventions in its female protagonist. Catherine is a professional writer who insists upon treating both the story we see unfold and Nick as her material, to be manipulated into whatever shape best expresses her vision. When Nick (and thus the story line that comes to us through him) fails to account for events, the failure is directly attributable to Catherine's narrative, whose exigencies consistently dominate the action.

In the opening sequence we see a woman astride a man tied to the bedposts. At what appears to be the moment of climax for them both, she stabs him to death with an icepick. We cannot see her face. The scene then changes to introduce Nick as an investigating police detective. Nick begins the investigation by focusing on Catherine, the victim's lover. His suspicions are aroused by his discovery that she wrote a book describing an identical murder. Although she does defend herself, after a fashion, by asking whether anyone would so blatantly announce her own murderous plot in advance, she also tauntingly proves, over and over, that she is capable of just such an audacious gesture. Exhibiting her vagina to an interrogation room full of hostile policemen, socializing with her friend Hazel and teasing her lover Roxy (both multiple murderers), and toying outrageously with Nick, she luxuriates in her own power, her obvious sense of invulnerability. As she plots out her next novel, which she jeeringly describes to Nick as his "own story," Catherine leads him on a wild chase of "clues" that bring him to shoot his sometime girlfriend, the police psychologist Beth Garner (Jeanne Tripplehorn), who had once, we are told, rejected Catherine's advances and whom we have seen trying to free Nick from his enthralled passion for Catherine. In the last scene, Catherine is once again on top of her lover, now Nick, and seems to be trying to decide when to use the icepick.

The film suggests that Catherine causes the violent deaths of many people: Johnny Boz, whom we see stabbed to death in the first scene; Nilsen, an Internal Affairs officer who sold Catherine information about Nick's therapy sessions with Beth; Nick's partner, Gus; and Beth. We may also surmise that before the drama opens Catherine has also killed her parents, her academic advisor in college, and Beth's husband. Part of the confusion of the plot comes from the lack of reasonable motivation for these murders. As soon as a motive is implied, evidence appears that questions it. For instance, one might think that Catherine murdered her parents to get their money. (She is the heiress to one hundred million dollars.) However, they died when she was a child and could not gain autonomy, which complicates accounting for the killings that way. Her murder of Nilsen at first seems clear-cut; he was investigating her past. But the question of how he could have done her any harm without also revealing his own guilt in selling her confidential police files is left unanswered. Other murders, including Boz's and Gus's, seem absolutely unmotivated. Catherine, too, seems troubled by these unreasonable crimes. She is said to use knowledge gained from her college double major in English and psychology to explore the violence that flows out of her, befriending and studying multiple murderers and "novelizing" her own crimes.

Whereas the noir heroine is conventionally shallow, mercenary, and calculating, less deep than she seems, Catherine has nothing to gain from her plotting but an insight into the construction of her own identity. Traditional noir heroines are figures for the mystery of the body of woman, that is, the terrible mystery of the *thing* of beauty whose surface draws out the soul through the eyes. Catherine is a new thing in noir, woman as active creator of images. Her manipulation of the world extends beyond presenting her beauty as a lure; she makes Nick as much as she makes herself. As an author, she contemplates a world recreated in her image. Because she is in the process of enmeshing Nick in her fiction, she makes him contemplate the mystery of her mind, just as she does. He becomes her reader.

The more Nick strives to resolve her mystery—that is, to contain the mystery of her within the police report he is trying to write—the more surely he is reduced to a character within the story she is writing. In fact, it is in this respect that the absence of voice-over is most conspicuous, because the concept of an exterior and containing text, put together retrospectively by the detective, is essential to the truth claims of the contemporary mystery story. Since Nick gives us no overview, we must turn to Catherine for one. While Catherine's novel might be considered to belong to the mystery genre, its mystery cannot be unraveled according to genre conventions.

By the conclusion we know that Catherine was the murderer we saw from the back in the first scene, but the only explanation we ever get of why she stabbed her lover during the sex act is that this action provides a conclusion to her story about him as the object of her sexual desire. If one were to insist upon retrospectively reconstructing the plot in order to give each murder a motive, one might come up with something like this: At college Catherine becomes obsessed with Beth. (Beth tells this version of their relationship to Nick.) Catherine then kills her advisor, a psychology professor, because he realizes that her feelings about Beth are abnormal and dangerous. Catherine continues to pursue Beth, and, when Beth marries, Catherine kills her husband. Then, several years later, after Beth and Nick become lovers, Catherine gets Nick's attention by murdering Johnny Boz, having first detailed the murder in a book and then seduced Boz. Although by the time Catherine's book is published, Nick has already lost interest in Beth, Catherine buys information from Nilsen that enables her to seduce Nick, kills Nilsen, and frames Nick for the crime. She then lures Gus and Beth to a setup so that she can kill him while making it look as if Beth is responsible, thus causing Nick to kill her. This version of the murders does reflect a somewhat warped sense of poetic justice, but it seems completely improbable both because the number of murders is absurdly excessive if the aim is simply to punish Beth, and most strikingly because Catherine never shows any emotion about Beth at all. Ultimately, the only reason we are given for Catherine's elaborate machinations to get Nick at icepick-point is that she has written the story that way.

Many film reviewers commented on the inadequacy of the film's plot. Terrence Rafferty's complaint that "they tell us who the killer is and leave everything else unexplained" is typical (83). This general dissatisfaction with the film's narrative may be due to its ignoring the usual noir plot questions about criminal women's motivations. Catherine's murderess friends' crimes are described as resulting from impulses as inexplicable as they were irresistible. Throughout the film, characters comment on Catherine's lack of motivation for the murders of which she is suspected. Catherine explains, "I'm a writer, I use people for what I write. Let the world beware." When Nick ask her to substitute a marriage for the murder at the end of her new novel, she says, "It wouldn't sell. Someone has to die."

This statement opens up a new frame of interpretation, one in which Catherine figures most significantly not as a noir murderess but as an author. Killing and making love are not sequential means to an end in *Basic Instinct;* plot has become an end in itself for the plotting heroine. Her answer to Nick directs our attention away from the idea that she as woman, the mysterious feminine, is the secret source of death. Instead, the film suggests that cultural and narrative conventions constrain her actions and explain the story's deadly secret.

Among the unanswered questions raised by the film is what the eponymous basic instinct is. A plausible, but crucially only partial, answer is that it is heterosexuality, since Nick and Catherine seem to struggle against and eventually romantically succumb to their attraction to each other. Visual images suggest that we are watching nature working in its rawest form. For instance, Catherine attracts Nick by displaying her body to him. She does this first in the most conventional (and hackneyed) film noir style by undressing in front of a mirror angled so that he can watch her, while thinking himself unobserved. Her next move breaks with traditions outside of pornography. During her police interrogation, she commands his attention with the sort of direct sexual remarks that psychologists tend to categorize as "inappropriate" and then spreads her legs. Her short white skirt rides up and her vulva is visible. Her expression is triumphant. Despite her degree in psychology, she is obviously unaffected by theories of female genital lack. Her certainty that there is something there, and moreover something the sight of which will give her power over the male, seems more confidently animal than intellectual. She positively sneers with superiority as she displays the power between her legs.

The film's redefinition of heterosexual "instinct" continues with Nick's reaction to Catherine's pursuit of him. He is unable to resist submitting to her. Water imagery, which has traditionally been sexualized in film as in literature, is played against close shots of ice to dramatize the power dynamics between Nick and the woman who is writing his story. The waves crashing on the shore at her Stinson Beach house and the deluge of rain outside her Pacific Heights house alternate with and inflect scenes in which she wields the icepick to break ice blocks, as she will shatter Nick's carefully maintained icy veneer. He gladly, and literally, puts the icepick into her hands.

In both the major narrative and Nick's own vision, he is identified with Catherine. Other characters remark that Nick is "as crazy as she is," and if he solves the crime it will be because "it takes one to know one." Nick makes a few feeble attempts to differentiate himself from her but soon gives in to full identification. This is most apparent in their parallel interrogation scenes. The set piece scene in which she wisecracks and spreads her legs as she is questioned about Boz's murder begins with the comment "This session's being taped." Later, when Nick is questioned, in the same room, about Nilsen's murder, it is as if the tape is being played back, as Nick repeats Catherine's defiant lines verbatim. This odd scene resonates with what is perhaps the strangest line in the film. In an earlier scene, set in a diner, Gus realizes that Nick is having an affair with Catherine and tries to warn him away from further sexual involvement. Nick remarks that he is not afraid of her. One might expect the foul-mouthed Gus to deliver the hard-boiled cliché "that's just your dick talking," but instead he says, "that's just her pussy talking."

If Nick relishes his role as stand-in for the contemptuously communicative vagina, Catherine insists on the difference between him and herself. She often reminds him of his fictional and her metafictional status. She consistently reminds the audience that we are in a postfeminist world of noir, where woman has access to the script. She not only creates the story in which he is a character, she also knows why the story must be as it is.

What determines the story's conclusion is the open secret at the film's core. To understand why the story must end with betrayal or rejection of heterosexual love is to begin to understand why homophobes would feel it necessary to teach children to despise homosexuality, rather than simply treating heterosexuality as if it were the only possible form of sexual expression. The film suggests that the conventions of fiction demand that we see heterosexual love as more fatal illusion than basic instinct. Before dismissing this message as aberrant and discontinuous with literary tradition, we might note that included among the earliest meanings of "romantic" listed by the OED are "having no foundation in fact," "having no real existence," and "going beyond what is customary or practical." These definitions raise some troubling questions about the evolution of the word "romance," which, since the middle of the nineteenth century, has slowly shifted in meaning so that to everyone except literary critics it now seems to signify nothing but flowery love stories. "Romantic" likewise has come to mean sentimentalized sexual desire. Since both terms are associated with such low-culture forms as greeting cards, formula novels, and "easy listening" songs, it would seem that the combination of the concept of romance with that of love results in a fantastical construction, one fundamentally divorced from the harsher principles of what we term reality.

Counter to what one might expect, given the dominant culture's demonization of homosexual relations, heterosexual love is particularly culturally marked as unreal. Expressed lack of belief in the ability of erotic love to bring about new worlds of experience is not simply part of the general cynicism currently considered a realistic attitude toward life. It also reflects the logical consequences of a specific part of heterosexist ideology: belief in the inevitability of a war between the sexes as long as civilization interferes with purely natural behavior, conceived of as unthinking acceptance of a gender hierarchy that males dominate. Heterosexist ideology cannot allow for an egalitarian resolution of the conflict between men and women, because such a resolution would be deemed unnatural. Female dominance is deemed even more perverse. Therefore no possibilities are left open for narratives about love except obvious fantasy that romanticizes away conflict (as the woman submits to masculine control that is always magically gratifying her desires) or "realist" representation of unresolvable battle.[7] For this reason, heterosexuality within patriarchal discourse inevitably becomes a battle site for women who refuse passivity. As long as heterosexuality was the only speakable option, when the penalty for rejecting it was death at worst and silencing and extreme marginalization at best, texts could mark themselves as sophisticated by doubting the possibility of heterosexual love without suggesting that they advocated anything else. The only recognized area of representation of love outside high culture's seriousness was low culture's "romantic" heterosexual fantasy.[8]

Pornography, women's romance, and horror films are all scorned as what Linda Williams calls "body genres," genres that stimulate physical responses (Williams 2–5). Traditionally, as the mind is understood to be in opposition to the body, the former is considered the site of reason and the latter of unreason. Consequently, body genres are deemed debased not simply because they stimulate the senses of the audience, providing an intimate service, but because they pander to our craving for the pleasures of unreason. Along these same lines, romance and pornography are also both often criticized for offering unrealistic wish fulfillment. If we recognize that so-called romantic love is radically incompatible with art that has pretensions to either realism or seriousness, we can see why horror and suspense films with a central love story so frequently attempt to redeem themselves as art with the sort of surprisingly open conclusion (The End . . . Or is it?) that *Basic Instinct* presents in exaggerated fashion.

Basic Instinct's conclusion follows a full fade to black from Catherine's tender embrace of Nick after his suggestion that they "live [together] happily ever after." After the blackout, the picture returns suddenly and, as ominous music on the soundtrack wells up more and more floridly, the camera tracks down from the entwined couple on the bed to an extreme close-up of the icepick under it. This narrative refusal to endorse romance is placed in a world where "pussies" talk and women write, where homosexuality has been spoken aloud and so must be recognized even by those who wish it did not exist.

Catherine's combination of bisexuality and murderousness has been read by many critics as a negative depiction of lesbianism harkening back to fifties film stigmatizations of lesbians as deranged and violent.[9] That Catherine's lover Roxy killed her two younger brothers, and that Catherine's friend (and possibly lover) Hazel killed her husband and three children, are seen as further indications that the plot crudely equates rejection of the traditional feminine role with viciousness. However, one might keep in mind that while all three women have killed their way out of the family, Catherine, unlike Roxy and Hazel, has not completely rejected heterosexuality. She is represented not just as a bisexual, but as that special creature, the San Franciscan bisexual.[10]

Wright calls Verhoeven's choice to film in San Francisco "ridiculously insensitive" to The City's existence as "a sanctuary of sorts for gay and lesbian people" (120). However, the choice of setting can be understood differently if we take into account Verhoeven's social-commentary films made in the Netherlands, especially the youth-culture film *Spetters* (1980). A main theme in this film is a teenager's struggle to find a positive identity as a masochistically inclined gay man against the backdrop of the unrelenting homophobia of his friends, family, and community. The use of locale in *Spetters* often seems like an exhaustive hunt for some niche in which homosexuality will be tolerated. The only free space the young man is able to find is the cramped bunk of a tiny trailer. *Basic Instinct* similarly makes emphatic reference to its location in nearly every scene, but also, in contrast, frequently informs viewers that homosexuality and bisexuality are neither illegal nor socially stigmatized in the San Francisco Bay Area. We might therefore read Catherine as a very contemporary figure, one who could not have existed openly in other times or places. Unlike the seeming bisexuals of fifties cinema whom we are invited to see as sneaky homosexuals whose "bisexuality" is itself alternately a disguise and the revelation of hidden evil, Catherine is not one-within-the-other but both/and.

The figure of the bisexual is often taken as representing confused gender identification. But it can also be read in a way similar to the figure of the mulatto as described by Hazel Carby: "as a convention . . . that enabled the exploration in fiction of relations that were socially proscribed. The mulatto figure is a narrative device of mediation, allowing a fictional exploration of the relation between the races while offering an imaginary expression of the relation between them" (84).[11] Catherine, as a bisexual, similarly brings two worlds of gender identification into contact. On one hand, she embodies dissonance. That her body holds heterosexuality and homosexuality in tension gives the lie to the dominant culture's reading of both identities, since, as Eve Sedgwick points out, above all else "'sexual identity' is supposed to organize [difference] into a seamless and univocal whole" (*Tendencies* 8). In this modality, Catherine's identity multivocally speaks the impossibility of absolute heterosexuality. On the other hand, Catherine as bisexual plays a mediating role, inviting us to look at her not only in comparison to the contextualizing characters Roxy and Hazel but in contrast to her foil and the other suspect in Johnny Boz's murder, Beth.

Played by Jeanne Tripplehorn in a wide-eyed pouty little girl style, Beth is the anti-essentialists' nightmare woman, a whining embodiment of stereotypical femininity, always defined by powerless maternal flutterings or helpless dependence. As both his psychologist and his girlfriend, Beth scurries supportively after Nick. We are led to read her as an animalistically "natural" heterosexual woman by such plot details as her seemingly involuntary submissive response to Nick's sexual violence and by dialogue like Gus's comment on her devotion to Nick, "She mates for life." But other details problematize this sort of reading. For instance, two scenes stress her inability to experience orgasm with a man. Nick attributes this to her tension and lack of self-knowledge, not characteristics one would expect in a natural woman. More subtly, her worship of the rebellious male is presented as darkly comic through her almost fetishistic attachment to the plastic Bart Simpson on her key ring. She strokes this toy during stressful encounters and it causes her death when Nick mistakes it for a gun hidden in her pocket. In relation to Catherine's story, Beth's seems a tragedy that is based on her rejection of female bonding in favor of self-destructive attachment to the role of the good girl who can rebel only through identification with the rebel hero. Catherine, whose basic instinct seems to be to kill whatever male comes too close, is conversely defined simply as the sort of survivor whose success comes from understanding culture's script—and who better than she who parodically rewrites it?

The rivalry over narrative control between Beth and Catherine, each of whom competes to persuade Nick of her truth, is reminiscent of the struggle in Marleen Gorris's *A Question of Silence* (*De Stilte Rond Christine M.,* 1983) between Janine the psychiatrist and Christine the murderess. Because Gorris and Verhoeven are the two Dutch filmmakers best known internationally, it is tempting to compare the two films, especially since both use detective story motifs in narrating an apparently motiveless murder. The configuration of female characters is also similar. Both films pit a lone female psycho-therapist against a trio of closely bonded murderous women.

Gorris's story is informed by collectivist feminist values. In contrast to Verhoeven's, it dramatizes the change in consciousness of the "male-identified" woman as the psychiatrist Janine is drawn into a complicitous understanding of the murderesses' need to kill a man who represents patriarchal power to them. Where Gorris's film emphasizes women's enforced silence, Verhoeven's dwells on the dangers women's writing poses to a therapist depicted as the handmaiden of patriarchy. Where Gorris, in pseudo-documentary style, locates the battle between men and women within the material world and its institutions, Verhoeven continually refers to the battle's foundation in textuality and its conventions. Thus her film's climax comes in a court of law, while his occurs in a writer's study strewn with manuscript pages. The films are alike in their insistence that, as Geetha Ramanathan says of *A Question of Silence,* "the price a female pays for claiming subject status in a violently patristic society [is] murder. For each of the women has to write her name in blood to write it at all" (69).

Basic Instinct resembles most of Verhoeven's earlier films in its wittily self-conscious engagement with the tradition of depicting heterosexual desire as paradoxically both irresistible and deathly. While I am not arguing for a reading of *Basic Instinct* based on auteur theory, the director's previous work is made more relevant to this discussion by his much publicized refusal to allow Joe Eszterhas to revise his screenplay in response to criticism from gay groups. Eleven other films directed by Verhoeven have been released in the United States to date. In subject matter and approach these films span several genres. Although *Katie's Passion (Keeje Tipple,* 1975) includes some classically naturalistic depiction of poverty in the turn-of-the-century Netherlands, both it and *Turkish Delight* (1973) might be best described as "sexploitation" films, as is clearly the case with *Showgirls* (1995). *Soldier of Orange* (1977) is a serious historical film about resistance to and collaboration with the Nazis in Holland during World War II. *Flesh and Blood* (1985), also a historical drama, less seriously frames class conflict in the Middle Ages in terms of a competition between a renegade soldier and a young nobleman over a pretty little princess. *Spetters* examines the interactions of five young people involved in various countercultural activities in contemporary Holland. *The Fourth Man* (1983), also set in present-day Holland, combines surrealism and film noir conventions to tell the story of a bisexual man's flirtation with a deadly widow and her fiancé. (Taubin calls *Basic Instinct* "a remake" of this film [36].) Three of Verhoeven's American films, *RoboCop* (1987), *Total Recall* (1990), and *Starship Troopers* (1997), are science fiction dystopias. Of all of these films only two, *Katie's Passion* and *RoboCop,* do not represent heterosexuality as a direct threat to life. *Soldier of Orange, Flesh and Blood, Spetters,* and *The Fourth Man* explicitly contrast homosexual unions with heterosexual ones, valorizing the former as more honorable. Even in the latter two films, where the portrayal of homosexuality is less schematically that of a contrasting good, it is still depicted as creating relationships in which altruistic alliance is possible. Although on this evidence one might be tempted to exonerate Verhoeven from the usual charges of heterosexism, in *Basic Instinct* he uses Catherine to explain an aesthetics perfectly consistent with the sexual politics of Western tradition, which is also evident in all his work.

Catherine's little lectures on literary convention emphasize the compulsion, basic to all but the lowest art, to represent heterosexuality as dangerous and distasteful for both partners. The film visually echoes these values. The sophistication that our culture equates with denial of the possibility of fulfilling heterosexual love lavishly varnishes the hard surface of every scene. A claustrophobic imitativeness visually marks Nick's relations to the women. The audience is teased by the remarkably perfect color coordination of Nick's wardrobe to each of the two women's in their shared scenes. For instance, in the notorious violent sex scene with Beth, they both wear identical shades of olive brown and olive green, with his underpants rather arrestingly, because so unusually, matched to her skirt. His shift into identification with Catherine is coded into their next scene together by the shift of the color range to steel blue and dark taupe, as if the cloth for their clothes had been cut from the same dye lots. Never has heterosexuality appeared more as a prefabricated life *style.*

*Basic Instinct'*s design, as well as its color palette, reifies heterosexuality's discontents into visible patterns of unease. In aerial shots especially reminiscent of *Vertigo,* we see Nick's world as a puzzle in which Northern Californian coastal roads and the stairwell of his apartment building are mazes he must work his way through in search of the woman and the secret. Nick's desire for certainty and closure appears in his (ungratified) demand that Catherine affirm his sense of their sexual encounter as an experiential peak, "the fuck of the century." His struggle for narrative control is also evident in his insistence that he become her only lover, and, above all else, his commitment to "nailing her" by solving the murder case. The case remains open and she remains free as he circles around and around, the hilly locale enhancing, as in *Vertigo,* the sense of much movement yielding very little progress.

The first close-up of one of Catherine's novels similarly paradoxically evokes both movement and stasis. The book, entitled *Love Hurts,* is one of those garish productions in which a window cut through the front cover reveals the center of the mystery, in this case a bloodied male corpse tied to the bedposts, and, when one opens up the book, a second cover inside reveals the solution, in this case a picture of the murderess. The simple suggestion, open me up and you will see the answer, is simultaneously belied by the author's name in large letters above the picture, Catherine Woolf. Catherine's pen name seems so offensively inappropriate to an obvious and trashy genre novel that it can hardly fail to make the viewer wonder what she can mean by it. We jump ahead to knowledge; we jump back to question.

In this sort of semiotic play with the viewer, the film de-emphasizes Nick's identity crisis in favor of an admiring contemplation of Catherine's richly full presence. Like the landscape before our eyes, she is twisty and obscure, difficult to read, but omnipresent. All roads lead back to San Francisco and to that exemplary San Franciscan, Catherine. Her meaning extends visually beyond being the key to the mystery. In this way, the film differs greatly from the classics to which it refers. As Tania Modleski says, the structure of *Vertigo* implies that "femininity in our culture is largely a male construct" and, in doing so, taps into a source of male terror, because "if woman, who is posited as she whom man must know and possess in order to guarantee his truth and his identity, does not exist, then in some important sense he does not exist either, but rather is faced with the possibility of his own nothingness" (91). Katherine and Lee Horsley argue that a form of "neo-noir" focusing "on the strong, independent woman" and opening the genre to "complex explorations of female identity" gained ascendancy in the 1980s and '90s (374, 398). *Basic Instinct,* in contrast to the earlier noir form, identifies authorship as female and femininity as the creation of women, thus positing that the woman who creates can exist beyond the narrative frame. Rather than the man fading as he destroys the woman he has made, in this film male presence is shown being effaced by the inscription of the woman-writer's name, written in his blood.

Basic Instinct parodies, through self-referentiality, the dominant aesthetics of our era, which, as Jane Tompkins shows, define legitimate art in contrast to "sentimentality" (20–23). Comic love stories can end with marriage because their pretensions to realism are already undercut by their frivolous tone. A story that demands to be taken seriously as art cannot go too far in indulging fantasies of romantic resolution. The aesthetics of seriousness implicitly demand conflation of the death drive and heterosexual libido because the idea that heterosexual desire can be satisfied is automatically dismissed as delusion. By this logic, to seek to satisfy heterosexual desire is to deliberately maintain a state of delusion, to willfully divorce oneself from reality, from the real, and hence from the world or life. Because it is given that heterosexual satisfaction cannot exist in the world, the pursuit of it becomes a yearning to leave the world. If this seems exaggerated, one might remember the vast number of serious love stories considered "great" that end with the death of at least one of the lovers.

Lynda Hart's interpretation of *Basic Instinct* is particularly instructive in revealing ways that a reading can be constructed by the preconception that heterosexuality is always antithetical to female and mutual pleasure. Hart understands the linkage between "the film's homophobia" and its representation of "the power and pleasure of heteropatriarchy" as "inadvertently" revealing the contents of "*the* masculine imaginary" (125, 130; emphasis mine). Throughout *Fatal Women,* Hart uses terms like "heteropatriarchy," "phallocratic libidinal economics," and "heterosexist patriarchy" interchangeably with "heterosexuality." She seems to believe that all heterosexual desire is phallocentric and thus essentially inimical to the very existence of women as subjects.

Hart's book opens with a reading of Freud's essay "On Narcissism," from which she concludes that men and women cannot enjoy amorous mutuality, and that, in fact, what we call heterosexuality is really a sort of misrecognition of a displaced homoerotic impulse. Since Freud first posits male love as object-directed (while he sees female love as self-directed) and then goes on to say that what a man really loves in a woman is an image of his earlier self as complete (not needing an Other), Hart takes the theory to be an exposure of the essential inability of humans to love those who are gendered otherwise than themselves (23). Questions left unanswered include why we must assume that binary gender difference based on genitalia is the most important source of identification with others,[12] and, perhaps more importantly, why we must assume that psychoanalysis has the final word on pleasure and desire.

However, if we push these questions aside, it is easy to see why Hart decides that the plot inconsistencies in *Basic Instinct* disclose "the comedy of heterosexuality—the 'non-sense' of the sexual relationship" (130). Since to Hart there is only one possible "male heterosexual imaginary," it is inconceivable that Verhoeven might depart from reiteration of patriarchal narrative. The most he can do to unsettle it is to accidentally exaggerate so greatly that his film "renders visible the systemic homophobia of masculine heterosexual desire," and through "[m]aking these often inarticulated mechanisms readable," the film "perversely inscribes a challenge to the patriarchal symbolic to own up to what it conceals in order to maintain itself" (134). For Hart, the film is placed in the "little room" of patriarchal enjoyment of women, a closeted space in itself, bounded, if troubled, by the others it must exclude to define itself.

But what if heterosexual desire and patriarchy were not always and everywhere identical? What if the film does not, as Hart claims, show us a deviant woman who, in the end, "accedes to the order of heterosexuality" by accepting subordination to the man (132), but instead shows us Catherine literally holding on to Nick while also holding on to her control of the relationship in the only way the narrative of seriousness allows, by reaching for the instrument of his death? In reading the film's ending as a would-be moment of horror and tragedy rather than a misguided comic resolution, we might see in it a critique of the incorporation of a new form of homophobia into a specific variety of heterosexuality, one that is heterophobic at its core. Such a vision of the film transforms the bedroom to which the action always returns from a guarded space to an "everywhere," quite different from the paradise imagined by John Donne in the poem that gives this section its title, a horizon at which we see the convergence of a myriad of contending forces that make up contemporary sexual attitudes.

In *Basic Instinct* the description of a possible future in which Nick and Catherine will "fuck like minks, raise rug rats, and live happily ever after" is repeated three times and dismissed three times. The first time Gus asks if this is Nick's goal, and then comments disgustedly, "Oh, man!" The second time, Nick proposes it to Catherine, who comments that she hates "rug rats." The third time, when Nick omits the mention of children, we are left to believe that Catherine accepts this comic resolution, until we see the icepick. Being serious and being realistic are euphemisms for being pessimistic in matters of love and romance, so for the film to move firmly into seriousness at its conclusion, it must promise to prick the romantic bubble. Because the story is placed in a context in which women irrepressibly create and choose, a world in which homosexuality has been spoken and cannot be unsaid, Catherine's rival narrative demands that, as a bisexual woman, she must puncture an opening in the heterosexual closure that would "nail" her down. Her face full of tender regret, she must still provide the ending that will transform her love story into art.[13]

At the moment when Catherine is most Nick's lover she is also more graphically than ever before revealed as the film's primary murderer. Because at the very moment that the film shows us the possibility of heterosexual love, the culture's (not the film's) script contemptuously codes the love as comedy, a coding that can only be effaced by the spectacle of woman not desiring but destroying man, the spectacle of woman as frighteningly, penetratively sexual in a way that cannot be separated from murder. It is this very specific positioning of the story within and also through Catherine's meta-fictional commentary and against twentieth-century conventions in the representation of heterosexual love, rather than a transhistorical masculine imaginary, that determines Catherine's assumption of the role of fatal woman as "phallic" lesbian. Because she is a San Franciscan, without a Heritage Foundation sex-ed class or an OCA to instruct her about how much worse homosexuality is than heterosexuality, she is left with that alternative when she has followed the cultural dictate to kill the man she loves. The only catch is that, because the marriage-plot always pursues her, she cannot inhabit lesbianism except as a killer of men.

Basic Instinct suggests that homophobia does not come only from a fear of losing the sense of identity based on belief in gender difference. It suggests that homophobia arises as much from a fear that if ordinary logic and literary realism both dictate that heterosexuality is incompatible with anything but love-death, then homosexual love might be left as the only sane choice. By equating heterosexual desire with death and thus placing a nondeadly heterosexual pleasure in the realm of the unthinkable, of unreason, the film reveals why homophobes must insist that homosexuality is a fate *worse* than death. In other words, the film shows that homophobia may be as much the product of our culture's devaluation of heterosexuality as it is of our culture's devaluation of homosexuality.

Basic Instinct shines a bright light into the corner where culture has desire boxed, death in every direction it turns. That the film stimulated rage against traditional representations of gender difference was the inevitable result of a design that foregrounds the naturalization of masochism, fatalism, and despair in artistic treatments of heterosexual relations, while recognizing the existence of homosexuality as a hated and feared alternative. Our anger, like the film's own, might best be directed toward this tradition, this message, rather than the messenger that discloses it, because art's endless reiterations that heterosexuality is both basic instinct and deadly madness do much to create the need to maintain the heterosexual couple through compulsion.

KILLERS ON THE ROAD

If we move beyond the idea that heterosexuality is inevitably cast by the psyche into the same forms across time and place, it is perhaps evident that American culture, although far from the only one characterized by heterophobia, gives this mindset its own special inflection. In my pursuit of horizon visions, I will now leave the in-folded space of the bedroom imag(in)ed through film as the claustrophobic enclosure of the noir and pass swiftly through some of the terrain covered by the closely related genre of the murderous road saga. My section title derives from two earlier titles, first James Ellroy's pulp novel *Killer on the Road* (1986) and second the 1995 British film *Butterfly Kiss* (directed by Michael Winterbottom), also released under the title *Killer on the Road*. While it is beyond the scope of this book to present a detailed comparison of British and American treatments of the erotic, I hope that the following very brief survey of a genre's development in the American cinema will throw into relief what is strikingly different in at least this one British film that belongs, albeit loosely, to the same genre. This comparison raises a few provocative questions about ways film conventions gender fantasies of escape from societal constraints.

Because of the current American love ethos, I cannot assume that my readers approach films about escape from domesticity with the same sense I have that they are seeing divinest sense, the only possible response to a smothering culture. And so, before plunging into what may seem like the maelstrom of madness, I will stop to contemplate an assessment, one which I am not alone in considering especially astute, of what has gone wrong with America. In 1976, with its first publication (a revised version came out in 1992), Tibor Scitovsky's *The Joyless Economy: The Psychology of Human Satisfaction* made a tremendous impact in the field of economics because of its challenge to the valorization of increase that dominates American business practice and its regulation.

Prior to Scitovsky's book, the most prevalent philosophy in American economics was that rational individuals will budget their resources to meet all of their needs to an equal extent. If they lack the money or energy to satisfy all their needs, they will try to distribute money and effort to attain as much general comfort as possible. Scitovsky uses statistics from behavioral psychology to challenge this dubious conclusion. He maintains that once people, or other animals, begin a pleasurable activity they stick with it, because the desire to increase the intensity of pleasure easily overweighs concerns about the future. Consequently, it is extremely difficult to convince people to follow a course of action that limits the intensity of their experience of pleasure, even if that course of action is the most rational one.

Although Scitovsky does not explicitly draw the following conclusion, this is one obvious reason that our affluent American society is, as he points out, obsessed with "laws and regulations which curb our freedom of choice and impose the narrow path of approved behavior by turning deviant behavior into crimes" (215). His view of the narrowness of this path is expressed with a quotation: "With the possible exception of 16th century Geneva under John Calvin, America has the most moralistic criminal law that the world has ever witnessed" (Scitovsky 215, quoting Morris and Hawkins 15). The pressure to channel eroticism into the formation of bourgeois earning and spending units counteracts the urge to seek intense pleasure rather than comfort. Our moralistic laws establish a regime of domesticity in place of the pursuit of pleasure that might otherwise unsettle a consumerist society that depends upon its citizens' choosing to expend their energies mostly on making money and acquiring manufactured goods. And finally even consumerism is voided of pleasure, becoming instead of entertainment an activity to signify the residue of wealth that is not spent. As Deleuze and Guattari argue, "something new occurs with the rise of the bourgeoisie: the disappearance of enjoyment as an end [so that now] the sole end is abstract wealth and its realization in forms other than consumption" (*Anti-Oedipus* 254).

Much of Scitovsky's book is devoted to showing how much less interested Americans seem to be than Europeans in pursuing pleasurable sensations through activities like eating gourmet food, conversing, looking at art, listening to music, and, of course, having sexual adventures, and how much more highly Americans seem to value domestic comfort and insulation from the rest of the world, except the nuclear family. Like Deleuze and Guattari, Scitovsky sees nothing natural here, but instead a territorialization of the American pleasure drive to serve "the bias of our consumer pattern" (150). Although Scitovsky's emphasis is on the damage done to men, he understands the gendering of consumerism as a vicious twist holding in place enforced domesticity. And so he sees "the end of sexism" and the breakdown of separate spheres and gender roles as a possible cure for America's joylessness. Because women's work has traditionally been more varied than men's and so offered more stimulation, he believes women may still have the ability to resist total capitulation to a life in which attaining wealth and minimizing distraction are deemed the only valid human goals (283).

Scitovsky's view may seem somewhat counterintuitive if we follow tradition in understanding women as those who benefit most by domesticity and are thus most deeply invested in maintaining it as stably as possible. Here, again, a radical break with conventional thought about gender difference is necessary in order to see a new possibility. Rather than analyzing subject positions in the terms of psychoanalysis, which always conceives of subjectivity in terms of lack, one must follow theorists like Deleuze and Guattari to consider how subjectivity can oppose capitalist paradigms and how women can model such subjectivity. To Deleuze and Guattari desire has nothing to do with lack; instead, it is a constructive force producing both subjectivity and connection. They accuse capitalism of reorganizing desire, or in their terms of deterritorializing and reterritorializing it, to impede the fluid, multivalent rhizomatic connections that desire would otherwise make between humans and their world. Capitalism keeps desire tightly restrained within the nuclear family. The excess is channeled into commodity exchange.

Instead of advocating a politics based on investment in identities that express group interests, as in the strategic essentialism advocated by some 1980s feminists, Deleuze and Guattari urge the transformation of culture and institutions through local political interventions and "the creation of group-subjects that form transverse connections between deterritorialized flows that are no longer subject to the constraints of commodity exchange" (Bogue 103–104). Because women are denied subjectivity within the dominant discourses of capitalist society and relegated to the position of other, Deleuze and Guattari see the potential for attaining the vision of the outsider in what they call becoming-woman, becoming-child, becoming-animal, becoming-imperceptible. These temporary identifications with the others of official male subjectivity serve as strategies to create a nomadic subjectivity always open to connectivity. Brian Massumi points out that "'Nomad thought' does not immure itself in the edifice of an ordered interiority, it moves freely in an element of exteriority. It does not repose on identity, it rides on difference" (xii). Thus the woman who knows herself as a subject, lacking nothing and filled with desire, becomes the consummate nomadic figure.

Filmmakers have overwhelmingly sided with Scitovsky and Deleuze and Guattari in looking to women to provide not only the inspiration for an escape from the American home, but a model of nomadic subjectivity as well. While Angry Young Men have typically fled from domestic woman, the genre I am referring to as "killers on the road" has a different, less binary response to women, because they inspire the flight and because they act, at the very least, as accomplices. The killers-on-the-road film often has undertones of a flight from gender difference.

In the most conservative of these films, at least from a feminist perspective, binary gender difference is maintained, but conventional gender roles are questioned, even if they are ultimately reinscribed. In *Bonnie and Clyde* (1967), probably the most famous film in this genre, Bonnie's aggressiveness both as an outlaw and as a lover and Clyde's shy impotence code them as sexual outlaws, although they themselves seem to yearn for reintegration into the ordinary world with which their poverty and their crimes have put them at war. A more extreme version of the aggressive woman leading a timid man astray appears in *Gun Crazy* (1950; first released in 1949 as *Deadly Is the Female*), where the crime spree begins because the gentle hero, Bart, falls helplessly in love with Laurie, a carnival tough, when she points her gun at him. Here, as in *Bonnie and Clyde*, the lawless passion is presented as tragedy. They, or at least he, may long to settle into a happy little home, but through a lengthy dramatization of their flight we are shown that there is no place in the world that can accommodate such as them. At the end of the road, back in his hometown, Bart feels compelled to shoot Laurie to keep her from killing his childhood friend, now turned sheriff. He is then shot himself. *Deadly Is the Female,* indeed.

Interestingly, killers-on-the-road films in which women function as demonic others always seem to end tragically, suggesting, as does *Basic Instinct,* that there is something in female rebellion that our culture finds much more antithetical than male rebellion to domestic resolution. Perhaps it seems unbelievable that women, once released from the home, would voluntarily submit to being immured there again, while a man who has tasted the joys of domesticity might be expected to want to return for periodic visits, which is all our society would require of him. Certainly, the films in which women spark the crime rampage attribute to them the attitude of the stereotypical escaped prisoner: "They'll never capture me alive!"

It seems easier for American cinema to imagine a man who represents the demonic other being enfolded back into comic domesticity at the end, the perfect example of this being Oliver Stone's *Natural Born Killers* (1994). The film is fraught with extreme tensions involving gender that are too numerous to explore here at any length. Among the many ways it troubles traditional ideas of binary gender is that the soundtrack (composed by Trent Reznor, about whom I will say much more in a subsequent chapter) showcases two angry, hard-rock songs by women, Patti Smith's "Rock N Roll Nigger" and L7's "Shitlist." The songs are unique among the soundtrack album's twenty-seven offerings in that in each one the rebellious voice gives no indication that she needs to offer an explanation of her rejection of American society. Smith's song simply asks, "Do you like the world around you?/ Are you ready to behave?" Her answer is, "Outside of society, that's where I want to be." On the soundtrack the song is prefaced with lines from Smith's "Babelogue," including "I'm an American artist and I have no guilt. I seek pleasure," with the obvious implication that this is what places her outside society. "Shitlist" is more brutally combative, with those on the (s)hit list explained only as "the squares who get me pissed."

These songs help complete the characterization of Mallory (Juliette Lewis) as an irascible psychotic. Her characterization needs all the help it can get because she looks as tiny and fragile as a small child next to her massively pumped-up co-star Woody Harrelson (as Mickey). In addition, Mallory is depicted as an incest victim, and almost all of her violence is directed against men who respond to her sexual posturing and coarse advances, giving the impression that it is the male ability to feel sexual arousal that she hates. Unlike the inexplicable wildness associated with the femaleness of Catherine Tramell, Bonnie Parker, Laurie, and the women rockers, Mallory's murderous rages seem symptomatic of a damaged sexuality, so her resistance has a normative explanation. Therefore it is comic, but oddly logical, to see her in the last scene happily immersed in maternity and wifely duties as the runaways still roam the highways, but now with a brood of kids in a comfy mobile home. Not only do cultural standards of seriousness and anti-romanticism demand that this narrative be reconciled with romantic love only as comedy, Mallory's traditional relation to Mickey as her protector and the dominant partner in their sex life, as well as their crimes, also tells us that their recuperation into domesticity is possible. Weirdly, since she is after all a serial killer, she is the good woman whose love redeems the even less ethical Mickey.

Another type of killers-on-the-road film goes further in troubling gender, often to the point of a real horizon vision, by effecting a resignification of at least one of the traditionally recognized genders. These could be called angry-girl (or in one case, angry-queer-boy) films, because they concentrate on the transformation of female or feminized victims into avengers. In *Natural Born Killers,* Mallory may see her own story this way; that is, she may believe that she is punishing males for "flirting" (as she calls it). However, she seems in full accord with the film's depiction of ideal masculinity as sexual domination of women, as is evident when, in a would-be comic scene, Mickey asserts his right to torture and rape a female hostage as if such behavior were simply an instance of sexual freedom, and Mallory critiques it only as infidelity. The film undercuts the sense of victimization it attributes to Mallory by showing us that the men she attacks tend to be smaller, weaker, and less aggressive than Mickey, as if she were punishing each one for not being the powerful rescuer she desperately needs in order to survive. Oliver Stone's film seems to attribute female rage to (most) men's failure as father figures, while some other killers-on-the-road films are more thoroughly anti-patriarchal, showing us feminized avengers who can hold their own.

Tamra Davis's 1992 remake of *Gun Crazy* as *Guncrazy* does more than join together the title words; it conflates Bart's sensitivity and sweetness with the violence and hard independence of Laurie in its heroine, Anita (Drew Barrymore), a quintessential girl-culture icon, the incest victim who fights back but otherwise remains feminine. Almost the same could be said of Thelma (Geena Davis) in Ridley Scott's 1991 film *Thelma and Louise,* although, as Lynda Hart points out, both women's journeys are "figured as precisely a *flight* from femininity" (72; emphasis Hart's). In contrast to Hart, however, who reads Thelma's sexual interlude with J.D. (Brad Pitt) "just a day after she has been sexually assaulted by a man in a bar as improbable at best" (75), I see this as one of the moments when the film's concept of gender is most revisionary.

Thelma, and Anita in *Guncrazy,* are heterosexual women of a type almost never seen previously in mainstream film, and only occasionally represented in feminist independent films like Monika Treut's *My Father's Coming,* featuring the irrepressible Annie Sprinkle. The sexuality of these women does not cave in under patriarchal pressure but remains a powerful force through which they express subjectivity. Thelma's encounter with Harlan, the man who tries to rape her, begins consensually and only turns violent when he refuses to respond to her but instead tries, until fatally interrupted by Louise (Susan Sarandon), to force her to submit to him. The whole incident with J.D., from the moment when Thelma first ogles his buttocks to her discovery that she has paid in cash for her use of him, attests to the possibility that heterosexuality could be about what women want (and can get) from men. His coding as a male prostitute, seen, desired, picked up, enjoyed for a night, and paid for (although not willingly), may have something to do with Brad Pitt's rapid rise to fame after the film's release.

The night with J.D. works narratively to construct a female who can function as a subject with men as well as in the separate world of women. Her surname of Dickinson, especially as opposed to Louise's boyish Sawyer, draws on the poet's legend to mark her with the potential for repressed, agoraphobic femininity. The addition of Thelma's girlish mannerisms to this already overdetermined femininity makes the film's resignification of femininity even more extreme. Thelma's character, like Anita's, anticipates the Girl Power movement.

One might make a similar argument about the ways Gregg Araki's *The Living End* (1992) re-envisions homosexuality. Roy Grundmann contrasts this film, about two young HIV-positive gay men on a crime spree, to *Basic Instinct,* claiming that, unlike the more mainstream film, Araki's film can metaphorically equate gay sex with criminality and death without "demonizing" gay characters because it addresses a different audience than the heterosexual film. Grundmann assumes heterosexuals uniformly decide that "heterosexual irresponsibility is OK (and therefore not irresponsible) and gay irresponsibility isn't." In his view the depiction of the rough and risky sex enjoyed by Luke (Mike Dytri) and Jon (Craig Gilmore) "allows the film to create a monogamous screen romance and still bridge the gap to . . . the kind of gay promiscuity, with its park sex and pickups, blow jobs and beloved backroom bonding, that heterosexuals secretly envy" (27). Perhaps a more accurate explanation of the film's crossover appeal to heterosexual audiences might be that it evokes the sexual freedom many of us enjoyed when we were young but that we were later taught was incompatible with love, because the majority of Americans of all sexual persuasions now publicly insist love means endless homemaking.

Perhaps heterosexist audiences and reviewers are more comfortable with depictions of heterosexuals engaging in extreme and dangerous sex acts and committing crimes, not because these criminals are being placed on a hierarchy above gays and thus considered "OK," but because this is the way conservative discourses on sex and love already understand any heterosexuality that is not domesticated and primarily familial: as deathly criminality. As the abstinence programs teach, heterosex outside financially stable marriage is inherently harmful to society and individuals. Luke and Jon do, as Grundmann says, "transcend their couple status" by being gay, but their transcendence may have more to do with the greater willingness of heterosexual, as well as homosexual, audiences to imagine and empathize with a gay couple who love each other yet do not settle down than with a heterosexual couple who make the same choice, because, since there are few places in America where gay couples are legally allowed to make homes together, gay lovers who remain "outside of society" can be seen as making the best of their situation rather than viciously choosing to reject domesticity (27). It seems worth noting that there are few, if any, American films in the killers-on-the-road genre in which a wild couple is "left on the road in limbo," as Luke and Jon are (28). The heterosexual couples generally must either convert to domesticity or disappear over the horizon of what is imaginable, as Thelma and Louise do at the Grand Canyon, or Laurie and Bart do when their bodies sink into the obscurity of a white mist.

Nonetheless, Grundmann is right to argue that when mainstream films conflate criminality and sexual wildness in gay characters, those characters do appear demonized. Whoever cannot be assimilated into the dominant culture's domestic narrative is almost always portrayed as inhumanly bad within mainstream media, whether we are looking at advice columns, relationship self-help books, (anti-)sex education, voter's pamphlets, film noir, or action thrillers. The late-twentieth-century version of the love that dare not speak its name is romantic passion that somehow fails to inspire in people a desire to buy a car and then a house, have a family, invest for retirement, and so on. And gay love (quite unfairly, as the advocates of gay marriage remind us) is stigmatized as particularly resistant to such taming. Araki's homosexualization of the killers-on-the-road genre from within gay culture represents a paradigm shift not because, as Grundmann claims, Luke and Jon are "a queer version of Bonnie and Clyde" (26), but because they are different from Bonnie and Clyde, not outlaws because they are outcasts, as "sexual deviants" are often depicted in mainstream films like *Dog Day Afternoon* (directed by Sidney Lumet, 1975). Instead, in a brilliant reversal, Luke and Jon are outcasts because they have contempt for the law, because, as Pedro Almodóvar puts it in his marvelous film of the same name, they obey only the *Law of Desire* (1987).

The thematic originality of Araki's film inheres in his refusal to treat obedience to this law as a compulsion that inevitably sets the characters against society and Nature. For a sharp contrast one might look at James Ellroy's novel *Killer on the Road,* which centers on the homosexual panic of one serial killer in love with another. At his first meeting with Ross, Martin, the protagonist, feels panic "coming on, naked and ugly" (146). Because both disavow their homosexuality, they cannot go on the road together. "Panic and unnamed desires keep [Ross] shut out but close" and "Martin tearing cross-country in flight from real sex" (177). After their only sexual encounter with each other, Martin understands that Ross is "rationalizing, running from what it made us, made *him*" (241). Their love is figured as an impossibility from which Martin can only retreat into "the sanctity of my madness" (280). Martin's direct narrative, which constitutes a little over half the book, figures all feelings of love and empathy as threats to individual identity. But the book as a whole tells us with the unsubtle repetitiveness characteristic of pulp fiction that this is a particularly "queer" perspective.

While audiences may choose to read Araki's characters similarly as alienated and criminalized because of their homosexuality, the film itself resists this by showing us that neither Luke nor the more conventional Jon is worried about being gay or in flight from it. The problems facing them are the virus that has infected them and the homophobic society from which none of us can escape. As Grundmann says, "AIDS is the epicenter of the film's rage" (26), but they seem equally furious at anything that gets in the way of their continuous pursuit of pleasure. The film might have treated their homosexuality as incidental to their social situation, just as, for example, in *My Beautiful Laundrette* (directed by Stephen Frears, 1985) the two protagonists' homosexuality seems less of an impediment to their love affair than their racially linked ideological differences. However, this is not the case in *The Living End.* Instead, Jon and Luke's rebellion is constituted in opposition to a homophobic world, with the fugitives' shooting of a gang of gaybashers providing one of the film's most exciting and satisfying moments.

This moment connects *The Living End* to films like *Guncrazy* and *Thelma and Louise* in that each makes a sustained attack on the idea that femininity or male gayness means receptive passivity and endless victimization. Albert Johnson notes, "Thelma and Louise's ultimate gestures of feminine liberation are exemplified . . . by their domination" of macho men like the truck driver and the state trooper, not to mention Harlan (23). None of these films can fully challenge binary gender difference, because it is essential to the plots and the emotional impact of the crimes. To the extent that viewers can identify with the protagonists, it is because they are fighting back against those who threaten them because of their perceived gender difference, which they themselves accept as real. While this difference receives a revisionary valorization (girls and gays are tougher than macho men), the difference labeled "effeminacy" remains in place and in contrast to a masculinity perceived as patriarchal and bad.

But it is possible to travel even further down the road, and to see more at the horizon than these films do. Michael Winterbottom's *Butterfly Kiss* (1995) is possibly the first ungendered killer-on-the-road movie. The central couple, Miriam (Mi/Me) and Eunice (Eu/You), are, as their cutesy nicknames suggest, universalized. The murders they commit have no apparent motives in common. It is left unclear, for example, whether Eu (Amanda Plummer) kills a man who picks her up hitchhiking and a woman whom she picks up in a cafeteria to get their vehicles or because they responded to her sexual overtures, or both. She kills a trucker because he is sexually forcing himself on Mi (Saskia Reeves), who has changed her mind in the middle of the sexual encounter. Mi kills her neighbor, Mr. McDermot, because he is sodomizing Eu, although apparently consensually. At the film's conclusion, Mi kills Eu at her request, after tenderly unfastening all the body chains Eu has previously always worn.

Once again, an unchained woman is quickly translated into a dead woman, but here the word "woman" seems superfluous. While they make love shortly after meeting and continue to act as lovers throughout the film, the two never mention lesbianism or talk about their desire for each other as being forbidden or deemed bad. Both are religious and seem to think that, if anything, heterosexual sex is less moral than what they do sexually together, which neither speaks of as sinful or wrong. Neither expresses any unhappiness over being a woman or any consciousness that women are treated differently than men in Britain (where the film is set) or anywhere on earth. Neither seems to suffer in any way related to gender difference or to homophobia.

Eu closely resembles the Misfit in Flannery O'Connor's classic killers-on-the-road story, "A Good Man Is Hard to Find," especially when she gives her haunting speech about the absence of God being evidenced by her own continued existence as an unpunished murderer. Mi apparently inhabits the space of madness; her framing narrative comes from a ward in a prison hospital, visions of which alternate in flashforward with the road saga. So, although both protagonists do seem insane, they do not fit any cultural stereotypes either of insane women or of insane lesbians. There seems no way in which the script would need to be changed if the two central roles were played by males.

Why, then, did Winterbottom decide to cast two women in these roles? Is it a homophobic move? I would argue that making the two protagonists the same biological sex is, instead, a necessity, given what is currently culturally readable through conventions in film. Making the film about a male and a female would be problematic and risk regendering the killers. If Eu were the male, Mr. McDermot's murder would then seem homophobic, as when Joe Buck turns on his male client in John Schlesinger's *Midnight Cowboy* (1969), and Mi's tranced collusion with Eu's crimes would seem traditionally feminine rather than part of her eerily displaced rage. If Mi's role were played by a male, the killing of Eu would seem misogynist, as does Bart's killing of Laurie at the end of *Gun Crazy*.

The difficulty of avoiding reinscription of binary gender difference in a killers-on-the-road movie with a male and female as the central characters suggests that while film audiences are apparently in some ways culturally ready for ungendering, they are not yet ready to actually perceive bodies marked with different biological sexual characteristics as sites from which contrastive gender difference can disappear. My favorite moment in *Natural Born Killers* comes in the midst of a parody of on-the-street interviews, when a beautiful youth of the blond androgynous type so loved by the Elizabethans expresses his fantasy of being "Mickey *and* Mallory."

This distinctly young and millennial fluidity of identification sheds light on Carol Clover's comment on *Thelma and Louise* that "a real corner in gender representation has been turned in mainstream film history," but that the same corner was turned much earlier in "so-called exploitation cinema," in the films that are traditionally discussed as being made exclusively for teen audiences, where "cross-gender imaginings" flow freely in all directions ("Crossing Over" 22). The killers-on-the-road genre has moved slowly (and inconsistently) away from the domestic enclosure of the noir and toward that horizon where the sharper eyes of the young can pick out more than their elders can, where some vision can penetrate beyond binarity to the dissolution of gender. Still, as I will argue in the following chapters, it is in the cultural products made by and for the young, and especially in the combination of music and visuals they seem to prefer to conventional songs and narratives, that contemporary ungendering as serious drama, rather than as a Bakhtinian carnivalesque that ultimately reinscribes through reversal, is most completely, most flexibly achieved.

good for
Tori article +
Riot Grrrl Reh Response

PART II
MILLENNIAL SEXSTYLES
THE VIOLENT BEAR IT AWAY

GLASS-SLIPPER BOYS, RUBY-SLIPPER GIRLS

In 1990, utterly disgruntled by traditional academe, I took a position as a member of
the foundational faculty at a new branch campus of a land grant university. A "senior
college," this branch campus offers only upper-division and graduate classes. My intention was to get out from under the mass of immutable introductory curricula and bu-
reaucratic rules that had constrained my teaching and research at other schools
and achieve some, albeit limited and personal, power to renew what higher education
might be. What I found was a near overwhelming amount of work in every area of
program and faculty development, but also an exciting opportunity to understand better what negotiations and compromises inform the workings of a college and its relations with the community that supplies it with the majority of its students. For the first
five years, our classrooms and offices were temporarily housed in one building on a
community-college campus, as we waited for the completion of our permanent site.
Because of the smallness of the start-up faculty, the cramped quarters, and the unusually heavy load of committee work outside our departments, I spent more time than I
ever had before with academics in other disciplines, especially the social sciences. My
interest, as a close reader, in slang and jargon made me seize upon one phrase popular
among my colleagues in social sciences that I half-joked summed up my experience as
an academic: "cognitive dissonance."

great personal narrative re: cognitive dissonance of academe

The source of my "cognitive dissonance" was the clash between the two worlds
where I spent most of my time. A couple of years after I arrived in Portland, I began to

realize something about myself that left me stunned for a few years. Up until then, I had always expected that, in the fullness of time, I would turn into a typical American adult in that I would begin to desire material security and the large, expensive objects that signify it: a car, a house, furniture, appliances. From observing those around me, I expected that one day I would feel the desire to own such things become so intense that I would find it possible to defer the attainment of immediate pleasures in order to have these things instead. Rather than wanting to be at rock clubs as fast as a cab could carry me, for instance, I would be content to drive around for half an hour looking for a parking spot where it would be safe to leave a nice car. And rather than waste money paying to see hot bands live about once a month, I would prefer to save up so that I could afford a car. On weekends, instead of taking every minute I could steal from reading, writing, and grading to dash out of my tiny apartment and spend hours in desultory conversations about edgy art with hip young things in coffee houses, I would prefer to stay in a house of my own, renovating it into a showplace.

My concept of how I would attain American maturity was that it would be similar to my experience of sexual awakening, through observation of French kissing when I was twelve years old. One day I would see people spending evenings and weekends redecorating their kitchens and I would feel nothing but revulsion. A few days later, I would be mysteriously possessed by an irresistible desire to have a kitchen of my own. However, time passed, I turned forty, and I still felt that car ownership would be an insupportable burden of responsibility, home ownership worse than a prison sentence. "Freedom" continued to be represented in my own mind by not-too-distant recollections of hitchhiking down the highway with no possessions except what I could fit into a cardboard suitcase, or by images of myself dancing in a trance as the disco lights strobed around me, unconcerned about anything beyond the physical sensations of the moment. And worst of all for a prognosis of financial success in later life, my ideal male continued to be a smart-aleck with a pretty face who knows all about current bands rather than a man in a suit who knows all about investment banking. My failure to experience the reorientation of priorities associated with maturing and becoming a professional means that I have continued to spend my recreational time hanging out in public spaces with people in their late teens and early twenties, because they are interested in the same things I am, the cheap and easy countercultural pleasures often described as youth cultures: "street" fashions, new bands, disorganized political activities, unfunded and unrecognized art, dancing, and aimlessly exploratory conversation.

Of course, instead of making jokes about cognitive dissonance, I could have simply recognized my situation as postmodern; after all, I am an academic specializing in the analysis of twentieth-century representation. However, despite the shared postmodernity of our condition, I could not help observing that the majority of my fellow academics did not seem to be experiencing the same inability to commit to material possessions that dogs my days. My own postmodernity seems to have a specifically rock 'n' roll–inflected flavor, if Lawrence Grossberg is right in seeing as one of "the historical conditions of rock's possibility" a postmodernity that inheres in the feeling that it is impossible to value what "social languages of signification" describe as valuable, "impossible to invest in those meanings that supposedly make sense of life. And similarly, . . . impossible to find a structure of meaning that makes sense of what matters" ("Is Anybody Listening?" 49)—outside youth's rock cultures, that is.[1]

As I indicated in this book's introduction, my young friends made me feel reimbursed for the dues one must pay in order to enjoy any freedom in a culture that punishes deviant desires mercilessly and deems deviant all desires that do not tend toward consumerist domesticity. Still, my movement back and forth from their company to the atmosphere created by scholarly writings and talks in my field caused me to experience a fierce disorientation. For example, I returned from a pleasant afternoon with an eighteen-year-old friend in a local café, during which she had talked quite a bit about her plans for the future and her determination not to be sidetracked from her goal of distinguishing herself as a rock musician by overvaluing romance and security, to find in my mailbox a publisher's catalog containing the following description of Master Richard de Fournival's *Bestiary of Love and Response:* "the work is more than a love argument between a man and a woman in the thirteenth century, it reflects problems that are universal to every age: the divergence of male and female expectations, 'love,' sexual dominance, sexual roles, and sexual exploitation" (18). This little bit of text seems to me typical of late-twentieth-century academic writing on gender and sexuality in its insistence on the existence of transhistorical and transcultural truths, its dismissive relegation of love to quotation marks, and its focus on dominance and exploitation as inevitable problems between men and women, and especially in its obvious attribution of conflict between lovers not to the differences that naturally occur between all humans beings but to gender differences. Leaving aside the vexing question of why the expectations of a man and a woman in love with each other would diverge any more than the expectations of two men or two women in love with each other, I was still left wondering, what exactly *are* these "problems that are universal to every age"?

My young friend had just told me about her struggle to balance her need for sexual pleasure with her need for artistic expression. I gather from her that "sexual dominance" is a term she is most familiar with in reference to the sort of dominatrix displays popular at rock club fetish nights, and "sexual exploitation" might be something she would associate with professional pitfalls, such as a record company executive trying to talk her into wearing sexier clothing to perform, but that she would see as having no immediate application to her relationship with her lover, since they both equally enjoy their physical contact. Moreover, her familiarity with homosexual couples causes her to think of gender as not necessarily relevant to intrarelational power struggles. She does see "the divergence of male and female expectations" as a problem in love (or "love"), but perhaps in a sense that would be surprising to Master Richard. Like most of the young women with whom I discussed these matters, she believes that males want commitment and security, while females need freedom and experimentation. To move from her world to that of the catalog is disorienting, to say the least. I have often felt that the only way I could adhere to the academic world's apparent central assumptions about gender would be to leave my other world entirely and forget about it completely.

To illustrate the gravity of this problem, I turn once more to the nomad in film and hope, through relating a brief personal anecdote, to suggest what has been at stake for me. In 1986, I saw a rather obscure horror film, *Nomads,* directed by John McTiernan. After repeated viewings of this film, which captured my imagination to an extent that few do, I began recommending it to my friends. The film's plot is fairly simple. A French anthropologist moves to Los Angeles, where he attempts to settle down in a bland suburb with his wife. Their domesticity is soon interrupted by visits from a pack of sinister black-leather-clad, motorcycle-riding supernatural creatures, played by hipster character actors including Adam Ant and Mary Woronov. Fascinated by their apparent nihilism, the anthropologist trails them through a night landscape and then makes contact. The nomads proceed to terrorize the couple, invading first their antiseptic-looking neighborhood and then their pristine white house. In the climactic scene, the husband and wife move into deeper recesses of their home as the nomads close in. Finally, he is carried away. In the last scene, we see the nomads on the move again out on the open road, the husband, now attired like them, riding along. I read the film as a cautionary tale divided against itself. While promoting a sort of Nietzschean warning against looking into the abyss, it also figures suburban domesticity as a wasteland to which the nomadic life presents a glamorous alternative.

At the time I saw the film, I was writing my dissertation, a study that transgressed the boundaries of academic feminism in its positive re-evaluation of Lawrence's relation to women's literature, but I was also working covertly on a much more transgressive book inspired by my personal experience of San Franciscan underground sexual communities. Filled with anxieties about my ability to mimic bourgeois affect well enough to assimilate into the professorial class, I found tremendous appeal in the fantasy that in the midst of some interview with members of a local S/M club, I might be carried away by nomads. At the end of each of my viewings of the film I would shut my eyes and envision myself side by side with Mary Woronov, riding a Harley toward the vanishing point, with my equally delighted darling clinging to the back of my leather jacket.

However, a number of the friends in academe to whom I recommended the film reacted entirely differently. The most typical response was that the film was a disgustingly sexist portrayal of male refusal to grow up and a subsequent hatred of women given violent expression. The wide gap between these readings must be attributed, at least in part, to the power that Freudian paradigms (Oedipalization, as Deleuze and Guattari call it) have over thought in Western cultures. If we can only think of subjectivity in terms of the gender roles of the traditional nuclear family, it makes sense to assume that the female nomads are men-in-effect and that Woman is represented by the domestically invested wife. According to this system of interpretation, the film becomes a fantasy about the fun a man can have scaring the woman to whom he owes a protective attitude and then deserting her. I have two points in telling this story. First, I hope it illustrates how impossible it was becoming for me, even in graduate school, to make my interpretations of popular cultural artifacts compatible enough with the feminist discourses then academically dominant that they could be understood as anything other than a willful assent to misogyny. And second, I hope it shows just how profoundly I would have had to give up on everything that signifies freedom to me had I renounced my nomad dreams.

Instead, in 1995, with the idea of transforming myself into an independent rock 'n' roll critic, I began to set up meetings with young people, during which I questioned them so that I could learn more about their reception of specific developments in rock 'n' roll–related subcultures that interested me as subjects for analysis. But as the meetings continued I became fascinated with the ideas incidentally revealed about sexuality, love, and gender identity. Instead of giving up on writing academic cultural criticism and trying to become a rock 'n' roll critic, I decided to begin to record my young friends' remarks about love, sexuality, and gender identity, and to examine that record for patterns that might help me better understand significant differences between their vision and the academy's.

As the record grew, I began a series of unofficial and informal interviews with other young people between the ages of thirteen and twenty-five who identified themselves as serious rock 'n' roll fans or as belonging to alternative rock 'n' roll cultures. Like Grossberg, I began to conclude that "rock is a [Deleuzian] deterritorializing machine," because "rock's politics are defined by its identification of the stability of everyday life with boredom," and, as a result, it creates "lines of flight into new mattering maps" ("Is Anybody Listening?" 51–52). Finally, a way out of here into a discursive community that might give me a language in which to articulate my feminism! ✔

nice exuberance

But I was unsure how to study such a community in order to learn its semiology. At this point I considered various research methods, including applying for permission to conduct official research on human subjects and putting together a properly demographically representative survey. But the unofficial and unfiltered conversations I was already having with the young provided me with information so rich and interesting that I decided to continue following the casual, snowball method, asking my "informants" only whether they would mind being anonymously quoted in my book and if they knew any other young people who might like to talk to me. A flood of contacts followed.

After spending a significant part of every week for two and a half years talking, listening, and frequently taking notes about rock 'n' roll, sexuality, and gender with over a hundred young people, including some I met on the Internet, on the streets, in clubs, on buses, even in airports, and many more to whom my young friends introduced me, I realized that for the very first time in my life I had found a group of people the majority of whom identified as heterosexuals who had codes of behavior I could actually understand.[2] This diminishment of my own alienation is the strongest sign I have seen that a cultural paradigm shift around sex and gender is taking place. Of course, I do not expect other scholars to be convinced by this sort of anecdotal evidence, nor by such a small and unscientific sampling of young people. And, as one of these young people told me after describing the many differences between her sex life and that of her sister, "to say there's a norm for this generation is misleading because everyone's so different and we accept different things." What does seem worth note is that my "interviews" consistently reflected patterns that are also apparent in popular cultural products such as films successful with those who identify with a specific youth culture, books written for a youth-culture market, advice columns for the young and hip, and, above all else, so-called alternative rock 'n' roll, as I shall discuss in the chapters that follow.

The more I questioned my young friends and informants about their views of sexuality and gender, the more completely I understood how profoundly the politics of my place and times determined my inability to find theories within feminism that I could unreservedly apply to my own life experiences and the art that most engaged me. Contrasting what the majority of feminist literary theorists professed to believe with what my informants told me, I was able to formulate a new analysis of those commonalities within feminist thought that continue to unsettle my efforts to situate myself as a feminist critic.

Although feminist theory within literary studies has been the location of numerous battles in the last twenty years, mostly centering on gender identity, especially as it impacts on experiences of sexuality, there have always been some substantial areas of agreement. Because some of these areas of agreement are the areas from which I must perforce depart, I will concentrate on them in the discussion that follows, while hoping that the reader will keep in mind that there are other areas of agreement in feminism that easily encompass my own beliefs and that I recognize that I am not alone in being a "dissident" academic feminist theorist; that is, I am not the only one in disagreement with what the vast majority profess to believe. Otherwise I would not continue to consider myself a feminist.

For the sake of brevity, I will call the discourse that is most familiar to critics and theorists and that is most often represented in anthologies and metacritical overviews majoritist academic feminism. To me, majoritist academic feminism can be understood to include both the writings of a large number of women who argue that gender difference is inescapable, basically unalterable (because it is coded into all symbologies and even into the structure of the mind) and also the writings of another large group of women who argue that gender difference is for the most part a cultural construct that has changed over time and can change more, and that thus calls for feminist intervention. Both groups belong to majoritist feminism to the extent that they agree with a few premises that have remained constant from the beginnings of feminist theory up to the present. These fundamental ideas of majoritist feminism are:

1) Men dominate or attempt to dominate all their relations with women except in very extraordinary circumstances, and any male articulation of another view of gender relations is obvious disinformation meant to justify misogynist attitudes and behavior. If this first claim about majoritist feminism seems overstated, I invite my reader to consider that Robyn Wiegman describes her own writing on the construction of Black masculinity in terms of a sexist and racist rhetorical category of "women and blacks" as "disloyal to feminism's moratorium on reading the category of men as anything other than patriarchal privilege" (82). I expected my own work on male masochism to meet with this sort of resistance, because the position of a volitional slave is ambiguous, but surely Wiegman's need to justify discussing the male victims of lynching as something

other than powerful patriarchs suggests that there were severe problems with the paradigms current in the most powerful academic feminisms as late as *American Anatomies'* publication in 1995.

2) A defining characteristic of women is a powerful, conscious craving for tenderness and emotional closeness, while almost all men have been successfully conditioned to reject emotional intimacy in favor of dominance.

3) Women generally fear physical violence from men so much that this fear determines the course of their lives in many respects.

4) The physiology of sexual response in men and women is enormously different. Heterosexual men experience sexuality as a straightforward matter, becoming aroused by visual stimuli and achieving orgasm easily following the insertion of the penis into the vagina. In contrast, women cannot become sexually aroused enough to be ready for penetrative sex without receiving substantial preparatory direct clitoral stimulation. Heterosexual women, except a minority too small to be significant, experience great difficulty reaching orgasm during coition, or simply cannot reach orgasm this way under any circumstances. Biological essentialists are far from being the only feminists who take this position. Linda Grant sums up a popular constructionist view: "Women failed to derive the pleasure they needed from sex not because they were incapable of sexual response or psychologically repressed, but because their orgasm was more complex and had, for too long, been subject to male interpretations of what it should resemble." She goes on to excuse men, to some extent, because in her view "male climax is much of a muchness," and thus these identical sexual subjects without complexity could not hope to understand the needs of women (185–186).

5) These differences, and pervasive male refusal to recognize them, render heterosexual intercourse more often than not emotionally and physically unsatisfying for women, no matter what their sexual orientation.

6) As a result of all of these fundamental gender differences, the sexual revolution failed women by removing traditional defenses against pressure to have sex and leaving women more vulnerable than ever to male sexual exploitation.

A good example of the effect of such standard feminist thinking on an otherwise well-informed and intelligent study is Joan Jacob Brumberg's *The Body Project,* a history of body images and body management of American female adolescents from the nineteenth century to the late 1990s. Toward the end of the book, when Brumberg offers suggestions to improve the lives of girls, she concentrates on opposing the "pro-sex argument" that girls under twenty "should be totally autonomous in their sexual decision making" (208). Brumberg argues that this is unrealistic because "teenagers do not always understand their own self-interest" (208–209). Very true (and not just of teenagers). However, Brumberg does not show a similar anxiety to protect girls from other risky adult activities, such as too early driving, an activity insurance companies continue to believe that most adolescents are emotionally unprepared to engage in safely. Nor does she take into account that a satisfying sex life often counteracts the media-instilled body disgust that might otherwise cause young girls to suffer from the life-threatening "body projects" she describes, such as anorexia and hyper-exercise mania. One of the case histories she offers is of a girl in the 1920s who, at eighteen, achieved a satisfying relationship with "a handsome neighbor who was a year younger than she" and of whom she wrote in her diary, "the only way he really attracts me is physically" (154–155). Apparently due to her own interpretive frame, Brumberg cannot recognize the significance of the details this girl provided. Sex was better for her when she was in control and felt powerful physical desire for her partner, and her pleasure had little or nothing to do with other sources of positive self-image.

Young girls continue to tell older, would-be helpful feminists that what they want is control over their own lives, including their sex lives. Most of us translate this to mean that they need our protection and we should control them. Unless we can examine the narrative about sex from which majoritist feminism works, I see little chance of a useful intergenerational dialogue.

The apparent deep agreement on the six ideas detailed above, which results in their status as foundational assumptions of majoritist feminist discourse, has caused an odd disjunction between what most second-wave feminist theorists say about gender relations and sexuality and what currently popular countercultures concerned with gender issues often seem to be saying to us. To provide a sense of the magnitude of this disjunction, I will summarize a bit from my interviews, using the much more extensive interview work of Paula Kamen as a reality check, and then will move on to briefly consider a few films very popular with the young but otherwise very different that all suggest similar visions.

First: Few of my informants believed men currently dominate all their relations with women. Instead, while male economic power and superior physical strength were seen as realities that impacted on many situations, these were not considered determinants of roles in courtship or sexual activity, except in that female anger about social subordination was deemed an important factor to be dealt with, usually through propitiating gestures on the part of the courting male. Almost all the men described "anger at men" as a characteristic female attitude, and had developed or were working on strategies for defusing it. None saw avoiding angry women as an option, since women's anger was seen as generally reasonable, even if unfairly directed at them. Instead, a certain degree of self-assertion was universally seen as necessary to female desirability.

In interviews with male Columbia University students, Kamen was told such things as "You have to marry a woman who won't let you get away with shit" and "I'll try to marry a woman who won't let me get away with anything, or I'll feel guilty" (151). Among the working-class young men I talked with, attitudes were strikingly similar. Two self-described conservatives, both in their mid-twenties, described their ideal woman as "strong and confident," in the words of one, and "aggressive and independent" according to the other. Both described male need to dominate the relationship as a sign of weakness. "I'm confident in myself, so don't need to do that," said one.

All of the young women said that they usually felt they were the one most in control in their sexual and romantic relationships with men. None apparently saw this as particularly unusual, but instead attributed it to their "having what he wants," as one put it. When I leapt to the conclusion that this meant they manipulated their partners by withholding sex, they soon disabused me of this notion by defining what men most want from women as reassurance and affection. In contrast, girls get the emotional support they need from their female and gay male friends. Such views of gender difference and the propitiation it requires of males were strongly represented in 1999 boy band hits like 'N Sync's "I Drive Myself Crazy," the video of which dramatizes various situations in which a young man annoys or offends his girlfriend by doing such things as talking on the telephone and motioning for her to be quiet, depicting them as disastrous events that not only cause her to dump him, but cause him unbearable agonized repentance.

Second: The concept of courtship as a contest in which romantic and sentimental females try to preserve chastity and hold out for love while horny males try to entice them into casual sexual activities appeared to be utterly alien to my informants. Just as females were generally assumed to be angry, males were generally assumed to be romantic. Young males interviewed expressed little anxiety about getting sex from females but worried that sexual relations would be impersonal or accompanied by distrust and contempt.[3] Courtship was seen as a space of negotiation in which males must prove their worthiness to be loved and respected as human beings, rather than used for sexual pleasure and then discarded.[4] A substantial number of young men said, in exactly these words, "I have no interest in the one-night stand," a sexual behavior that, incidentally, they associated with the previous generation. Males expressed desire for "intimacy," "emotional closeness," "a soul mate," "true love." Many named the attainment of such a relationship as their goal in life, and a few confided their dreams of a happy home complete with children. As one mid-twenties rock guitarist put it, "Without romantic love, sex seems pointless. I want love for life, and I think that deep down that's what everyone wants but they won't admit it."

Rather amazingly, those "who won't admit it" were generally seen by both sexes as predominantly female. Every young woman I interviewed, including three single mothers, expressed fear of being "tied down" by love and so kept from realizing their dreams, which invariably centered on either artistic achievement or material success—or a combination of the two—rather than love and family. As Kamen says, "Twenty-five years after the outbreak of civil war for women's rights in this country, a great declaration of independence is being drafted" (160). As she did, and in keeping with the findings of the Institute for Women's Policy Research that she cites, I discovered that among young women, "instead of being considered a privilege of womanhood, dependence is now more often feared as a trap" (161). Like Kamen, I found that some of the young women I talked with were so afraid of emotional dependence that they ended any relationships that aroused such feelings in them (162).

The female fear of dependence seems symbolically represented in the portrait of the domestic abuser frequently offered by young women in response to my question, "what kind of man would you see as a potential threat?" Most replied that such a man would be "too intense," and then went on to describe someone who "is always saying he loves you," "clings on you, hugging and kissing you," "says he needs you all the time," and makes a large number of romantic gestures. A twenty-two-year-old college senior who was engaged to be married as soon as he graduated described the trepidation he felt over giving his fiancée a gift of flowers, because he felt she might see this as a sneaky attempt to gain power over her through conventional romance. He solved the problem by "pretending I bought them for myself, because a guy can want flowers, then I put them near her so she could share them."

While my male informants typically indulged in glass-slipper fantasies of finding the ideal mate and living happily ever after (in part because their ideal mate's personality is closer to that of the wicked stepmother who makes her needs known than that of submissive little Cinderella), my female informants typically had ruby-slipper fantasies. Like the gay men who made Dorothy's ruby slippers a cultural icon, these young women dreamed of improvisational identities to which mobility and self-determination were more important than security and permanence in love. Yes, "there's no place like home," but to discover that "we're [not] in Kansas anymore" provides the exhilaration for which one lives.

Third: Unlike Katie Roiphe, my unwanted companion in skepticism about Take Back the Night marches, I did not find that young women who identified as feminist were consumed by terror of rape.[5] In fact, as an educator, I sometimes felt apprehensive about the degree of their bravado, and wondered whether I should try to impress on them the need for caution. All my young female informants expressed very strongly their belief that they could fight back effectively against men, even women who were physically quite small. A few showed me their biceps and claimed they would "deck" or "knock out" male aggressors. Others said that a lover might hit them once, but then "I'm outta there!" Battered women who stayed with their abusers were pitied by women and men alike, but were seen as uninformed about "options" or victims of "low self-esteem." Rape victims were often deemed insufficiently alert or "too trusting." Young women who confessed to having been sexually harassed, beaten, or raped invariably drew from their experience the lesson that, as one delicate and feminine woman put it, "next time a guy even starts with me, I'll kick him in the balls as hard as I can."

However, the women with whom I spoke were far from seeing all men as potential attackers. At millennium's end, there is an apparent shift away from the dichotomous representation of gender difference so typical of second-wave feminism, in which female sexuality is deemed sensual and gentle and male sexuality is most often figured as invasive and predatory. Almost all the young women I interviewed saw their own sexuality as inherently aggressive, using terms like "leap on him" to describe how they made advances to males. They often expressed the view that both males who offered unwanted attentions to them and males who aroused their own desire "better watch out." This attitude is perfectly exemplified in the songs of the all-girl (and all-Donna) 1990s Punk rock group The Donnas.

Fourth: All of my informants had heard that male and female sexual responses were radically different, usually as part of sex education provided by an older woman, but sometimes through watching television. The males accepted that they must work at sex to give a female partner pleasure. The majority of both heterosexual women and lesbians with whom I spoke expressed doubt that they personally responded differently to sexual stimuli than the average male in their age group. Their own experiences suggested to them that, while this difference might hold for women my age because we had been raised at a time when female sexual expression was inhibited, it did not hold for them.

One area in which they were anxious about sexual response was in revealing the intensity of their arousal in situations where they felt strongly and wanted emotional reciprocation from the object of their attraction. Not one young woman I talked with had experienced such demonstrations of sincere desire as being seen negatively by the object of her desire, whether that person was male or female; however, all had been told by authoritative older advisors (parents, advice columnists, etc.) that they must "play it cool" and conceal their eagerness for sex if they expected relationships to yield real pleasure. The best relationships, they were told repeatedly, were those in which the girl showed little sexual desire. It seems to me that if we really want younger women to have satisfying sex lives we must stop telling them this nonsense. Of course, showing that you desire someone gives that person some power over you, but conversely, if you feel so little that you are able to conceal your attraction from its object, then it hardly seems reasonable to expect that you will be able to experience intense pleasure with that person.

Fifth: Among my informants, neither males nor females expected heterosexual intercourse necessarily to be less satisfying for women than for men. If these young people were cognizant of what Elizabeth Grosz calls "the social and representational constraints mitigating against any structural possibility of reciprocity" ("Animal Sex" 279), they saw these constraints as acting upon others less "in touch with their own sexuality" than themselves. All the females with whom I spoke expressed some variation on the idea that finding one's partner very physically appealing and having some familiarity with one's own body and desires were, for both sexes, the two necessary prerequisites to sexual satisfaction, not, as most second-wave feminists seem to take for granted, specific acts of clitoral stimulation that are assumed to result in intense orgasm for all women.

Males emphasized the need for clear communication, for which almost all took sole responsibility, saying such things as "you need to find out what she wants" or "women all want different stuff; you have to ask her." Both lesbians and heterosexual women suggested that women who were nonorgasmic with compliant male partners of their own choosing should "question their sexual identity" and consider whether they were really lesbians. They seemed to define female heterosexuality as a tendency to be aroused sexually by looking at and having intimate contact with attractive males. They also seemed to regard lesbianism as being as much of a legitimate and wholesome sexual identification as heterosexuality. Rather than implying some slur on the women that they believed might be lesbians, they saw the choice as outside morality, often saying things like "some people like chocolate and some like strawberry" or "we are all different in what we need."

Surprisingly, given the many totalizing references to "male desire" and "the male sexual imaginary" in the feminist theory most of my informants were compelled to read for classes, almost all the young women and men with whom I spoke recognized that not all males desire the same sexual activities. Most of those with any sexual experience at all had engaged in a substantial amount of experimentation with sexual practices usually considered alternative to genital intercourse, including, in a number of cases, sadomasochistic role-playing. I was initially surprised also to hear that many young people (male as well as female) described their only sexual practice as "cuddling," and more surprised when I learned that for most of them this meant mutual masturbation preceded or accompanied by very diverse types of stimulation.

The language gap here, which confuses many adults, seems attributable to a difference in values. Many women of my generation see heterosexual activity as a competition in which women can only attain pleasure if they manipulate men into acting affectionate by withholding the sexual pleasures men seek. They create an opposition between sexualized touching and nonsexualized physical affection, which is deemed the only purely loving physical interchange men and women can have. The young people with whom I talked had trouble understanding this distinction, since they assumed that everyone enjoys sexual activities and wants to reach orgasm (and can reach it). In such a context, "cuddling," as they understand the word, is a means of avoiding the necessity of birth control and disease protection while still enjoying intimacy as fully as possible. Conservative Christian young people often saw cuddling/masturbation and oral sex as means of preserving the "virginity" their churches taught them was important.

Another enormous and confusing generation gap in semantics concerns the terms "abuse" and "perversion." Most of the young people with whom I spoke interpreted the messages about child molestation that they had been receiving since elementary school as meaning that any sexual contact with their bodies constituted "abuse." Because, in the view of most young people, adults in authority are unconcerned about whether other adults hurt them physically, as long as this contact is not sexualized, the young do not usually seem to associate the term "abuse" with doing an injury. Instead, they sometimes use it to connote a sexual contact that may well be welcomed and enjoyed, as when the Victorians referred to masturbation as "self-abuse." In their conversations it sometimes refers to caressing between two people of the same age. The irony of this situation is not lost on all of them, as was illustrated in Silverchair's 1997 hit song "Abuse Me" ("abuse me more, I like it").

What the young do generally take from their instruction about "abuse" is that adults consider sex to be "evil" in itself, a type of wrongdoing justified only by "love," which exclusively refers to domestic bonding, hence the impossibility of a love of which the main components are physical attraction and arousal. The ever-increasing social vigilance about sexual contact between minors and adults also conveys the message that the healthy, normal, and natural situation is for everyone under the age of eighteen to be completely devoid of sexual desires, since older people apparently believe it impossible for the young to initiate sex. Thus the young tend to refer to all intense desire that is either directed at them or *felt by them* as "perversion." In Alanis Morrissette's enormously popular song "You Oughta Know," the question about a new girlfriend, "Is she perverted like me?" seems to refer to the singer's willingness to have oral sex in the back row of a movie theater, a common practice of youth for at least the last fifty years. My informants regularly referred to themselves as "perverts," usually defining the term, when asked, as did one young man who explained, "when I look at women I sometimes think sexual thoughts."

It would be a mistake, however, to think that the young are tormented by the "perversion" and "abuse" that fill their lives. The young people with whom I talked were obviously pleased by this indication of their own ability to resist the adult agenda of sexlessness. They seem to enjoy shocking us as much as many of us in the 1960s relished offending grown-ups. When I innocently remarked to some young women that the name of the popular swing band Cherry Poppin' Daddies might be offensive to some, who would erroneously take it to connote father-daughter incest, they all laughingly told me they were well aware of its connotation. Their outlaw desire is something they own in the face of an adult culture that would deny it to them. In this sense, to paraphrase the famous claim of Kurt Cobain (fronting Nirvana), every one of them is queer. One thirteen-year-old virginal girl happily told me of her knowledge of various sexual practices, concluding, "as I get older I'll try all these things and find out if I am a lesbian or heterosexual or whatever." When I asked her how she would know, she told me that she would be able to tell by what caused her to have an orgasm—"duh!"[6]

Sixth: None of my informants agreed with prominent feminist theorists that the sexual revolution had failed *women,* although several of the young men in their twenties complained that it had encouraged a style of sexual interaction that left out emotions entirely. In keeping with their interest in relationships that could lead to marriage and family, males were generally more negative about the sexual revolution, equating it with a sex life organized around the club scene and one-night stands. Over half of the young men with whom I spoke mentioned fathers' abdication of parental responsibility in this context and talked about the emotional and economic damage divorce had done to them and their mothers. The ones who did think of the sexual revolution as largely beneficial talked about how they felt it had diminished homophobia or freed women to discover what pleased them sexually, often praising the way it had made communication about sexual desires easier for women.

Interestingly, all of the young men who had experienced a relationship with a woman that set a standard for them (and a number of them described themselves as still longing for reunion with such an ex-girlfriend) described her as sexually knowledgeable. Where once males seemed to see sexual initiation by a more experienced female as a stage they would pass through on the way to their true love, an innocent girl whom they would initiate, now many seem to view the more experienced woman as the ideal partner, as is illustrated in the popular youth cult film *Chasing Amy.* The only problem is preventing her from moving on.

In my discussions of the sexual revolution with young women, they also seemed to see it as enabling a life of casual sexual encounters, but most of them deemed this a potentially useful approach to managing their sexuality, as they continued to forcefully assert their refusal to be duped by romantic love or dominated by males. Females were more positive generally about 1960s sexual liberation than males, associating it with availability of birth control and education about disease prevention, and ultimately with power in sexual situations. My favorite remark, from a twenty-year-old female Marilyn Manson fan and snowboarding enthusiast, is "Sexual liberation was a good thing for women, because I can't imagine sitting there all demure saying, 'yes, sir' to men—I wouldn't like that at all."

What makes these young people so different from the generations that have preceded them? Their concepts of gender relations, like those of previous generations, are founded on ideas about gender difference, since gender can only be significant in determining identity if one believes gender-related differences are meaningful. But for my informants gender difference had a meaning far removed from the naturalized binarity taken by second-wave feminism to be central to twentieth-century thought. One question I asked everyone to whom I talked for this project was, "Do you think there are differences between men and women?" If they answered yes (and several did not), I asked them to elaborate and then followed up with the question, "What do you think causes these differences?" The biggest surprise was that very few males or females said there were intrinsic differences other than in genitalia. Otherwise gender was simply a matter of societal expectations, according to the majority. Typical responses from men were "no, there's really no difference," "I believe we socialize our children into masculine and feminine roles respective to their sex," "it's cultural expectation mostly," and my favorite, "women may pretend to be different in order to jerk you around." Only one male I interviewed believed in biologically determined gender differences and referred to many conventional ideas, such as that women were "more romantic," but he stressed that media representation distorted and exaggerated these differences. Interestingly, this informant was gay and said he had never had a sexual relationship with a woman. He told me that his concept of female difference came from observation.

My conclusions about these young men were similar to those expressed about male audience members by Leslie Mah of the radical lesbian band Tribe 8: "boys don't have the same attitude that I encountered even five years ago . . . younger kids seem different" (Juno 45).[7] It also seems worth noting that while Tribe 8 expressed pleasure at seeing heterosexual males become more willing to listen to and accept women as musicians on their work's merits, they expressed frustration with "'70s" feminists like those who protested their appearance at the Michigan Womyn's Music Festival without first giving them a hearing (43–44). (Tribe 8 were protested because their music represents women as aggressively sexual and sometimes violent.)

The young women I interviewed were slightly more likely to profess belief in gender difference than men were, but only when it reflected favorably on their sex, as in a frequent claim that "women have more sense" or "girls have more courage." But such chauvinistic statements were often followed by laughing denials, such as "I'm just kidding, you know." Males tended to joke from time to time in response to this question, as well, and also in ways favorable to women, saying things like "deadlier than the male." More typical were responses like "gender, sex, and race difference are all lies," "we are exactly the same in our feelings," and "they try to make you think so, but it's not true."

A few of the most conservative young men argued strongly that the sexes differed in many respects, but each one, when asked to what these differences could be attributed, replied without hesitation, "the media." As I sat rather stunned by this, they went on to elaborate on ways that they felt television in particular inculcated "false images" in women, leading them to believe that they were morally superior to men, instead of being men's moral equals, as all felt to be the true situation.

One could find many explanations for the differences in basic assumptions about gender relations between my young informants and the feminists of my generation. Ironically, the main reason for the changes in attitudes about gender that most sharply separate young women and men from the feminists of the previous generation is probably that second-wave "feminism has been injected into the mainstream of America and given it a transfusion of values, expectations, and ambitions" (Kamen 144).

Almost all the young people with whom I spoke believed that misogyny was outdated and unhip. The younger the person, the more she or he seemed to associate stereotypical gender-role playing and the attitudes about difference that accompany it with "old people." Young people who continued to act out such roles or to do things that indicated a belief in patriarchal concepts of differences, such as females deferring to males or males physically dominating females, were derided as being very much behind the times. Although date rape and other problems in gender relations between the young were mentioned during a number of these discussions, the attitude of my informants was always that such behaviors were indicative of a failure to change with the times, and the criminals in these cases were often described as "unevolved." Many of my informants parodied macho posturing or femme fluttering for my entertainment as we talked, and a substantial number attributed such behaviors to their grandparents' generation. One fifteen-year-old girl asked me whether people had ever really "believed all that shit," and then flattered me by asking, "or were you, like, born yet when they did?"

I could have spent a lifetime talking to young people like this, just asking them about their views of love, sex, and gender, and never tired of hearing their responses. But as those born after 1975 especially like to say, "I had to ask myself"—are the ideas of these charming young people represented in the cultural products that they consume? Because, if that is not the case, it would seem inevitable that they will eventually "mature" into attitudes similar to those that have laid such a big chill on my own once seemingly free-spirited generation. In order to answer that question I started to ask my informants not only about their musical interests, which will be discussed in the two chapters that follow, but about their favorite recent films, as well.

Two enormously popular films, *Scream* (1996) and *Titanic* (1997), whose commercial success has been attributed by most film critics to their appeal to the young, very obviously depict the types I describe as ruby-slipper girls and glass-slipper boys, as even the briefest plot summaries reveal. *Scream* cleverly parodies a large number of horror film conventions, but centers on the "Final Girl" phenomenon described by Carol Clover. In Clover's view the two most important aspects of this heroine's personality, intrinsic to the logic of her survival, are her virginity and her boyishness (*Men*,

Women, and Chain Saws 39–40). Clover deems this bisexualizing of the heroine essential to the figure's function "as a vehicle for [the young male audience member's] own sadomasochistic fantasies," and thus feels that for feminists to "applaud the Final Girl as a feminist development [is] a particularly grotesque expression of wishful thinking" (53).[8]

Wes Craven's *Scream* playfully reverses the pattern Clover attributes to horror films. In a neofeminist twist, *Scream's* plot teaches the heroine, Sidney (Neve Campbell), that the ideal of female chastity to which she has been clinging since her promiscuous mother's murder is "totally bogus." After choosing to have sex and initiating it, she discovers that her romantic and seemingly sweet boyfriend Billy (Skeet Ulrich) is a psychotic killer responsible for her mother's death and now planning to murder her as well for failing his chastity test. Unable to get protection from the men who should, according to the cultural script, be providing it (her father, the policemen, her other admirer) this aggressive girl kills the murderer and triumphs. That Sidney is defined partly through contrast with her ineffectual and virginal male friend, Randy (Jamie Kennedy), a horror film buff, points up her function as an identificatory figure for girls (or grrls), not as a stand-in for a male viewer. The horror-film fanboy, as Craven depicts him, is rule-bound and hopelessly old-fashioned about sex, while the girl enthusiast is interested in becoming a woman who wins. The film's—and its sequel's—enormous success with young women suggests that Craven's assessment of his female audience was correct.

A further *fin de siècle* twist on the Final Girl horror story appears in *The Devil's Advocate,* in which the *hero's* rejection of nonromantic sexuality redeems him. Urged by his Satanic sire (Al Pacino) to copulate with his own sister in order to produce the Antichrist, the half-demonic protagonist (Keanu Reeves) looks up from her writhing nude body to ask plaintively, "What about love?" The Satan figure's impatient dismissal of its importance clearly provokes his son into exercising free will in order to go over to the human side. This film, which has a large cult following among the young, suggests that if one side of the new gender equation is that girls are no longer deemed evil for choosing sexual experimentation, a boy's holding out for true love constitutes his saving grace.

This new double standard is perhaps nowhere more in evidence than in the megablockbuster *Titanic.* Katha Pollitt wittily heralds it as the advent of a new women's movement, "romantic feminism" (9). The feminist dimension of the plot of *Titanic* is summed up neatly in its most publicized image: brave young woman at the front of the ship, supportive male behind her. Nor is the crucifixion image suggested by their spread arms entirely unrealized as an element of the film, because Jack (Leonardo DiCaprio), the hero, exists to redeem the life of the heroine Rose (Kate Winslet), dying that she may live; and, in a very *nineteen*-nineties updated mode, living does not mean mere survival, but instead realization of her every adventurous dream. While Pollitt seems skeptical about the film's portrayal of "costless liberation," she does see it as a contradiction of the general media assumption that "feminism is over and retro is *de retour*." She also observes that Jack's death is read by its female audience as necessary, because "'otherwise,'" as she quotes a friend saying, "'he would have disappointed her down the road.'"

How did we get to the point where the two films with the most demonstrable appeal to the young both depict her boyfriend's death as necessary to the heroine's self-actualization? Tracing some changes in film depictions of romance suggests that this resolution to the feminist problem of narrating youthful love is not anomalous. In the interests of brevity, I will do so here by looking at three films that did well at the box office or in video rentals with young audiences and that emerged as having strong appeal for my young cultural informants.

My own views of the films will, of course, color my interpretations of their spectator appeal, because, as Judith Mayne claims in "Paradoxes of Spectatorship," universalizing descriptions of spectator response are always at risk of being nothing more than "displaced representations of the critic's own" (163). However, through lengthy discussions with my young friends before and after viewing the films, I have attempted to keep in focus the differences in the ways we see. Each of the films is in the love-and-courtship genre, with the main plot concerning a heterosexual couple's resolution of romantic problems.

In 1996 the film I was most often urged by my young friends to see, because it was considered a "cool" love story, was *Jerry Maguire.* Directed by Cameron Crowe, it stars Tom Cruise as a sports agent whose career problems center on a massive "twenty-something" identity crisis during which he almost loses the love of his wife and business partner Dorothy, played by Renée Zellweger. While the film is traditional in its high valuation of a marriage defined by the man's career and conventionally gendered through his love of football, it has many elements that mark it as a late-twentieth-century product successfully aimed at the young. Perhaps most objectionable from a feminist perspective is the organization of Jerry's moral redemption around his realization that his wife is valuable as an adjunct to his personality.

Jerry is the subject, as is established not only by the title and plot but by the number of point-of-view shots from his perspective. Thus his recognition that Dorothy "completes" him makes narrative sense, while still recalling the patriarchal dyad of male subject and female object. More interestingly, though, the word "completes" marks him as essentially incomplete, lacking. He gets the idea from an encounter with another couple in an elevator. The man is signing to a woman with whom he is obviously in love. It is unclear whether only one or both of them are deaf/mute, but because the man is the one doing the signing, he appears to be. Jerry cannot decode their communication (another indication of his incompleteness), but Dorothy does and translates it as the phrase he will repeat to her near the end of the film, when he returns to save their marriage: "you complete me."

The film also suggests that maleness is incompleteness in other ways. Jerry's role is often that of a secondary or supporting player, although the film is very much Cruise's star vehicle. His job as a sports agent requires him to take a supportive, and often subordinate, role in relation to his client, Rod Tidwell, played by Cuba Gooding Jr. Tidwell comes off, in contrast, as a very powerful African American man defined by his huge family, his passionate relationship with his wife, and the courage ("heart") that makes him wildly successful as a wide receiver despite his relatively small stature. Tidwell must learn from the more ingratiating and soft-spoken Jerry how to court the public, to take the warmth he lavishes on his family and offer it to the team and fans as well, losing the aggressive "attitude" that characterizes his earlier behavior. In turn, he functions as a relationship standard for Jerry, who admires and envies his behavior with his devoted, but strong and rather pushy, wife.

All the women in the film are markedly aggressive, and all except Dorothy are characteristically angry. Tidwell's wife, although mainly sweet to her husband with the exception of occasional admonishments, shouts a lot and, in one scene, hits and shoves her brother-in-law because his criticisms of his brother annoy her. Dorothy's sister belongs to a divorced women's support group, which seems to be meeting continuously for the duration of the film. It stands as a sort of representative female norm: angry women full of complaints and determined to fight men to the end. Dorothy agrees with their assessment of men as "the enemy," but confesses that she cannot avoid loving the enemy. She is the only submissive woman in the film, longing to subordinate her life to that of her male love object. When Jerry is kicked out of his agency for writing a mission statement urging his colleagues to serve rather than exploit the athletes they represent, she is the only one who accepts his invitation to go with him.

Jerry, however, distinguishes himself as the most submissive person in the film. In his interactions with the athletes, most of whom tower over him, he stresses his sincere desire to serve them, to "be there for them." He accepts betrayals and disappointments from other men with very little fuss, and without any threats or apparent anger. With women he is absolutely abject. He is described as afraid to be alone, a weakness showcased when, for his bachelor party, his friends screen a home movie of his old girlfriends explaining his inability to say "no" or disappoint them. Dorothy's attraction to him is sparked by her overhearing him telling another woman how he became engaged by accident because his fiancée expected a proposal and he did not want to let her down. Later he proposes to Dorothy so as not to hurt her feelings or those of her son. When he breaks up with his first fiancée, because he cannot make money as fast as she wants him to, she beats him up, punching him twice in the face and once in the stomach. He never defends himself and later wears dark glasses to conceal his battered, bruised face. He jokes to Dorothy that he is lucky he did not "buy her the ring she wanted," because his face is so cut and bleeding from the smaller diamond he did give her. When Dorothy tells him she wants a divorce, he accepts it with bowed head. When he does return to her to tell her he will not leave, he cries as he explains that he does love and need her. The ubiquitous women's group watches without comment.

If women in the film are mostly angry mothers, traditional dominant fathers are replaced by sensitive mentoring father figures. We are told that Jerry's own father deserted him, but we see many flashbacks to the avuncular sports agent who trained him and transmitted a philosophy of love, connection, and emotion as the basis of success. Jerry himself becomes such a kindly mentoring figure to Dorothy's son, whose father is dead. Equally kindly to his small son, Tidwell is an exemplary family-oriented African

American Dad, a dramatized rebuttal of the white mainstream's lament that Black men shirk family responsibilities. To the extent the film is aimed at a female audience that will enjoy its romantic plot, the pleasures offered seem to be fantasies of men who function well as selfless, gentle fathers; who are lonely and vulnerable because of their beauty; whose need for female approval is so great that they cannot oppose giving women whatever they ask for; and who consequently submit to verbal abuse and beating from women without any retaliation, even verbal.

To the extent that the film is aimed at a male audience that will enjoy its references to football and AFC Championship suspense, the pleasures offered seem to be the fantasy that integrity and a soft, unassuming manner attract gentle, supportive women; that one can find a beautiful and smart woman who wants only to work in support of her husband's projects; and that total passivity will result in being pursued by beautiful women who want sex *and* lasting relationships. In addition is the fantasy that a man can attain great wealth simply through getting in touch with his feelings, as long as those feelings include insecurity and neediness and exclude any sort of anger and aggression.

While *Jerry Maguire* does offer African American audiences the charm of Cuba Gooding Jr. and, in his characterization of Tidwell, the satisfaction of a role model with whom few could take exception, this film was not especially popular with the young African Americans with whom I spoke. Perhaps his embodiment of the perfect father was too old-fashioned to intersect with their fantasies. Far more popular was the "in-your-face" comedy *Booty Call*.

This 1997 film, directed by Jeff Pollack, is relentlessly witty, mostly due to the "signifying," rapid-fire creative insults and exaggerated self-promotion, that dominates almost every verbal exchange in the film, but also because of its ample visual jokes. Placing itself in hip-hop culture through its play with language as well as the self-stylings of the more daring of the two contrasting couples, *Booty Call* follows rap music in mocking American social pieties. This mockery is expressed through deliberate assaults on liberalism, as in the deployment of members of other minorities as exotic or clownish figures, but also in the defiant ridiculousness of many of the main characters' most "Black" attributes, such as the names of the more sexually confident pair, Bunz (Jamie Foxx) and Listerine (Vivica A. Fox). What sets the film apart from other, more sedate visions of young, urban African American romance, such as *Love Jones* (also released in 1997), is its depiction of sex as a field of negotiation in which both genders are equally eager to experience physical pleasure.

The rather slight plot hinges on the young men's search for latex condoms through the dangers and annoyances of an unaccommodating city. While achieving lasting love is suggested as a possibility for both couples, and seems more likely for the more timid pair, protection against venereal disease is the only issue the film seems to take seriously. Notable challenges to traditional views of gender difference include the straightforward treatment of young women's interest in sex as an end in itself, the underlying assumption that it is appropriate for women to control sexual interactions, the presumption of solidarity between women, and the lack of moralistic lessons about the necessity of love and trust to sexual pleasure.

Instead of the last, the film offers us delightful moments as the shyer of the two women, Nikki (Tamala Jones), develops under Listerine's tutelage into an aggressive, even dominating lover. "What's my name?" Nikki imagines herself harshly demanding of her sexually overwhelmed boyfriend in a fantasy about releasing her deeper emotions. Both the men and the film itself appear to consider female sexual dominance the clearest, and most attractive, manifestation of female passion. It is through actualizing her fantasy of control that Nikki is able to slow down the *romantic* advances of her aptly named suitor, Rushon, enough to appreciate him sexually and thus relax and consider committing herself to a long-term relationship.

Addicted to Love, a film that won the favor of a diverse group of my young friends that included both sexes and four races, also takes a playful attitude toward essential tenets of contemporary liberalism. Its major targets seem to be "love addiction" and "stalking," two pathologies newly created in the Foucauldian sense. Matthew Broderick plays Sam, a jilted lover who squats in the vacant building next door to his former fiancée's home and sets up elaborate surveillance equipment so as to observe her life with her new French lover; he is an indisputable stalker, but the most innocuous specimen imaginable. The gentle loser persona conveyed by his hopeful-puppy expression is borne out in his inability to do any real harm deliberately, even when egged on by Maggie, the Frenchman's rejected girlfriend. In contrast to the frighteningly vindictive Maggie, played with demonic panache by Meg Ryan, Sam prefers moping and hoping to vengeance, and reads his own character as incomplete, even "empty," without love. His descriptions of what love means to him seem taken right out of the pages of self-help guides to overcoming love addiction. But he is unwilling to try to eradicate the mindset that brings him so much pain. In the face of Maggie's corrosive scorn he can only feebly moan that without the excitement of love he and his life are meaningless.

A romantic comedy with more respect for therapy culture would certainly show Sam learning the lesson of self-sufficiency. Once he had realized that unrequited loving is an illness, and that we must not overvalue romance, he could be rewarded with an appropriately emotionally mature love object. Instead, *Addicted to Love* not only posits the addiction as unbreakable, it celebrates the transference of his passion from Linda to Maggie as a sort of upgrade. Where once he loved an unfaithful, shallow, and silly kindergarten teacher, by the end his hopes are fixed upon a violent and awesomely mean criminal with a strong resemblance, right down to her red leather costume, to the motorcycle bitch persona Chrissie Hynde developed in the early days of the rock group The Pretenders.

Maggie shows a smidgen of kindness, in a scene that parodies the great renunciations of 1940s women's weepies, by ordering him to leave her alone because she does not love him. She seems to be motivated to protect him from herself, because she is obviously too powerful ever to allow him equality in their relationship. He sadly leaves and then, while watching a Lassie film on the airplane home, experiences an epiphany. On the screen-within-a-screen, Timmy is threatening Lassie with a huge stick and telling her, "go away, I hate you!" It is all for Lassie's own good, to protect her from dog-catchers, but Lassie slinks back on her belly and crouches at Timmy's feet. Returning, he tells Maggie about this experience, concluding that he can only emulate Lassie. No matter how he is treated, he must accept it in the name of his god(dess), Love. The film's resolution occurs as Maggie enfolds him in her arms.

In recommending these films, my informants consistently described them both as "realistic" and as representing an image of "how I'd like it to be for me." I was also often told the films were "all about gender, how it is, all that stuff you ask about." Heterosexual males and females often described the films' protagonists, if of their own gender, as being either eerily "just like me," or models of "how I want to relate" to the opposite sex. They typically described the opposite-sex protagonists as exactly the sort of people they were looking for, or were already in love with. The only exception was that no one I spoke with expressed any enthusiasm for or identification with the character of Dorothy in *Jerry Maguire.* One young man did, however, admit that he longed to find a woman aggressive enough to complement his own passivity, and therefore he "could understand the concept" of being completed by another person.

Two current models of sexuality, as organizing principle and as disorganizing force, are represented in two recent films: *The Opposite of Sex* and *Species II.* Differences between the two are suggestive of the new generation gap. Both films show a contemporary awareness that heterosex is not the only option available. And in both films heterosexuality is viewed somewhat negatively in that it means procreation, and heterosexuals are by definition "breeders." But the former film is aimed at a mature liberal audience and takes the instructive, edifying attitude liberals seem to love, while the latter is pure sensationalism aimed, like all horror films, at the frivolous young.

The "serious" film represents the homosexual world as disordered, and not simply by the AIDS epidemic, which touches the hero's life through the death of his lover before the action begins. At the opening of the story, the hero has a new lover ten years younger than him, which is much discussed as a grave problem. His other problems include being hopelessly admired by his former lover's sister, who tries to live with him, and the invasion of his nice suburban home by his sixteen-year-old half-sister (Christina Ricci), a destructive, pregnant drifter.

All the characters seek love and ponder the purpose of sex as if they had never heard of, let alone experienced, orgasm. They are saved from meaningless chaos by the disclosure of the little sister's pregnancy, which magically causes her brother's lover to find a partner his own age, her brother to pair up with a sober, domestic man his age, his former lover's sister to marry and have a baby of her own, and the teen herself to settle down. These events mitigate the girl's intense and vulgarly expressed homophobia. Everyone learns that sex is permissible as long as its expression is strictly confined and disciplined by domesticity and familial caring. As Mandy Merck astutely observes, in discussing "post-AIDS authors . . . [who] *suburbanize* the gay novel, maintaining its object choice while domesticating its stories and settings," such moves neutralize homosexuality's disruptive effect on the rigid narrative of "'the family'" (45; emphasis Merck's).

Species II, unhampered by any imperatives except to achieve the utmost in sensation, opens on a homosocial world in which astronauts (one is female but is treated as a nongendered being by "the boys") are segregated from women due to the government's concern that the boys have been infected with a virus during their Mars flight and will transmit it sexually to others. Meanwhile in a supposedly impregnable glass case a female alien (Natashia Henstridge) lives in a simulacrum of a bourgeois bachelor-girl apartment. She is dressed in Laura Ashley–type frocks by her female scientist-protector and overseen by an all-female staff, lest her alien breeding drive be aroused. Heterosexuality is figured, in seemingly unconscious response to William Burroughs's famous claim about language, as a disease from outer space.

In the film's best scene, one of the astronauts, infected with the alien virus, enters the female alien's compound and she gets a whiff of him; her head rises like a racehorse's and she crashes through the walls of her glass case to get some sex. Chaos follows as Earth's human population is threatened with extinction should the aliens, who have no interest in anything but sex, be allowed to breed. The specter is raised of a society devoted to nothing except (hetero)sexual pleasure.

Programs for social change that issue from agreement with majoritist feminist views of sexuality, like Judith Butler's in *The Psychic Life of Power,* seem to me inadequate when I view them from within such cultural contexts as are represented by these films. I have no doubt that, as Butler claims, "gay melancholia . . . contains anger that can be translated into political expression," or even that it is possible that such expression could bring us all to realize that "there is no necessary reason for identification to oppose desire, or for desire to be fueled by repudiation" (*Psychic Life* 147, 149). However, the mechanisms through which normative subjectivity is produced seem to me unlikely to be changed by gay activism alone, for the very reason that it is not gay desire alone that fills the mainstream with terror, but also heterosexual desire. As *The Opposite of Sex* and *Species II* both, in their own ways, graphically illustrate, attacks on homosexuality mask hostility to desire itself, which is always coded first by the dominant heterosexual majority as heterosexual. As long as the bursting forth of the daughter from her glass coffin in pursuit of sex rather than of love and marriage is seen as crisis, and finding one's place in the world means finding a house and settling down and away from sexual adventurism, gay anger at exclusion does not seem likely to effect any great reversal of the system by which we are recognized as subjects according to the degree of our renunciation of desire.

All of the young people, gay, lesbian, and heterosexual, with whom I discussed *Species II* and *The Opposite of Sex* found the former entertaining and amusing and the latter mainly annoying. They confessed themselves unable to understand what the audience was meant to make of Christina Ricci's character. Were we to identify with her revulsion against homosexuals and then learn along with her that they could be just as proper and dull as heterosexuals? In contrast, we all shared enthusiasm for the breaking-out scene in *Species II,* with many of my informants informing me that, like me, they found it a hilarious metaphor for sexual awakening.

Cognizance of young people's visions of romantic love and sexual pleasure, in which uncontrollable, irrational passion is the only force capable of even temporarily bridging the chasm between glass-slipper boys and ruby-slipper girls, can help orient older readers of other artistic expressions, such as independent music, that are pro-duced and consumed within youth subcultures. In what is perhaps the best guide ever written for culture critics attempting to analyze the things loved and created by the young, Donna Gaines writes, "Kids are operating in different linguistic, sartorial, and mythic systems from adults. Sometimes we can translate" (229). It is with similarly modest expectations that I go on to look closely at some permutations of independent rock 'n' roll cultures at the end of the twentieth century.

CLOSER TO GENDER DISSOLUTION

As part of her 1996 *Village Voice* parody of the *New Yorker*'s traditional New Year's poem on "the year that was," Ellen Willis wrote:

This was the year that turned the heat
Upon the "cultural elite,"
Defined by Bennett and his mates
As anyone who celebrates
The sound of rap or Nine Inch Nails

The humor in Willis's verse derives from standards of seriousness generally agreed upon among intellectuals, which mark music popular with the young as lacking much cultural weight. What is most popular, especially among teenagers, critics usually deem both transient and insignificant. Sometimes one concedes that the music may reach an apex of anti-meaning, with a temporary and unintended deconstructive effect. For example, in *Blissed Out,* Simon Reynolds says that one can experience pop music as "a rupture/disruption in the signifying system that holds (a) culture together" (13). That popular music not only might do so for a moment that renders one relatively small group "blissed out," but also might serve as the register of a permanent cultural change, is a more difficult idea to defend. Claiming that, in addition to temporarily undermining familiar systems of signification, rock 'n' roll signifies in ways that go beyond the re-packaging of tired sexual stereotypes for new consumers puts one at risk of seeming as ridiculously overwrought as the conservatives Willis mocks. Yet to uncover what is particularly unsettling to conservatism about the celebration not simply of the sound of some currently popular music but also of the sense that can be made of its lyrics and performances entails taking that risk. So to paraphrase Reynolds's introductory claim— "This book is an argument about bliss; it is an argument about noise" (13)—this chapter is an argument about cultural absurdity, about the explosion of those nineteenth-century categories of gender identity described so notably by Foucault, and about what happens when categories of identity break down so far that they cannot be put back together again to make a culture readable in the old ways. This chapter celebrates Nine Inch Nails.

In recent years many theorists of postmodernism have addressed its apparent unsettling effect on concepts of gender difference, perhaps none more influentially than Judith Butler. If one begins with the premise, common to theories of subjectivity developed in response to psychoanalysis, that gender difference is the primary departure point for identity formation, the radicality of Butler's conclusions in *Gender Trouble* is apparent. Responding to revisionist work in biology and the history of science, Butler advances the thesis that sex difference is just as much a construct as gender difference. While acknowledging that human beings differ biologically from each other, she recognizes no need to organize the myriad physical differences into two basic groups correlating to male and female identity. She declares: "There is no gender identity behind the expressions of gender; that identity is performatively constituted by the very 'expressions' that are said to be its results" (25). Consequently she suggests that only if we believe in such beings as biologically constituted men and women does discussion of their respective possession of masculine and feminine attributes make sense. In the absence of such naturalizing figures, the incoherence and instability of the signifiers "masculine" and "feminine" are revealed. She ends her study by looking forward to a time when "cultural configurations of sex and gender might proliferate, or, rather, their present proliferation might then become articulable within the discourses that establish intelligible cultural life, confounding the very binarism of sex, and exposing its fundamental unnaturalness" (149). In other words, Butler seems to be anticipating a time when, in actual lived experience, the fragmentation of sex and gender roles beyond the traditional contrastive pairing of an apparently coherent masculinity and femininity might reach such proportions that a multiplicity of diverse representations of gender would spill over into the public sphere. We could imagine that this public presence of genders too diverse and plentiful to fit binary categorization would completely overwhelm all the old definitions of femininity and masculinity, thus bringing about a new age in which it would become possible to conceptualize subjectivity without reference to gender.[1]

Hopeful signs of the beginning of this explosion of gender difference into illegibility began to appear in the last decade in some pretty unlikely places. One of the most unlikely of these places must be rock 'n' roll music videos featuring male performers, although the video form has regularly been harshly criticized as conventionally sexist. However, a great many rock 'n' roll performances of gender, now plentifully available on television, suggest otherwise. In order to explain how I am able to entertain the hope that we are currently crossing the threshold of an age in which gender difference will no longer be a very meaningful concept, I will first look at the relation between what might be called a rock 'n' roll aesthetic and the performance of female-dominant, male-submissive S/M, and then I will trace the not unrelated representation of gender in alternative music videos up through what I see as its dissolution in the work of Trent Reznor, otherwise known as Nine Inch Nails.[2]

In *Feminine Endings,* Susan McClary argues that "the Western musical tradition" is characterized by exclusion, expulsion, or neutralizing containment of women and the feminine. Where female strength is represented, from opera to rock 'n' roll, a "desire-dread-purge mechanism prevails," whereby the aggressive(ly) female element is either brought under masculine control or destroyed (152). McClary goes on to praise Madonna's resistance to this hegemonic pattern in her music videos. The resistance McClary describes here and that can also be seen in the performances of many female rockers, from riot grrls to pop stars, is undeniably important, not least in that it is being articulated by women. However, elsewhere in the vast world of rock 'n' roll performances something else, possibly equally significant but apparently less evident to most people working in gender studies, is taking place. My critical foray into that other world of musical resistance will begin obliquely, with a side trip to a place where performance art and rock 'n' roll are indistinguishable.

Andrea Juno and Stacy Wakefield's book *Bob Flanagan: Supermasochist* features two photographs arranged diagonally to fill half of page 92. The picture at the upper left shows Flanagan holding a microphone up to another man, who is playing a drum. It is captioned "With Mike Kelley and our improvisational noise band, Idiot Bliss, Los Angeles, 1984." The picture at the lower right, captioned "Finding SM messages wherever we look, Los Angeles, 1984," shows Flanagan lounging against a stereo store's display window. His pose is emblematically that of the hip rebel: long, thin body leaning backward, knee bent and foot resting on the toes, middle three fingers of each hand inside the pockets of his tight jeans, head cocked to one side, faint enigmatic smile, and eyes turned to the side. His sightline draws our attention to a poster advertisement in the window. In the foreground of the poster is a drawing of a woman in dominatrix regalia with a long whip dragging on the ground. She stands in front of massive, stacked stereo speakers. A legend at the top of the poster reads "TOUGH TO BEAT." Obviously, the surface message of this photograph is comic. Flanagan, a performance artist who specialized in displays of his own extreme masochistic practices, was certainly tough yet was anything but hard to beat, as the book's previous 91 pages of text and photos show.

But this particular display is a little more complicated than a simple visual joke. To analyze the photographic display in terms of female aggression and its traditional containment (as characteristic of literary and visual arts as it is of music), first consider that everything we see here is shaped by women: the photography was done by Sheree Rose, Flanagan's lover and mistress, and the page design by Juno and Wakefield. The arrangement of the pictures creates a diagonal sightline from Kelley's arms in the first to the second, in which Flanagan's body angle points to the dominatrix figure. Her apparent containment between the two masculinized images of music-making (guys in a noise band and the huge stereo speakers) is seriously undercut by Flanagan's nonchalant contradiction of the advertisement's suggestion that consuming "big," loud music is a male activity that defeats female aggression. If tough, cool rockers in noise bands are easy for women to beat and proud of it, then the relationship between rock 'n' roll and femaleness must be a little less continuous with the (male) dominant Western tradition than it initially seems.

Flanagan is indisputably "deviant," but in this particular case perhaps he does not deviate as far from the standard as one might think. Rock 'n' roll itself is a paradoxical enunciation of rebellion. Because socialization is achieved through appeals to the emotions and especially through the inculcation of guilt, rock embraces an ethos of "cool" in order to rebel against society. That is, rock must be uncaring; it must express the negativity, the sarcasm, the refusal to be manipulated by others that characterize the attitude we call "cool." As we all know, the cool person is self-contained and self-controlled, smiling that ironic little smile and gazing through half-closed eyes as if at nothing.

But as we also all know, sulking around in black does not constitute as annoying a rebellion against the powers that be as a great blast of dissonant noise does. The difference between silent coolness and rock 'n' roll is analogous to the difference between depression and anger. Where cool is turned inward, rock assaults the outside world. As numerous critics have pointed out, "authenticity" is the most important standard by which fans evaluate rock, and the authenticity effect is created by seemingly unrestrained displays of emotion.[3] Authentic or cool bands generally make a lot of noise; they scream and throw themselves around; they enact a complete rejection of control. Thus rock's central performative paradox comes from the incompatibility of coolness with emotionality, yet the necessity of demonstrating both. Like Flanagan, who simultaneously defies and submits, whose very submission is presented as an act of defiance, rock 'n' roll gestures paradoxically in ways that can radically redefine masculinity's relation to power and control, and thus to subjectivity.

The question of to whom rock 'n' roll performance and video are addressed has received a relatively large amount of attention. Yet each rock performance is created as much in defiance of insulted, unwilling listeners, the ones who can hear only noise in it, as it is in identification with the admiring audience who deliberately consume it. The structure of rock's address is triangulated. It says to its fans, I am like you in that I am not like those squares. For this reason, rock's self-positioning is vitally relevant to its fans' identity construction, in ways that are inherently involved with power relations.

It is hard to imagine a cultural moment when Bakhtin's and Foucault's theories hit closer to home for academic critics than when we turned to writing about music videos. This relatively new practice we have taken on not only draws on our knowledge of the carnivalesque, it places us at the center of the carnival as rulers of misrule, authoritative clowns, just as it puts us in the uncomfortable position of formulating a discourse on power that conceals its confessional aspects even as it constitutes a confession. Most of us experience little apparent difficulty writing about other popular cultural forms with the requisite degree of analytical distance, a distance that allows us to delineate our speaking positions in relation to a text that is seen as exterior to and nonidentical to those positions. But for those of us born during the baby boom or later, rock 'n' roll inhabits a place closer to the imagined center of selfhood.

For, as Jane Flax argues, even constructionists who categorically reject the notion of a unitary self still produce theories that seem to "presuppose" a "core self" that enables our own resistant vision (210, 218–219). The question always raised by any theory that claims that identity is formed by and within culture is, what then allows some of us to resist simply playing out the cultural script, what enables some of us to consciously and deliberately trouble the categories? The most naive and perhaps first answer to that question is usually "something inside myself." Since rock has always attempted to articulate that something that makes every young person feel different from the others, the relation of rock 'n' roll to the imagined identity core is profound, perhaps as profound as the relation of gender, so that to think about rock 'n' roll videos is to think about gender in ways that can call up some of our deepest, most unsettling feelings. This is the reason that music videos have tremendous power to challenge the construction and naturalization of binary gender difference.

Music video brought previously compartmentalized fields of study and areas of unanalyzed pleasure into collision for many critics. When worlds collide, both fragmentation and fusion result. This phenomenon is reflected in the music video criticism of the last decade, which, as Lawrence Grossberg points out, privileges this new form diversely "as the *ultimate* example: of commodification, of the incorporation of authenticity and resistance, of textual and psychological schizophrenia, of the 'postmodern' disappearance of reality, and of new forms of resistance" ("Media Economy" 185; emphasis Grossberg's). It is telling that in this short list the word "resistance" occurs twice. For most of us now writing some form of cultural criticism, rock 'n' roll is strongly associated with our own experiences of what, no matter how our later assimilation of theory would call the term into question, we once considered individuation. The birth of our adolescent sense of self was probably accompanied in most cases by a simultaneous burst of stereo noise and a parental shout of disgust. Later, while we disciplined ourselves to sit for hours in libraries and in front of computer terminals moving nothing but our eyes and fingers, many of us have continued to maintain a secret life of resistance through our identification with shrieking, posturing rock 'n' roll rebels. This half-hidden, intellectually denied life shows itself in the passion that has invested arguments about to what extent the resistance to hegemonic ideology articulated on the surface of most rock videos can be taken as meaningful.

Some analysis of rock videos' participation in consumer culture seems, therefore, especially necessary to any serious, rather than merely laudatory, commentary on their role in political resistance. Andrew Goodwin stresses the role of music videos as promotional devices for performances and audio recordings of the songs, as well as for lines of associated products (28), but he explains that what "makes the music video text an extremely complex and unusual cultural artifact" is its ability to "both *exceed* and *contain* the commodity it advertises" (47; emphasis Goodwin's). One mode of such excess that he singles out for criticism is the videos' frequent participation in "a reactionary vision of consumerism" based on a "simplistic and banal [use of] gender roles" (185). This reiteration of stereotypes goes beyond advertising the intended commodities by attempting also to sell a concept of gender.

However, as Goodwin shows throughout his study of MTV, the conventionally sexist concept of gender is far from the only one proffered by music video, and just as videos effectively sell us what they intend to sell, they have also endowed popular culture with some interestingly subversive "by-products." Blaine Allan makes the point that "the music video normally addresses a problem posed by the institution of television itself, which characteristically transforms the commercial into the personal and emotional" (10). Music videos not only maintain pop music's traditional focus on "romance, identity, and expressions of emotion," they do so in dialogue with television's other forms, notably commercials themselves (11). Their representational slippages from conventionality thus cannot avoid affecting the medium as a whole. This is strikingly apparent when the video's topic, as is so often the case, is the gendered human body. In Grossberg's view a crisis in interpretation has been brought about by "new visual formations of youth culture." Their privileging of spectacle, which had formerly been secondary, over sound demonstrates "that authenticity is something that is always constructed" (204), and has inspired a new self-parodic attitude in rock 'n' roll performance. Grossberg explores this aspect of rock videos in terms of the special qualities of music as a Deleuzian deterritorialization resisting "the structures of meaning, will and emotion which society is constantly trying to impose upon the individual desire" (205). Considered together, these two visions of the political potential of rock videos suggest they will inevitability undermine gender binary as the bedrock of "authentic" identity. Because the reinterpretation of rock music as video foregrounds the music's constructedness as a commodity, its contexts, including its representation of gender/identity, are denaturalized.

Nonetheless, inside and outside the academic world, rock videos that feature male singers or all-male bands are still mostly discussed in terms of their reinforcement of normative images of exemplary masculinity and femininity. The most obvious reason for this is that we recognize what is articulable within the cultural discourses we know. With a will to see differently and some grounding in a countercultural or subaltern perspective, sophisticated audiences can often read against the grain of complex representations; in fact, the existence of this sort of space for resistant reading has traditionally been associated with aesthetic value in literary texts, and currently is valorized with such terms as dialogism. But rock 'n' roll is too often assumed to be both relatively simple and almost completely masculine in its self-presentation. The most comprehensive challenge to the idea that rock 'n' roll has been dominated by men and a masculine aesthetic is Gillian Gaar's history of women's rock music, *She's a Rebel,* which from the title onward stresses the double rebelliousness of women musicians who went against both the dominant culture (by creating rock 'n' roll) and the masculinized counterculture represented by rock.

In recent years rock 'n' roll's function as a register for rebellion has received considerable attention, as members of influential groups like the Centre for Contemporary Cultural Studies at Birmingham have undermined the elitist idea that popular culture is received uncritically by its mass audience, and introduced the practice of reading popular cultural products as sites of resistance to the dominant culture. But the specter of brainwashed masses swaying in the evil grip of one-note propaganda re-emerged with the movement of music videos from art houses to television when MTV began its cable broadcasts in 1981. Efforts by cultural critics like McClary, Goodwin, Grossberg, Frith, and E. Ann Kaplan to problematize this simplistic view of music video often leave undisturbed the standard accusation that videos promoting male musicians are misogynist. Even among MTV's most ardent academic defenders, such as bell hooks and Lisa Lewis, the basic assumption seems to be that music videos reinscribe conventional representations of gender difference.

In fact, Lewis's 1990 book, *Gender Politics and MTV,* is subtitled *Voicing the Difference.* In Lewis's view, music videos are addressed either to male or to female audiences. "Female-address videos" have value for feminists to the extent to which they subvert gender norms and "act as a social commentary on the regimen of female representation," but they are also limited by "the double standard that informs rock discourse" (141, 87). Lewis believes that female MTV stars have been able to begin the articulation of a woman-centered vision, through the creation of a subcultural context based on their own past work and the community provided by their fans. However, as she describes it, this articulation is limited to female artists and is defined by its reversal of values associated with males. For example, in Madonna's video *Open Your Heart,* Lewis claims that the central figure, an erotic dancer in a peepshow, succeeds in overcoming sexism because she "retreat[s] to a vision of life in which gender is undelineated" and regresses back to nonsexualized childhood (143). That the only way the video can represent a world that is not divided into masculine and feminine is by depicting its inhabitants as presexual children does not seem to trouble Lewis.

bell hooks's treatment of Madonna in her book *Outlaw Culture* is not so approving. While she praises Madonna's early work as symbolizing "unrepressed female creativity and power—sexy, seductive, serious, and strong" (11), hooks sees Madonna in the 1990s as enacting the role of "the white imperialist wielding patriarchal power to assert control over the realm of sexual difference" (21). Madonna's fall from being the darling of academic feminists could have been predicted by anyone who considered that because her feminism was situated in transgression of gender roles, it could have meaning only in relation to the gender norms it transgressed. Outlaw personas are always of necessity invested in the law they stand outside of. Madonna played with masculinity and femininity, often parodying them brilliantly, but she could not break down the separation between them because their existence as discrete entities was vital to the "sexy" shock effect intended by her reversal of codes. To leave gender difference entirely meant to leave sexuality, as she appears to do at the conclusion of *Open Your Heart.*

A similar phenomenon appears in Prince's songs that push gender difference to the vanishing point: at that moment, despite Prince's vaunted sexiness, sexual possibility also disappears. In a typical "gender confusion" song, "If I Was Your Girlfriend," Prince oscillates between gendered positions in relation to a female love object via the electronic creation (at 55 rpm) of a high, feminized version of his voice. As Reynolds points out, the effect is negation of any subject position from which to reach the beloved. "Sex for Prince isn't 'communication' or 'exchange' but something altogether more mystical: the dissolution of the very differences and identities that make communication and sex possible" (50). I would add to this that the girlfriend remains a fixed point with conventional feminine attributes such as vulnerability, while the aspiring lover dances himself into disembodiment around her. The outsider arrives, at last, outside the realm in which sexual contact with another person can happen.

Alternative music introduced the possibility of representing sexuality in ways distinct from the transgressive outlaw stances of more conventional rock. In critical terminology, "alternative music" is basically a catchall term for the independent rock 'n' roll that appeared in the wake of Punk. In the late 1990s those who confused alternative with Grunge pronounced it dead; however, its putative successors, such as Goth-Industrial, Ambient, and Techno, initially appeared in the category "alternative," featured on the MTV showcase "Alternative Nation." While Punk led to alternative, the music cultures associated with each style are very different from each other.

As most rock 'n' roll music critics assert, Punk rock, while never becoming popular enough in the United States to define an era, still opened space for radically new music styles. In what is probably the definitive academic work on British Punk, *Lipstick Traces,* Greil Marcus explains how the early Punk rock movement called into question "the old Frankfurt School critique of mass culture." By embracing their always already defeated subject position and proclaiming that there was no future, the Punks "turned Adorno's vision of modern life back upon itself . . . Punks were those who now *understood* themselves as people from whom the news of their not quite successful decease had been withheld for reasons of population policy" (74; emphasis mine). Knowing themselves as the walking corpses needed to fill roles in a consumer culture, they were unlikely to have much faith in sexual pleasure, let alone love. For what may have been the first time, a musical genre emerged that seemed categorically opposed to sex and love. Reynolds explains this in terms of Punk's central belief that "demystification was the route to enlightenment" (73). Early Punk portrayed desire as bait that only unconscious idiots take. In fact, if early Punk had genders, they could be described as those who are duped by sexuality and those who are not. Gaar gives a compelling account of women's shaping of "Punk Revolution" explicitly in resistance to a hostile music industry determined to reduce them to sex symbols (229–270).

Unfortunately for feminist musicians and fans, contempt for sexuality often translates into misogyny, because women remain culturally "the sex." As Gina Arnold remarks in her study of the development of alternative rock, *Route 666: On the Road to Nirvana,* in the late 1980s the American independent music scene seemed more misogynist than "the scenes that came before it" (121). Reynolds and Joy Press argue powerfully in *The Sex Revolts* that Punk rock made by men in both England and the United States was explicitly misogynist in all its manifestations (33–42). Their chapter

punk pedagogy

"Careers in Misogyny: The Stranglers and Malcolm McLaren" is an especially depressing corrective to Marcus's and Gaar's more approving accounts of the same period. I remain unconvinced that this period was quite as dismal as Reynolds and Press paint it, preferring Thomas Foster's view that Punk "has always represented an internal space of critique against rock music, which has not been feminist but which has provided a kind of critical space for women to intervene."

Still, it is obvious that an additional problem for feminists resulted in part from Punk's appropriation of styles from sadomasochistic subcultures. The one area in which Punk had immediate and lasting impact on the mainstream in the United States is fashion. Here Punk styles like black leather "fetish" clothing, dog (or slave) collars, wrist restraints, cock rings worn as bracelets, chains, and elaborate piercings, all borrowed from S/M rituals, rapidly began to define rock 'n' roll hipness. For Punks S/M was a parodic metaphor for the irredeemable corruption of desire by externally imposed structures of dominance and submission. The quintessential expression of this is X-ray Spex's 1977 hit "Oh Bondage, Up Yours," aptly described by Julie Burchill and Tony Parsons as an "anti-oppression song" (242). Poly Styrene, the singer, understood her song as a rejection of "consumerism" and of feeling "bound" by her own feelings (Savage 357).

This vision contrasts with that of many of S/M's serious practitioners, who describe it as a highly romantic and politically radical mode of self-expression. More traditionally (in a sense), these defenders of the practice understand S/M as sex-positive because they envision all sexuality that deviates from heteronormativity as potentially liberatory. When S/M practitioners eroticize and thus emphasize voluntary renunciation of power, they inevitably disrupt conventional gender categories; this disruption most commonly results in an association of masochism with male subjectivity.[4] In contrast, because Punk S/M was a dramatization of victimization rather than a mode of imagining resistance to official assignments of power, it almost always envisioned the masochist as female. Consequently, Punk participated in the development of a musical symbology in which sexuality was figured as male-dominant female-submissive sadomasochism. When music videos were developed for the teenage male MTV audience by rockers whose relationship to consumer culture was not critical, but defined by a fairly simple desire to become rock stars, it was inevitable that they would draw upon that symbology to fill the screen with images of women in bondage.

It is in this context that music videos like Nine Inch Nails's *Closer* are so deviant. They recover a prior S/M vision in which masochistic practice emblematizes men's resistance to conventional gender roles. In order to highlight the most astonishing aspects of *Closer*'s assault on gender difference, I must locate it in a context that does more justice to what music television has now become than my discussion up to this point has. Traditional gender roles have been assailed by music videos in the last few years, almost as frequently as they have been reinforced. Role-reversal videos have been wildly successful, as was beautifully exemplified by Salt-N-Pepa's female-voyeuristic *Shoop*. And in alternative videos like Jane's Addiction's *Been Caught Stealing*, cross-dressing has been celebrated as liberation rather than sneered at as decadence or flaunted, in Heavy-Metal style, as an invitation to battle.[5] The Chemical Brothers' *Block*

Rockin' Beats locates the point of convergence of gender—and race—differences in the figure of the disco diva as the center of anti-authoritarianism.[6] But, like the revolutionary early Madonna videos, such work still depends on the legibility of those binary opposites "masculine" and "feminine"; even while it posits them as poles that any subject can choose to occupy, it still maintains them and the distance between them.

What happens in the work of alternative rockers can be noticeably different. The rising band PJ Harvey is a case in point, as can be illustrated by a quick look at their song "50ft Queenie." To the extent to which the song's lyrics have a topic it seems to be freedom from confining form. In this song Polly Jean Harvey, fronting the band, represents herself as a thing, perhaps female in that it is "one big queen," but perhaps not in that it is also "the king of the world." Those eminent videologists, Beavis and Butthead, watch the video and ask each other, "Did she say fifty-foot weenie?" The song does have overtones of phallic presence in that the singer primarily asserts power and proclaims authority based on a constantly growing size, from twenty inches long to fifty, and then leaping to fifty feet. Bringing together *The Attack of the 50 Ft. Woman* of camp horror-poster fame and the Lacanian phallus, which is the biological property of no one, "50ft Queenie" undermines the gender grounding of rock stances. The power source here does not ultimately appear in the form of the penis, but of the Queenie itself, a thing composed through the fusion of animal desire (including the desire for presence) and an augmenting technology, a screaming cyborg with a skinny androgynous form and a guitar in place of genitalia.

Assault on gender difference through a technologically mediated presence typifies Polly Jean Harvey's self-presentation, as is evident on the cover of the *4-Track Demos* CD, which shows her in a bikini in a mock glamour-girl pose with a camera slung directly over her crotch, the partially telescoped lens positioned as neither hole nor protrusion, but something of both. The band PJ Harvey's music is excitingly suggestive of the sort of cyborg feminism outlined in Donna Haraway's "A Manifesto for Cyborgs" in its embrace of technology as a means of disrupting the signs of gender. One might consider also the use of multiple voice tracks, including the falsetto choruses and vocal echoes provided by percussionist Rob Ellis, to construct the composite identity implied in the band's name. Unlike Gene Santoro, I do not find this identity "uniquely female" (716), but instead uniquely resistant to limitation within animal gender categories. Dispersed over the surface of objects, PJ Harvey's gender eludes biological determinism.

The Afghan Whigs, who incidentally covered some of Harvey's songs in two of their concert tours, take deterritorialization of desire somewhat further. The startlingly masochistic song "My Curse" on their CD *Gentlemen* does little to disrupt gender because it is sung by a woman (Marcy Mays) in a guest performance, although Mays's husky voice could be mistaken for a man's and even for lead singer Greg Dulli's. Still, while the invitation to "Hurt me, baby" is lamentably appropriate enough for a woman following conventional rock 'n' roll gender roles, the direction to "zip me down, kiss me there" does not work anatomically if we are imagining a woman in jeans. Likewise the reference to "your perfume" suggests a female addressee. The repeated disclaimer, "And slave I only use as a word to describe the special way I feel for you," seems a little too arch for an abjected woman, and a little too much like Dulli's characteristically self-parodying tone for the song to be as easily attributed to Mays. However, we hear what we are conditioned to hear: a woman begging for pain and sexual violation.

The CD, therefore, heightened the impact of Greg Dulli's performance on his 1995 tour, when he used "My Curse" as a signature encore piece. The last line's reference to the occasion for the song's confession, as no longer wanting to "to lie about it, every time I came undressed," gained particular resonance. The conflict between the gendering of masochism on the CD, which is aimed at the largest audience, and the gendering of masochism in the more intimate atmosphere of the clubs the Whigs played on tour suggests not only a vision of gender as purely (and volitionally) performative but also that the performance of gender is determined to a large extent by the audience. In the Afghan Whigs's varied performances of "My Curse," gender is relocated from the contested space of bodies locked in sexual power struggle to the ear of the hearer. It has no material beginning or biological anchor; rather it floats free, transforming in relation to what touches it.

Whereas it is difficult to say what masculine and feminine mean or what sorts of subject positions they are associated with in some songs by bands like PJ Harvey and the Afghan Whigs, it is almost impossible to find anything that corresponds to known concepts of gender difference in the musical products of Nine Inch Nails. I would claim that it is completely impossible except for some evidence to the contrary. In a meeting on 18 May 1995 between representatives of Empowerment America, the National Political Congress of Black Women, and executives at Time Warner to discuss media encouragement of violence against women, Nine Inch Nails's song "Big Man with a Gun" was offered as an example of "gross, violent, offensive and misogynist lyrics" ("Fighting Words" 36).

The idea that Reznor's work represents the worst sort of self-indulgent masculinist violence is echoed in the *Village Voice,* where R. J. Smith, apparently inspired by the rumor that Timothy McVeigh was a Nine Inch Nails fan, calls Reznor "John Doe Number Two" and compares him to Hitler (64). Smith's criticisms of Reznor are instructive in that they reveal the difficulty, for anyone sensitive to gender issues, of avoiding reading violence and sadism as inescapably gendered masculine. Through analyzing Smith's interpretation of two videos, one can begin to see how a display of male masochism can be misread as the sign of male sadism.

Smith's particular target is the black-and-white music video *Hurt,* which juxtaposes newsreel footage of atrocities, including concentration camps, time-lapse film of a decaying animal corpse, and images of Reznor in performance assuming various poses of agony as accompaniment to a ballad of alarming self-hatred beginning with a reference to self-inflicted pain as a test "to see if i still feel," followed by an assertion that pain is all that continues to feel real. I would argue that the point here is not, as Smith suggests, that Reznor's psychic and self-inflicted physical pain are to be considered as significant as the sufferings of the victims of fascism, but that knowledge of the world's evil causes intense, agonizing alienation and despair.

Not a very original thought, but one that seems to lead Reznor to identifications unrelated to gender difference, as in the *Burn* video, also criticized by Smith. Here footage of Reznor holding his head and screaming is intercut with Holocaust images and near-narrative sequences of wife beating and child abuse (from the film *Natural Born Killers*) to the accompaniment of Reznor singing, "I never was a part of you." While Smith is right that wanting "to burn this whole thing down" is not a desire conducive to social peace and harmony, surely the identity of the "whole world" that is to be annihilated needs to be determined before we can make definitive statements about a song's politics, especially when "your institutions" are imagistically equated✔ with scenes of domestic violence in which mothers futilely strive to protect their children from rampaging patriarchs. Locating a speaking/singing position that can be fully attributed to Reznor within the dialogically arranged samples that make up his songs is also difficult, as they seem deliberately to defy the listener's need for order.

For illustration, let us turn to Timothy McVeigh's alleged favorite, "Head Like a Hole." The song begins with the assertion "god money i'll do anything for you" followed by a critique of capitalist culture to gladden the heart of any Marxist. We are warned that this god wants more than "everything" from one. It is unclear whether one persona is expressing the absolute submission to Mammon and another issuing the warning against selling out or whether the same speaker is to be understood to be conveying both the desire and the admonition. The admonition is answered by a voice of refusal: "no you can't take it." Things rapidly become even more confusing as the refrain ends "i'd rather die than give you control." A second chorus follows immediately, threatening, "you're going to get what you deserve." Note the difficulty of identifying any specific speaker or even separating out a certain number of speakers, a difficulty enhanced by Reznor's use of multiple separate and overlapped voice tracks.

More unanswerable questions block interpretation. Considering that the majority of the songs on the CD, *Pretty Hate Machine,* refer to masochistic submission as pleasurable, exactly how much of a threat is offered by the second chorus? One might think of the voice in "Sin" begging to get "the sentence" he "deserve[s]" while assuring his potential torturer that this is why he exists, or of "Maybe Just Once," in which the singer begs to "get what's coming to me" and also that the other "make it hurt."

The *Head Like a Hole* video adds to the confusion. There is a narrative of sorts among the rich mix of images in the video. We see Reznor fronting the band on a stage covered with great piles of recording tape in which he becomes tangled. He is lifted up in the tangle of tape, struggling furiously, until by the end he hangs upside down over the stage. The other most frequently repeated image accompanies the chorus: an indeterminate figure, seen in black-and-white negative, bows its head and dips its hair into a bowl of liquid, which is then thrown outward as the head rises. In the summer of 1994 a ferocious argument sprang up on the Internet over whether the bowing figure in the video is Reznor or a woman. This was deemed important to determining whether Reznor is sexist, but the undecidability of the speaking positions in the song or even of its tone would seem to render the issue of who is bowing moot, as some e-mailers pointed out. This is a graphic example of Nine Inch Nails's deflection of attempts to gender the voice(s) in the songs.

Later Nine Inch Nails work also resists gendering the addressee. Notably, the video for "The Perfect Drug" features Reznor as a Goth Edgar Allan Poe-esque figure haunted by and mourning the absence of an unglamorously androgynous little person. The presentation may cause the audience to see this indeterminate figure as confusing (male? female? adult? child? demon? angel?). But within the song's lyrics this manifestation of the beloved signifies not confusion but the clarity of painful revelation. Her(?) arrowlike, piercing presence tears the veils from his "stupid-eyed" face and causes him to "see the truth."

While gender difference and identification are elusive in Reznor's work, sexuality is generally emphatically evoked. The videos I have been discussing do not represent the full range of Nine Inch Nails's material, by any means. Somewhat more characteristic in subject matter is the video *Happiness in Slavery*, which was banned from MTV. Jonathan Gold calls the video "a torture-lashed essay on the ecstasy of submitting to ultimate control" (52). The refrain to the song "Happiness in Slavery" is "take it from me, i found, you can find happiness in slavery." The video, shot to resemble a black-and-white horror movie, features Bob Flanagan. He enters a room in a mysterious building and takes a seat in a torture machine that does various painful things to him, including apparently ripping off his penis, before grinding him up. Throughout the experience Flanagan's face exhibits expressions of orgasmic delight. Reznor begins the video singing in an iron cage such as professional dominatrixes use (an image he recycles in other videos, notably *Wish*). He watches Flanagan, until at the end he enters demurely dressed and solemnly re-enacts the ritual Flanagan had performed before entering the torture machine. In an interview Reznor explains the "key [to the video] being the person never looking afraid; knowing what was going to happen, yet willfully doing it" (Dunn 29).

This video could be defined as homoerotic because of its display of Flanagan's body and Reznor's voyeuristic role, and thus it could be argued that *Happiness in Slavery* is less genderless than monogendered. Its framing within the infamous, uncensored *Broken* video compilation, which alternates concert footage with a pseudo-snuff narrative in which one man tortures, rapes, and kills another, would also suggest such a reading. So would the so far unexplored but intriguingly possible influence on Nine Inch Nails of homoerotic fiction by Dennis Cooper, whose work reflects a fascination with male adolescent angst, extreme sadomasochism, and sex murders in which the teen boy victims comply in a last desperate attempt to connect with anyone. Among many similarities between Cooper's writings and Reznor's songs and videos is the title of Cooper's 1989 novel, *Closer*. However, the tension and anguish in Reznor's songs never seem to be located between men but rather within men. Masculinity appears as a horrific thing one finds within oneself: "something inside of me has opened up its eyes" ("Burn"). The framing in the video compilation *Broken*, through a narrative containing images that conflate the artist's diving into and being flushed down a toilet with a hypermasculinized murderer's willing acceptance of execution, suggests the necessity of eliminating masculinity, as a sort of filth or waste. Within this context the artist's destruction of his own masculinity constitutes release.

The *Happiness in Slavery* video could be seen as referring to masculinity's renunciation because it posits castration as a climactic moment in the rendering up of the flesh. Certainly it appears to be a rejection of stereotypical masculinity, even more emphatically than the *Burn* video. But Reznor's videos do far more than excise traditional masculinity; they work deconstructively as collections of self-consciously excessive signs, many pointing elsewhere than the familiar genders. Some point specifically to the world of hard-core S/M, in which gender as we know it can become irrelevant, as the genders S and M float free of masculine and feminine markers.[7] The reference in "Sin" to the speaker's longing for "your kiss, your fist" exemplifies such vividly sexual but ambiguously gendered moments in the songs.

Reznor's use of motifs from S/M subcultures is one of the most unusual things about his work. Unlike the Punk rockers of the 1970s and early '80s, Reznor does not seem to be treating sadomasochism as a metaphor for life under capitalism. Instead, despite the anger about sexuality that Reznor often projects, he seems quite sincere in his advocacy of the pleasures of submission. In comparison with the Heavy-Metal bands to which Nine Inch Nails has some resemblance (and one might note that Bob Flanagan also appears in Danzig's music video *It's Coming Down*), Reznor's tone toward the violently dominant female figures in his music suggests urgent longing rather than the "frantic terror" typical of Heavy-Metal "male victim" performances (Walser 163). Some of the most lyrical moments in his work seem to refer directly to female-dominant S/M scenes, as in "Sanctified," where the singer tells us he achieves that exalted state because "she walks me through the nicest parts of hell."

R. J. Smith and the delegation to Time Warner aside, Reznor is much more often identified with such masochistic personae than with exaggeratedly masculinist posturers like the speaker in "Big Man with a Gun." In stage performances, as in videos, Reznor is generally seen as presenting himself as a masochist. An apparently unintentionally comic moment of disjunction between attacks on Reznor as a figure epitomizing sexist violence and his self-presentation is provided in the illustration to an article in *Time* on William Bennett's critique of the media. Reznor appears in a series of pictures of controversial figures promoted by Time Warner.[8] The caption reads, "1994 The songs of Trent Reznor and the group Nine Inch Nails evoked paranoia, murder, and suicide" (Zoglin 39). The picture is a publicity head-and-shoulders shot of Reznor, his face raised with closed eyes and an enigmatic smile; he is wrapped in barbed wire. Hardly an image immediately recognizable as misogynist. One music magazine reviews a Nine Inch Nails concert: "People need artists to suffer for them. It's part masochism and part exorcism. . . . Trent Reznor suffers for us because of us, and we love him for it" (Dunn 26). Gold comments, "Reznor appears powerless onstage . . . martyred to the noise and to the crowd" (52). Eric Weisbard calls him "rock's reigning king of pain" (34). Reznor's much televised 1994 performance covered in mud at Woodstock II seemed perfectly suited to his enthusiastic embrace of abjection.

It may be necessary to explain here that I am not claiming knowledge of the private sexual practices, fantasies, or desires of the actual person named Trent Reznor. I am commenting only on the public self-presentation and the audience reception of this celebrity figure during the period of his greatest public activity, 1989–1997. Reznor's presentation of himself in interviews is instructive here. When pressed by one interviewer about his personal sexual practices, Reznor admits to some "masochism" and then says, understandably enough, "I'm somewhat uncomfortable talking about this too much" (Heath 143). In another interview he wittily responds to the interviewer's attempt to elicit affirmation that he is trying to help his fans by providing them with images of extreme sadomasochism: "I'm a public servant" (Berger and Lengvenis 51). This role is expanded upon more seriously when he tells Gold, "'I think Nine Inch Nails are big enough and mainstream enough to gently lead people into the back room a little bit, maybe show them some things it might have taken them a little longer to stumble into on their own'" (Gold 53). On the liner notes for *Pretty Hate Machine* Clive Barker is among those credited with "sounds and ideas (with all due respect)." In an interview conducted by the editor of the S/M fetish magazine *Skin Two,* Barker describes his film *Hellraiser,* which ends with a scene in which an ecstatic man is ripped to pieces by a torture machine, as a defense of consensual S/M (19–24). He emphasizes that his aim is to help his audience understand that "these are images of liberation, not of repression" (26).

With this in mind, the mainstreaming of Nine Inch Nails should give us pause. As Gold notes, *Pretty Hate Machine* (1989) was "the first rock & roll indie album to sell a million copies" (54). The *Closer* music video was indisputably one of MTV's most successful, with the CD *The Downward Spiral* rapidly making the charts as a result. Among many other honors, including *Rolling Stone* covers and Grammys, Reznor was voted "Artist of the Year" in the *Spin* 1996 poll and in 1997 he was their "Most Vital Artist in Music Today," headlining "the Spin Top 40." Whether his music was called alternative, Goth-Industrial, Electronic, or simply independent, it continued to receive lavish praise from critics even during Reznor's least productive period, 1995–1998. Reznor says of his career so far, "I like the challenge of flirting with the mainstream with Nine Inch Nails. I think we can do it honestly" (Bozza 62). By 1999, it is safe to say that flirtation has turned into a love affair, at least on the side of the general public. For 14 October 1999, less than a month after the 21 September release of *The Fragile, Rolling Stone* once again gave Reznor the cover, with a screaming headline, "NINE INCH NAILS Trent Reznor Reborn." It suggests something about cultural change that Reznor is the first male artist presenting himself as a (primarily) heterosexual masochist who has achieved major crossover success since Leopold von Sacher-Masoch, author of *Venus in Furs* (1870), in the late 1800s. And it is perhaps even more suggestive of his cultural significance that his former protégé, Marilyn Manson, continues to achieve enormous attention as he presents himself as a heterosexual-male willing victim in one video after another. The influence of Reznor's masochistic self-presentation is so pervasive, it would be impossible to list all the other bands' performances in which it is echoed.

To get just a snapshot of the last months of 1999, however, one might want to look at music videos as diverse as the Red Hot Chili Peppers' *Scar Tissue,* Limp Bizkit's *Nookie,* and Ricky Martin's *Livin' La Vida Loca,* in ascending order of their great popularity. The Red Hot Chili Peppers' comeback CD, *Californication,* was introduced with the release of a video in which we see the band members looking dazed and severely beaten, driving around the desert, to the tune of a mournful song about being shoved around by tough girls and consequently being physically and emotionally wounded. With their big bandages and somber expressions, the Peppers look as if those girls were much too tough for them. While they are a fairly traditional rock 'n' roll band in terms of their presentation of masculinity, they cannot compare in aggressiveness with the exaggeratedly sexist self-presentation of the Rap/rock group Limp Bizkit. At the beginning of July 1999, Limp Bizkit's *Nookie* temporarily broke the grip of the much softer Backstreet Boys on MTV's number one request spot. This litany of complaints and angry rejection of friends' conventional advice to dump the girl features the lines "she put my tender heart in a blender / and still I surrender." The song ends with an assertion that the singer will continue to submit to the will of this mean and unfaithful girl because he wants the sex she provides. In Ricky Martin's phenomenal pop hit *Livin' La Vida Loca*, the first image of him with the girl focuses on her pouring hot wax from a candle down his bare chest to his (apparently naked) crotch as he throws back his head in what looks like an expression of mixed pain and ecstasy. A representative lyric is "she'll take away your pain / like a bullet to your brain." While the videos and the lyrics present us with recognizable males and females, the behavior and attitudes attributed to them seem independent of traditional gender stereotypes. This pretty much covers the spectrum from men's hard rock to pop rock in the last year of the '90s. Although the sound of Reznor's music has little or no influence in the examples given here, his masochistic self-stylings and refusal to depict women as submissive, or as unattractive if aggressively selfish, are ubiquitously reiterated.

One of the things Nine Inch Nails's popularity suggests is that many people have become hungry for visions of intense, even violent, sexuality that are devoid of binary masculine/feminine gendering. That the Nine Inch Nails phenomenon belongs to a movement that has been growing for a long time within rock 'n' roll is suggested by Chrissie Hynde of The Pretenders, who sees herself as following after Patti Smith in pursuing "the genderless sexuality of it all" (Juno 191). The world of chaste cuddles and hugs and of sweet childlike androgynous presexuality seems to lack lasting appeal for many of us, yet the old genders and sex roles we have known so well fail to please either. That Reznor has not presented himself as homosexual, while refusing foreclosure of his sex-object choice, reinforces the message of his music and videos that gender is irrelevant to some forms of sexual pleasure. His offering himself up as masochistic object allows a different type of identification than did most previous sadomasochistic spectacles in mainstream media.

My curiosity about what Nine Inch Nails's fans heard in the music and saw in the videos led me beyond "lurking" on the Internet, eavesdropping on Usenet discussion groups, to actively seeking out fans. I put out a general call for informants at my own and other college campuses and I stopped people in Nine Inch Nails t-shirts and hats wherever I found them throughout 1995, 1996, and 1997. Among the remarks I found most interesting are these. One twenty-five-year-old male student explained that he identified with the way "Trent is always crushed, put down, and disillusioned" and that he liked the music's reflection of despair about traditional expressions of romantic love in dating and marriage: "that's like TV to us now," an unattainable fantasy because "the disguise is lifting." Conversely, a female fan, age twenty-one, believed the songs are about "[l]iving out your fantasies, Trent does it and says through performance that it is ok to live out your dreams and turn them into reality." However, she is not referring to conventional romantic love but is a practitioner of female-dominant S/M, as were several of the female fans I interviewed.

In contradiction to the common belief that young people appropriate S/M styles and paraphernalia without really understanding what practices these things represent, all but one of the fans under twenty-five with whom I spoke recognized bondage equipment in the videos without any prompting from me and also knew its exact uses. In addition, most readily recognized references to such sexual practices as fisting and knife play and gleefully described to me what was entailed.[9] A nineteen-year-old heterosexual male film major was inspired by Nine Inch Nails to make a video of himself in bondage because "to see myself on film in some sort of pain and suffering . . . is my way of letting out my emotion . . . that satisfies me just as Trent has through his music." Constants among all the fans' responses were dismissal of conventional concepts of gender difference, vehement dislike of misogyny, and a concept of themselves as unusual in terms of both their sexual preferences and their need to feel that love accompanied their own expressions of sexuality. Surprisingly, this was as true of the ones whose desires were fairly conventional as for those whose desires were decidedly outside the range of what is usually deemed ordinary. The more conventional informants expressed anxiety that they were more "old-fashioned" or "white-bread" than their contemporaries. And almost all of the young people anticipated problems ahead due to their rejection of traditional male-dominant/female-submissive sex roles.

All of the young people who considered themselves fans connected their enthusiasm for Nine Inch Nails to their frustration in trying to reconcile longings for a lasting love relationship with their cynicism about the traditional ways that such relationships have been institutionalized. They seemed to see Nine Inch Nails songs as expressing their fear, based on experience and observation, that marriage could not work to satisfy their emotional needs or even to accommodate their need to escape situations in which men hold power and women submit to it. (The male informants typically said things like "I don't even want to seem to her as if I am trying to be dominant," while all the females said they could not tolerate a relationship in which they felt subordinated.) One could easily understand Nine Inch Nails's music as explicitly opposed to the dream offered by mainstream culture that desire can be domesticated and made commensurate with patriarchal "family values."

The best example of a song that conveys this message to the fans is "Ringfinger." The version marketed to the largest audience, included as the last selection on *Pretty Hate Machine*, begins with a lament, evocative of traditional marital roles, of a man's inability to give the addressee everything she wants, despite working his "hands until they bleed." But the song then departs from its heteronormativity in asserting her dominance: "still you lead me and i follow." The subsequent lyrics alternate between emphasizing his subjection to her will and demanding as a payment her ring finger. As in most of Reznor's songs, images of the religious and demonic, written over with S/M eroticism, overdetermine this critique of the amorous exchange system (for example, in "Purest Feeling": "She could be a savior, with everything she does / or some kind of punishment for people just like us"). Thus the usual dichotomy between Faustian sexual arrangement and marital commitment is undermined.

"Twist," the demo version of "Ringfinger" and a performance remix available on the *Purest Feeling* CD, underscores the perversity of conventional love and commitment, suggesting that passion makes a mockery of vowed reciprocity, rendering desire frighteningly sacrificial no matter what rituals society chooses to dress it up in. In the demo and remix, S/M knife play symbolizes the woman's attention to Reznor, which undeniably touches him deeply but feels like a "switchblade" going in. "Wearing these chains" of helpless attraction, all he can do is invite her to "go a little deeper" and "twist" because, as he screams in the chorus, "I love the pain." Here, paradoxically, not only is virility slavery, but to be a subject is to be abject.

Popular culture forms, such as horror films, often use S/M reference to encourage cross-gender identifications, but often do so while leaving undisturbed the conventional heterosexual symbology in which, as Barbara Creed points out, "the abject body is identified with the feminine, which is socially denigrated, and the symbolic body with the masculine, which is socially valorized." Thus, while they "explore our darker desires, [they] do so at the expense of woman's abjected body" (131). Reznor's abjection is frequently configured in contrast to the imagined plenitude of a female figure who has the power to (re)shape him: "she's turning me into someone else" ("Sanctified"). Yet his abjection is also posited as his only possible speaking position.

Because it is the broken one who enunciates the lyrics we hear, his self-presentation challenges the border between abjection and subjectivity. This border has traditionally been equated with that which separates femininity and masculinity (Creed 121–122). Butler sees the "abject zones" as threatening a "dissolution of the subject itself" and consequently, while attractive, uninhabitable except in fantasy (*Bodies that Matter* 243 n2). But some fringe cultures suggest otherwise. Their valorization of those who absolutely renounce gender difference implicitly asserts that the zone of fantasmatic dissolution of masculinized subjectivity is also the site of the subject's rebirth as something hitherto unknown. The video "Closer," even in its censored TV form, probably did open a window into another possibility for many, just as Reznor said he hoped it might.

The exact form of the possibility offered is not easy to decode. As in "Head Like a Hole," it is hard to identify a speaker or speakers in the song "Closer." For instance, is the plaintive voice that cries out for "help" that of the same speaker who addresses "you" in the opening's sensually articulated accusation, "you let me violate you . . . desecrate you"? Or are we supposed to imagine two separate voices in a call-and-response pattern? What is the situation of the second persona addressed? Violated, desecrated, but also redemptively powerful and "the reason I stay alive"? And how exactly is the modifying phrase meant to be understood in the refrain "i want to fuck you like an animal"? Does it refer to the abandon with which the speaker wants to perform sexually or does it mean "as if you were an animal," that is, disregarding your humanity?[10]

One might read it as a borrowing from W.A.S.P.'s Heavy-Metal hit "Animal (Fuck Like a Beast)," or as a parodic response to it. In the first instance, one might assume Reznor's stance to parallel that of W.A.S.P., a band whose acronymic name (We Are Sexual Perverts) suggests both the sadistic image they cultivated through such demonstrations of misogyny as whipping a bound naked woman on stage and their naturalization of this behavior as appropriate to their position as members of the dominant race and class. Working from the opening reference to violating the sexual object in "Closer," one could read Reznor's song's refrain as a tribute to "Animal"'s celebration of rape and torture of women as the only adequate expression of male sexual arousal. However, a reading of the line in *Closer* as parody seems more reasonable since in Reznor's song abject pleas for help and howls of anguish replace the threats and boasts in "Animal (Fuck Like a Beast)."[11]

The semiotics of the music further intensify confusion, with multiple voice tracks and at least two singing styles, ranging literally from a whisper to a scream, adding to the impression of unreconstructably fragmented identity. Reznor's vocal styles here could be called, for convenience, the romantic and the harsh. The matching of the harsh voice to the lyrics correlates fairly well to what John Shepherd describes as stereotypical "cock rock," in that it oscillates between desperate self-pity and aggression (166–167). However, with the panting shouts of the main section interrupted by eight separate pleas of "help me" coming in on a separate voice-track loop, and all the lyrics enclosed by an auditory frame of romantic whispers, the song could hardly be described as an exclusionary refusal to allow "anyone in for completion" (Shepherd 167).

The distribution of lyrics to the softer, romantic voice disturbs rock 'n' roll stereotypes even more by beginning with boasting about what "you" allowed and ending with images of a speaker, who may or may not be the same, shattered, crawling, and gratefully receiving nurture, "drink[ing] the honey inside your hive." At this moment what is visualizable breaks down along with grammar: "through every forest, above the trees / within my stomach, scraped off my knees." The speaker is placed simultaneously inside his own body and hers and, at the same time, in and above "the forest." His identity seems to collapse into the other's. Rather than reaching closure through exclusion of the feminine, the lyrics close in a linguistic confusion like an embrace that dissolves, in a warm rush of honey, the distinction between masculine and feminine along with the border between inside and outside. Where are we, other than with him/her/it/them?

The multiple tracks of sampled music lay on further tangles of complexity. The hard drumbeat that apparently musically expresses the desire to fuck like an animal is heavily distorted so that it seems to be both heartbeat and machine sound (as the image of the steam engine–operated heart at the opening of the video suggests). Its disjunctive positioning between physicality and mechanism affirms the claim that "my whole existence is flawed." At the song's conclusion, the electronic distortion of the hard-driving beat, emphasized as the rhythmic tracks merge, is overwhelmed by a melody floating up, transcendently sweet.

Yet even here we cannot read this as mere code for the triumph of the feminine because the melody's vehicle is the keyboard, the instrument associated with Reznor himself through his fans' awareness of his other performances, not to mention the popular and much reproduced Nine Inch Nails t-shirt whose front is covered with an image of a keyboard. We actually see Reznor playing it as the video ends. But neither is this an instance of masculine mastery in the way that Reznor's notorious propensity to smash keyboards in concert might suggest. In fact, "even instruments themselves are conventionally gender-coded" by rock musicians, with the keyboard seen as the most feminine instrument (Walser 173), indeed, the only instrument that was always deemed appropriate for women to play (Gaar 17). When the sounds of the keyboard ultimately dominate the rest of the electronically generated sounds and computer-controlled samples in the mix as the song moves toward an open conclusion, trailing tinklingly away, meaning remains unresolved.

Reynolds and Press criticize Industrial/synthetic sound, like Nine Inch Nails's, as indicative of revulsion against the flesh, and specifically against female corporeality (91–101). It is in reference to this idea that the complexity added by the visual images in the *Closer* video are especially powerful in subverting rock 'n' roll's traditional gender coding. While the video does in some ways fit Reynolds and Press's description of "the industrial attitude [as] a drive to peel back reality's epidermis and expose the mess behind everyday facades," it departs radically from the model in not identifying "Woman" as "the privileged victim . . . of all this vivisection" (101). Instead, the video directly references vivisection in flashes of the "crucified" laboratory monkey, an image familiar from PETA pamphlets. Then it strongly associates these images with Reznor's own persona in cuts to him wailing about his pain in front of an open carcass on a meat hook. We also see him seemingly hurtling through space in a leather flight helmet, his face distorted in a scream, dangling on wires from the ceiling, and, in direct reference to S/M practice, suspended in bondage, wearing black leather opera gloves, and later tied to a chair in a ball gag (the latter is also shown in the mouth of a severed pig's head).

The extreme nexus of pain and pleasure evoked here is far in excess of the nonchalant "gender tourism" that, in Reynolds and Press's view, characterizes male rockers who adopt abject poses. They use the term, coined by Suzanne Moore, to describe the "dandies, slackers and would-be playthings" who, while not conforming to the cultural demands of normative masculinity, are still misogynist, and who opportunistically use the gender confusion of modern society to try to redefine the "true New Man" in contrast to violently subordinated woman (227). Perhaps the lack of any mention of Nine Inch Nails in their 410-page book, which covers many less popular alternative bands and performers, including some who have opened for Nine Inch Nails, says something about the difficulty of fitting Reznor into this schema.

In its insistent association of the position of abused beings and broken-open flesh with Reznor's own flesh and desires, the *Closer* video profoundly differs from the most typical use of S/M imagery in Gothic and Industrial styles, of which the film *The Crow* is probably the definitive example. *The Crow*'s conventional distribution of spirit and flesh and of rescuer and victim roles respectively to male and female figures illustrates a new ostensibly pro-woman masculinity that still keeps the figure of the male hero intact. In contrast, the singer of Reznor's song seems right to cry, "I broke apart my insides."

The video also visually subverts another convention, one older than those of rock 'n' roll. Made partially on grainy antique 1920s film stock in homage to Joel-Peter Witkin's "fetish photography" (Gold 52), the *Closer* video teasingly calls back early cinema. But with a difference. As Mary Ann Doane argues, cinema met the assault of modernity on the coherence of the masculine body by creating a visual "discourse which effectively constitutes itself as a denial of the body through the projection of contingency and embodiment onto the white woman or the racial other" (15). In this vicious move, the invisible "spectatorial position" of the white male body is ensured (15–20). Reznor's revisionary pseudo-document reverses the gesture. The video places his own body as spectacle at the center and includes the other potential voyeurs in the frame in slow, full-face shots of watchers, including some tight-lipped men Gold describes as "sneering industrialists straight out of a German expressionist print" (52). Reznor is also watched by a contemptuous domino-masked dominatrix. On what seems to be a giant turntable, widely differing forbidden male and female objects of desire slowly rotate, until near the end a Black man in minstrel-show drag holds the crown of his top hat to his mouth and in a puff of dust blows it all away, leaving us with nothing but the image of Reznor, who closes the video mournfully picking out notes on his keyboard with bandaged fingers. Knowing what our culture calls masculine and feminine seems little help in decoding this spectacle.

What may be more useful is knowing a little about cyborgs. Reznor's personae in videos like "Closer," and in his music generally, can be seen as part of a reaction against an earlier reaction formation, part of a succession of increasingly mechanized waves of resistance to the superman of the early twentieth century who used technology as a prosthesis to put back an imagined lost completeness. This figure, who found his most idealized form in the good cyborg of *Terminator 2* whose "mechanized" masculinity the film sentimentalizes as a lost perfection (Jeffords 260), is radically revised in the broken-open mess of wires, samples, tape, and undifferentiated human/animal flesh that is Nine Inch Nails. The speaker in "The Becoming" tells us that the part of him we once knew is gone because "all pain disappears it's the nature of my circuitry." Donna Haraway says, "The cyborg is resolutely committed to partiality, irony, intimacy, and perversity. It is oppositional, utopian, and completely without innocence" (192). (As Reznor sings in "Reptile," "i am so impure.") While Haraway obviously wrote her "Manifesto for Cyborgs" to inspire feminists, it often furnishes eerily apt descriptions of *Closer*'s tortured reach toward a union of humans, animals, and machines, its refusal of coherent gender positions, and its straining to achieve a vision that would "reverse and displace the hierarchical dualisms of naturalized identities" (Haraway 217).

Our knowledge that the music in *Closer* is electronically produced and arranged by computer does more than just create a darkly comic counterpoint to the song's articulation of a desire for natural(ized) pleasure. It marks the end of an era in which an informed and intelligent person could imagine having access to sexuality *as* an animal, and introduces us to the idea that the most we can hope is to have it *like* one. And finally it raises the question: what sort of self-deluding practice would such mimicry be?

Reznor's voices and the images that accompany them work as a denaturalizing ensemble that redefines consciousness of gender binarity as itself the state of disavowal. If "cyborg heteroglossia is one form of radical cultural politics" that can "cut the code" that would imprison us in language, what the *Closer* video may be showing us is not the "back room" of our gendered culture, but the beginning of a passageway out. For me, as Haraway says of "cyborg imagery," "This is a dream not of a common language, but of a powerful infidel heteroglossia" (223). In *Closer*'s cyborgian plea "help me become somebody else" we might well hear love articulating itself as it is so beautifully described by Elizabeth Grosz in "Animal Sex":

> Erotic desire is not simply a desire for recognition, the constitution of a message, an act of communication or exchange between subjects, a set of techniques for the transmission of intimacy; it is a mode of surface contact with things and substances, with a world, that engenders and induces transformations, intensifications, a becoming something other. (294)

When we look at rock videos like "Closer," hear songs like PJ Harvey's "50ft Queenie," or see performances like Greg Dulli's concert rendition of "My Curse," we face a world of gender trouble beyond inversion or reversal, beyond even ordered multivalence; we reach the realm where semiological systems determining sex and gender begin to break down. This is not new territory, or, in Deleuze and Guattari's terms, a new deterritorialization. The very reason that performative transsexualities and ritualistic sadomasochism have been of such interest to many academics is that they represent subcultures where the complication of gender can become so great as to explode binaries. The growth of gender studies out of women's studies and of queer studies out of gay and lesbian studies similarly reflects scholars' desires to explore places where binary gender difference dissolves. And it would seem that alternative rock's rocking of gender categories cannot rightly be called subcultural when it appears featured in one of MTV's "most popular videos of all time," as veejays frequently call "Closer." The commercialization of these songs and videos is certainly no cause for lamentation if, as Frith claims, an important "social function" of music "is to give us a way of managing the relationship between our public and private emotional lives" ("Toward an Aesthetic" 141). At the very least these recent developments in the representation of gender call for new critical and theoretical paradigms, ones no longer founded in the idea that masculinity and femininity must always be meaningful concepts.

ALTERNATIVE WOMEN
FROM CINDERELLA TO SPINDERELLA

One of the favorite poses of the second-wave feminist here at the end of the twentieth century seems to be exhausted scanning of the horizon for reinforcements, for younger women who have a complete enough commitment to feminism to carry on the struggle. The subtext of this self-representation is that we not only have a prior claim to feminist radicalism, but also continue to set the standard by which the usefulness of feminisms should be judged. The first implicit claim seems to me defensible, even reasonable. I am not inclined to debate, for example, Alice Echols's contention in the foreword to *Daring to be Bad* that "Twenty years after the first stirrings of radical feminism, we are still living with the disappointments, problems, and confusion of an unfinished revolution," (xiii) nor to call into question her conclusion that "If younger women see feminism as irrelevant, it is partly because the movement has managed to change the world" (293). Like bell hooks and others "who grew to womanhood at the peak of contemporary feminist movement," I remember when "sexual liberation was on the feminist agenda," and so I sigh to see "a new generation of women who are aggressively ahistorical and unaware of the long tradition of radical/revolutionary feminist thought that celebrates inclusiveness and liberatory sexuality" (*Outlaw Culture* 73–78). But I also see women of another kind in the new generation, women who dare to be different from what we so often were, and even from what the feminism of the 1960s and '70s placed under the rubric of "difference," women who in their apparent ahistorical ignorance of the fairy tales that have defined us may break into something new.

Just as women as a group have been traditionally understood in relation to men, who furnished the standard, second-wave feminists often see the third wave as most relevant in what they tell us about ourselves, and as deficient when they are not like us. An extreme example is provided by *Sexing the Millennium*. Here Linda Grant develops a narrative of feminism from her own experience. Beginning with her political awakening in college when she realized that she was not alone in being nonorgasmic and ending with her anger in middle age at not being able to get the kind of sex she wants, she concludes that her experiences are universal. The politically admirable realization that what she had considered her personal problem "could be collective, a failure not of the self but a social condition to be studied and solved in a collective manner" quickly translates into a conception of uniformly unsatisfying relations between women and men, which in turn leads her to the idea that binary gender difference determines sexual experience (13). The central problems, in her view, are that women can only enjoy sex with men whom they love and trust, while men are always promiscuous, and that "[w]omen are attracted to power, men to youth and beauty" (238–239). As a result, young women will always be disappointed and older heterosexual women are always left unable to profit from any relaxation of laws and mores that restrict sexual expression. Grant sternly warns that "until women find their own sexuality, what we will have is a single, hegemonic definition of pleasure, male sexuality: pornography, rape, the pursuit of younger and younger women, trophy wives, male fantasies structuring female consciousness and female libido" (16).[1] What of women who are happy with the sexual revolution that has already taken place and who feel they have already found their own sexuality? She is incredibly harsh about them if they happen to also be young: "1992 had become The Year of the Hardbody, the raunchy, voguishly libertarian postfeminist woman who . . . explore[d] the adventure playground of sex. With bravado and condoms, she stalked the club scene" (232). This monstrous young female's most notable characteristic is her inability to recognize the emptiness of her practices. Her "sex is formed of images and styles" (12). She pathetically apes the "San Francisco gay scene of the late seventies" without understanding that such behavior is "meaningless" and "not revolutionary at all" (235). And if she fails to change her ways, she will receive her comeuppance when she "hits forty, then fifty" (255). By framing her totalization of female sexuality as concern about the young, Grant manages both to erase the experience of dissenting feminist coevals, like me, and to ignore the likelihood that younger women's attitudes about love, gender, and sexuality are as experientially based as ours. I have discussed Grant's book at such length because it exemplifies a trend in second-wave feminism that continues to strengthen as we move into the new millennium.

In order to view the next generation of feminists a bit more clearly, I have found it useful to look at them within contexts provided by their own social activities, where they are the most visible females and thus define what female identification is, rather than when they are acting as the students or daughters of the women of my generation. If I look at the third-wave feminists in relation to the social movements I remember or in

our own context

telling us in

Great descriptive power

relation to the second-wave activists and theorists whose ideas shaped my professional life, the younger women often seem merely imitative at best, or, at worst, foolishly reactive, as when they proclaim themselves postfeminists. Disturbingly, they sometimes seem to have little of their own politically, and that little can seem framed in reaction against my own politics. However, in another context, the one defined by the movement that "Generation X" calls "Girl Culture" or, in its more extreme manifestations, "Riot Grrl" and the movement that the third-wave feminists I know refer to as their own, I feel that I understand them better. And "feel" does seem a more accurate term than "think" here.

As we dance together in a packed club to a band of women rockers, the raw, aggressive self-assertion that is redefining female identification electrifies the air around us. I begin to suspect that there is more here than the theories current in my field can account for. When it addresses heterosexuality, feminist theory has generally remained preoccupied with women's right to say no to men. Many cultural critics have commented on the powerful resistance to rape and other forms of violent sexualized oppression expressed in music made by riot grrls and female Punk rockers. Less remarked upon has been the trend in women's popular music toward increasingly violent representations of female sexuality, especially heterosexuality. This omission may seem odd because in mainstream music that receives heavy radio play, women in every rock genre adopted increasingly confrontational and even threatening sexual personae throughout the 1990s. From Meredith Brooks's soft rock song "Bitch," which asserts the singer's right to bitchiness, to Garbage's "Temptation Waits," which opens with frontwoman Shirley Manson singing, "I'll tell you something, I am a wolf but I like to wear sheep's clothing," femininity is styled as hard and aggressive. Some bands quite literally carry the banner for female aggressiveness, as was evidenced when one was flown over the notoriously soft-core 1999 Lilith Fair in Pasadena, California, bearing the legend, "BORED? TIRED? TRY L7." Donita Sparks, who fronts the band, explained, "We were just doing our part in the war against mediocrity" ("Random Notes" 32).

One reason for the discrepancy in focus in this area of cultural criticism may be that, in dealing with heterosex, academic feminisms tend to emphasize danger rather than pleasure. Because of our position, to some extent *in loco parentis* to younger women, female professors may be more pleased by and thus more interested in songs about women's refusal to fall victim to male sexual aggression than in songs about women's wish to violently impose their sexual desires on men. However, the latter genre, if we can consider it one, seems to me more important as a cultural phenomenon in that it is newer, constituting a break with traditional representation of women in rock 'n' roll.

Women are sometimes represented by men in popular music as sexually aggressive and consequently dangerous. This has been a traditional theme in folk ballads and in operas, such as Bizet's *Carmen* and Berg's *Lulu;* however, the narratives in these cases usually suggest that the woman is dangerous to the extent that she feels nothing. A woman's own experience of desire is almost always represented as a danger to her. Rock 'n' roll songs written and performed by men generally continue this tradition.[2] A dangerous woman in rock 'n' roll songs is usually one who arouses sexual feeling in others and uses it to gain nonsexual ends without feeling anything that endangers her control of herself.

In contrast, sentimental, romantic expressions have long been a staple of popular music made by women. Angela Y. Davis seems right to distinguish between the weepy, yearning style typical of early white female pop vocalists and the aggressive music of the Black blueswomen who knew, as Ida Cox sings, that "you never get nothing by being an angel child." Davis understands songs that some other feminists have read as masochistic, such as Bessie Smith's famous "Tain't Nobody's Bizness If I Do," as assertions of absolute control over one's own body in which the choice to accept violent treatment from a lover is compared to the woman's right to "choose to take her life" (252–253). The exaggerated quality, as well as the sexualization, of the examples of what is the singer's business and no one else's, Davis attributes to an ongoing reaction against the condition of enslaved women, whose awareness that their bodies were owned by others was most painfully evident in the way their sexuality was controlled and exploited. "Sovereignty in sexual matters marked an important difference between life during slavery and life after emancipation" (232).

After such events as the legalization of abortion and the gaining of economic power that has come from affirmative action, one might also apply to the condition of all American women Davis's important realization that "sexual freedom was . . . one of the most tangible ways in which the meaning of emancipation was expressed" (232). Just as economic dependence gave bourgeois women something not utterly unlike slave status in the marital breeding pair in times past, the current economic situation in which women can, and generally must, make serious financial contributions to their households frees women to assert themselves more sexually. And, as in the blues, that assertion becomes a mark as well as a result of freedom.

Janis Joplin's "Piece of My Heart" and Hole's "Violet" provide a useful comparison of popular song stylings of female sexuality at different points in white women's emancipation. It is important to remember, as Joplin acknowledged, that "Piece of My Heart," released in 1967 on Big Brother and the Holding Company's *Cheap Thrills* album, was a cover of Erma Franklin's Top 10 Rhythm and Blues hit. Inspired by both Franklin sisters and by Big Mama Thornton, as the R. Crumb album cover reflects, as well as by other classic African American singers, Joplin saw herself as a blues singer.[3] But unlike the Black blues singers whose representations of sexuality were in themselves political acts because they came out of a culture in which doing as one pleased with one's own body emblematized freedom from slavery, Joplin adopted the '60s posture that sexuality was an alternative to politicized violence of any kind. This is evident in her much quoted remark, "My music ain't supposed to make you want to riot! My music's supposed to make you want to fuck" (Gaar 106).

"Piece of My Heart" was a good choice of a blues song for Joplin because of its appropriateness as a vehicle for her timely "Make Love Not War" philosophy. Far from embracing violence as a part of sexuality or taking the masochistic attitude that pain is pleasurable, as critics often claim the song does, the lyrics repeatedly insist that the singer puts up with her lover's bad behavior because of the pleasure his lovemaking pro-vides. Her ability to endure his abuse, figured as infidelity rather than beating, is what makes her claim that she can show him how "tough" a woman can be.

The singer's invitations to her beloved to break off "another little piece of my heart" are followed by her rather defeatist admission that he knows he already has it. In other words, she belongs to him, not to herself. Although such posturing is not attractive from a feminist viewpoint, the song's original performance as a Black woman's message of love to a Black man still retains what Davis identifies as the postemancipation atti-tude to the extent that it is about African Americans' freedom from being commodities owned and manipulated by white masters. The message that love is what makes one person belong to another has subversive political power in this context. As a white woman's song it reinscribes traditional gender relations, particularly disturbingly in that Joplin's song's release coincided with the rise of second-wave feminism.

In contrast "Violet," as performed by Courtney Love fronting Hole, seems subver-sive through and through. Lucy O'Brien describes Courtney Love's sexuality as "a witch's parody" (166). Like her band's name, Love's self-presentation attempts both to acknowl-edge what femaleness has signified and to defiantly resignify it, much as Queer politics has done with that formerly pejorative term. Love is certainly what most feminist theo-rists, myself included, would call an essentialist, condemning female promiscuity and androgyny with explanations like "on a physical and mental level, sex is not the same for women as it is for men. And sexuality is also different. Or should be different" (Des Barres 203). Still, her understanding of female sexuality seems to be that it is a medium for angry confrontation.

In "Violet" Love's body becomes the battleground upon which she meets and de-feats males who would possess her. Purportedly the answer to a letter from a man with whom she was obsessed, in which he asked her what she would do if she got what she wanted, "Violet" replies that when she gets what she wants, she stops wanting it for-ever. The song title's implicit puns on the idea of being violated and also violating (*vio-laht* and *vio-layte*) are dramatized in the video, which replays her well-known past as a stripper through performances that are more threatening than erotic, as is her taunting scream, "come on take everything—I want you to." At the very moment of her offer, she reasserts her control, not unlike Bessie Smith challenging her listeners to deny that her body belongs to her, to destroy because it is she who so chooses.

Other alternative rockers go even further from mainstream norms in their repre-sentations of female sexuality. While male sexuality in women's music at best is sus-pect, and at worst simply figures all that is despised, female sexuality is represented with great frequency as violent and inherently sadistic. The Donnas, who exemplify this stance throughout their repertoire, characteristically warn a male object of desire, in "Searchin' the Streets," "Baby you better run." Among the most startling images of fe-male sexual aggression in popular songs are leering threats to injure the object of de-sire's penis. For example, in "Flower" Liz Phair threatens to take a young boy home and force "everything" on him, concluding, "I'll fuck you 'til your dick is blue." PJ Harvey's song title "Rub it 'Til It Bleeds" speaks for itself, but does not convey the playful sadism of the song in which she lures back the lover with her crooned "I was joking / Sweet Babe, let me stroke it" and then pounces on him again with a screaming chorus, "I'll rub it until it bleeds." The band's frontwoman Polly Jean also presents herself as capable of inflicting sex as punishment in "Rid of Me" with the threat to the would-be jilting boyfriend that he is not rid of her, because "I'll make you lick my injuries."

Phair's CD *Exile in Guyville* was promoted as a response to the Rolling Stones' *Exile on Main Street* and Polly Jean Harvey is often discussed as presenting herself through a masculine persona, "a drag king," according to Ann Powers ("Houses of the Holy" 328). But these songs go beyond simple appropriation, unlike, for example, Linda Ronstadt's cover of "Tumbling Dice," in which the chorus's exhortation "you gotta roll me" inevitably positions her as sexually at the mercy of others. In contrast, Phair intimates, as she sings about the pleasures of stalking and dominating pretty boys who look barely pubescent, that she will roll *him*. However, as a female Mick Jagger successor, I prefer Skin of Skunk Anansie, whose "Intellectualize My Blackness" can stand up against the Stones any day.

The difference between these rising performers and many female rockers of the past is in the former's perception of sex as a medium for the expression of power, rather than as the indirect means to power that it has traditionally been for sexually attractive women. In songs by Love, Phair, and Skin a woman's sexuality is not something she trades for money as a means of advancing herself into a position where she can have what she really wants. Sex is itself the object she wants, but only on her own terms, which include a profound exploration of her ability to manipulate both her own body and the male's. As such, sexual expression becomes aggressive and often violent, a force that cuts through cultural pressures rather than turning them away.

Such refiguration of women's desire and sexual practice may be partly complementary to the elaborate displays of masochism that have become a regular feature of male alternative rock 'n' roll culture, as discussed in the previous chapter, but it may also signal a paradigm shift in which sexuality is associated with destructive urges. Alternative youth culture shows a pronounced tendency toward *liebestod* narratives and eroticized death imagery (*The Crow* perfectly exemplifies this), as is especially apparent in Goth stylings. The impact of AIDS awareness and fear is obvious here, as it is in the current popularity of vampire stories and imagery, a trend also probably partially informed by the general desire of the young to act as if they believed, in defiance of all public warnings to the contrary, that oral sex cannot transmit disease. These recent cultural developments might suggest to those of us who are in a position to define feminist approaches an urgent need to address heterosex in something other than negative terms. We need more from sex education than a "just say no" approach that leaves those whose desires compel them to say "yes" without any plan of action other than alternating between denial and a sense of doom.

Over and over, we academics have asked what women would be if it were possible to conceive of ourselves other than in relation to men. In the midst of dancing at my favorite all-ages club, I always have the feeling that some of the grrls around me know the answer to this question. In order to situate my investigation into what female subjectivity might be coming to mean in the intensely charged space at the center of an emergent women's culture, I will therefore concentrate on some of the rock 'n' roll music performances and their receptions that appear especially popular with the new generation of feminists. I do not mean this focus to suggest that feminist understandings of gender are changing only within rock 'n' roll cultures, or even that this is the most important area in which change is taking place. Rather, my personal preferences dictate this chapter's topic in that while, like most adults, I have failed to move with the times in many ways, I love rock 'n' roll so passionately and it is such an essential part of my everyday life that it provides me with a familiar way of seeing youth culture as much from the inside as seems possible for a woman well past forty.

Due to the close relationship between popular music and identity formation so frequently noted by cultural critics, even a cursory look at the reception given by some young women to music performances of others suggests the magnitude of the shifts in communications between women and consequently in group perceptions of female subjectivity. To provide a quick frame for discussion of some recent developments in relations between female pop music performers and their female audiences and a few of the implications of these relations for feminist theory, I will begin by going back to my own wave to comment briefly on two different sorts of Cinderella-like response formations that have long been observable among feminism's more privileged practitioners, by which I mean the educated women who have collectively spoken for feminism in the last three decades. Looking at these response formations may illuminate the extent of the changes taking place in the formation of female subjectivity, because both of these second-wave responses to male domination of culture reify women's position as inescapably in relation to men. The first response I want to touch on is the one made to the historically subordinate position of women by many heterosexual women who, because of economic advantages, including the ability to support themselves comfortably, have had the least restriction in marital or partnership choices. I will then comment on what feminist theory has so far made of this cultural matter.

When Colette Dowling's self-help book *The Cinderella Complex* came out, it was greeted with annoyance by some feminist academics and other activists on the grounds that its critique of women's characteristic expectation of rescue by a high-status male represented a postfeminist repersonalizing of gender politics. While I agree with Wendy Simonds that the book is illogical and sexist in blaming women's passivity and related personality "inadequacies" for relationship failure (123), I also see the book as unintentionally offering some definition of a culturally important moment in that it contributes to the identification of a fairly pervasive problem for feminism in late-twentieth-century gender relations. As Simonds observes, capitalist ideology pervades the American approach to love and marriage, resulting not only in an unrealistic emphasis on the power of the individual but in insistence that sexual and romantic relations should be evaluated in terms of economic exchange. Moreover, both ideas are gendered in pernicious ways (201–203). Through an odd conflation of capitalist values and a feminism that emphasizes women's putatively better developed interiority comes an understanding of marital equity that is particularly dangerous for women. Wives are encouraged first to assume that they contribute a greater emotional investment to the marriage, and second, working from this assumption, to strive for fairness in terms of financial compensation from the husband (214). As a consequence, professional women who could easily have been financially independent can find themselves in marriages that are as economically skewed against them as are those of traditional housewives.

While I agree with Lynne Segal that "poorer women" are the main victims of the capitalist marriage economy, because they face social limitations that make it difficult for them to reject the conventional wifely role of economic dependence, they are far from being the only women whose more feminist goals have been hampered by "the ongoing reality of men's greater access to positions of status, economic security and power" (305–307). To put it bluntly, it does not take being stuck in the role of poor, dependent Cinderella to drive many women to assent to a form of marital prostitution. As I discuss in the opening chapter, self-help books and courtship guides indicate that, in the late twentieth century, the ability to carry a woman financially remains among the most important qualifications a significant number of women look for in a Prince Charming. As numerous surveys have demonstrated (and as most of us can confirm through anecdotal knowledge or a glance at the personals), most heterosexual women seek partners who are older, have more social prestige and money, and are in all particulars recognized by the most hegemonic forces in society as their female partners' superiors.

During the period when feminism was most concerned with debates over essentialism, the degree to which feminists played out the Cinderella role was a frequent topic of discussion outside the academic world. One of my most depressing recent experiences occurred as I went through a box of old issues of *Ms.* In the 1985 special issue on men, I found Barbara Ehrenreich pointing out "our own internalized problem: the deep feminine hankering to acquire status through contact with the men who already have it" (118).[4] Although most of us know women who show no inclination toward any such behavior, these exceptions still stand out more than they should, and over a decade after Ehrenreich's analysis of the situation, there is little evidence of substantial change.

This situation is especially important to feminist theory because our ability, after essentialism, to theorize about women as a group depends to a large extent on the existence of some recognizable sociological conditions that define such a group. Not only what is done to us, but what we do, helps to make meaningful the idea of all women sharing some political interests. So it is distressing to recognize that the practices of a large number of women continue to replicate the nineteenth-century pattern of subsuming social ambitions into romanticized marital relations. If, as Virginia Woolf said in *Three Guineas,* educated women constitute a specific social class, our class struggle, like that of our nineteenth-century precursors, has routinely been displaced onto a competition for the most financially promising princes, in which women's desire is suppressed in favor of social ambition. This behavior is so prevalent that many of the intellectual women (heterosexual and lesbian) who promulgate the most powerful discourses of feminism seem to accept as a given of female experience the most obvious side effect of this practice: woman's inability to conceive of herself as a subject rather than an object, except through identification with masculinity or through representation of lesbianism as nonfemininity.[5]

Among other things, this severely limited understanding of heterosexual female identification lends itself well to acceptance of the paradigms of psychoanalytic theory as a collection of transhistorical, transcultural truths. In a review of Teresa de Lauretis's *The Practice of Love,* Elizabeth Grosz asks, why do we begin theorizing gender relations with the assumption "that psychoanalysis has provided and should perhaps continue to provide an understanding of the subjective psyche, the structure of fantasy, and the modalities of desire and sexual pleasure"? ("The Labors of Love" 278–279). Majoritist feminist understanding of heterosexuality provides one answer.

The concept of an eternal feminine subject position, if not essence, is certainly suggested when Grosz herself includes in a discussion of what Derrida's work on "the signature" brings to theorizing sexual identity Nancy K. Miller's "recognition" that women do not have "a 'proper name'" in the sense that men do, and adds that "at best, women have the proper name only on loan or provisionally, borrowing it from the father or the husband, always potentially exchangeable for another name" (*Space, Time, and Perversion* 20–21). Was this a "recognition" in 1990, when Miller's text was published, and was it still one in 1995 when Grosz published hers? Census figures as well as my own observations of the marital customs of the young lead me to wonder whether such moments in the articulation of feminist theories deconstruct or reconstruct gender difference. Since it is becoming increasingly normal for women with professions or professional aspirations to retain their original surnames, as is suggested by the fact that ten percent of the women now marrying do so, why must we base descriptions of female subjectivity on the idea that a woman can never have a permanent signature? Only when we theorize the female heterosexual condition as passively waiting for the prince who will define her does the emphasis on the woman's name as a temporary placeholder make sense.

Which brings me to the second Cinderella-esque problem I want to address, the relation of feminist scholars to psychoanalytic discourse. For some time now, academic discussion of gender has been virtually required to have recourse to written theories of sexuality around which the great edifice of psychoanalytic paradigms has stood like a medieval castle. As Mary Caputi notes, fidelity to "psychoanalytic precepts" leaves us in a "conceptual impasse" because psychoanalytic theory is "undergirded by binary opposition" (145). However, into this impasse we have been forced, not by any biological or even linguistic imperative, but because Freudian and Neo-Freudian discourses have functioned for many of us as a sort of glass slipper; no matter how transparently ill-fitting we found them, we recognized that we had to insert ourselves into them before we could enter the castle whence came the rules that governed our lives as women in academe. Only from within the psychoanalytic could we attain the authority to speak.

The most extreme version of this situation was the edict enforced by academic journals in the 1980s that every discussion of sexuality take into account Lacan's theory that the law of the father structures "the symbolic," so that to speak and be heard women must not only depart from the maternal body (of knowledge) but also accept the psychoanalytically grounded concept of gender difference that makes intelligible this mapping of discourse through the family romance. No matter what our own sense of ourselves or our bodies was, we had to theorize as if we felt castrated in relation to the phallus as signifier, men as well as women, but women perhaps more so than men, since men at least have the penis, not to mention the social power associated with its possession.[6]

Even more problematic, the Freudian vision of a sexual "economics" traps feminist analysis of gender relations within a capitalist framework. Influenced by the Victorian discourse of sexual energy as capital that one "spends" in orgasm, Freud characteristically conceives of sexual relations as determined by limitation of libidinal resources. He places sexuality within a system where worth can only be understood in relation to scarcity or lack.[7] To understand sexuality in this way, as Deleuze and Guattari argue, means that one must see lack as intrinsic to desire, rather than taking their view that the sense of lack that permeates the Western consciousness is created by actual material circumstances reflecting political interests: "The deliberate creation of lack as a function of market economy is the art of the dominant class" (*Anti-Oedipus* 24–28). The scarcity model of sexual economics results in a paradigm that can work against women by personalizing political situations that inform our reading of our own desires, returning them always to the rules of an exchange economy and the limitations of the patriarchal family, telling us both that we desire an object (the imago of the parent) whom we can never attain and also that we can experience identity only as gender-related lack. "Such is always the case with Freud. Something common to the two sexes is required, but something that will be lacking in both, and that will distribute the lack in two nonsymmetrical series, establishing the exclusive use of disjunctions: you are girl *or* boy!" (*Anti-Oedipus* 59). Sexual difference is always maintained as a site of investments and payments. Among other things obscured by this financial model is the experience of what Deleuze and Guattari call revolutionary "group fantasy," in which desire, detached from any object, flows between the members of the group, making them pleasurably aware of the interconnectivity of subjects within a society, so that desire allows exploration of how we function together (62–63). Just as collectivity grounded the dream of feminism, so has academic focus on psychoanalytic theory deferred that dream's realization.[8]

It has seemed as if the most we could hope for was to find some way to make psychoanalytic terminology fit us without, like the stepsisters trying to get a foot into the slipper, having to cut off some part of ourselves. To be anti-psychoanalytic in feminist academe has been to be a disenfranchised stepsister, in a state of resistance, denial, or disavowal. And, to switch fairy tales, we have been no more able than Kafka's protagonist to enter the Castle on our own terms. In the wake of Foucault's *History of Sexuality,* a great shift slowly began as more and more critics proclaimed the death of psychoanalysis as the master narrative of sexuality. At roughly the same time as academic feminism has been creating Foucauldian genealogies of gendered identities, a new women's culture has emerged in which identity seems to be differently constructed, made from the stuff of new media of communication. Allowing some of these current cultural formations to inform the academy's ability to think otherwise could result in theories that do not have, or need, recourse to Freud's universalizing descriptions of the nineteenth-century bourgeoisie in order to discuss what it means to be designated a woman.

Freud's theories and their linchpin terms, such as "castration," "fetish," "disavowal," and "phallic mother," came out of his analysis of how the workings of a specific type of Western bourgeois patriarchal culture shaped identity and caused it to adhere to particular subject positions. An endless anxious vacillation between the desire for unified being and the desire to escape the boundaries of such unity into a fragmentation felt as freedom seems inevitable within a culture that creates dichotomous epistemological categories and insists that we either are mouthpieces for the words of the Fathers or else are outside signification and so have no language or authority. The crisis brought on by our sense of choice about which side of the dichotomy we can inhabit is what we have known as the modern condition. But what happens when familiar categories of identity move from a foundational, invisible status within ideology into the light and are examined as myths that no longer compel belief? Many theorists have followed Derrida, Foucault, and Deleuze and Guattari in seeking an answer to this question. Poststructuralism has re-examined subjectivity in reference to the death of the Cartesian subject within philosophical discourse and the cross-cultural erosion of the concept of masculinity as universality. Corresponding change in the category of femininity has received less attention—one might even say "less recognition," since most academic writings on changes in female subjectivity are articulated as speculations on what might come into being at some later time, during a sort of post-postmodernism.

My purpose in this chapter is to explore the possibility that in the last twenty years, as we second-wave feminists vigilantly scanned the horizon for the newest new woman, she has danced right under our noses. Looking forward to a transformation of "sexual difference," Hélène Cixous and Catherine Clément anticipate it occurring "in another time (in two or three hundred years?)" (83). But their contemporary readers can be more optimistic. Alluding to "The Laugh of the Medusa," in which Cixous famously urges women to "break out of the circles, don't remain within the psychoanalytic closure" in order to "launch" a new subjectivity, and predicts that "the new history is coming" (348, 346, 340), Liz Evans writes, "As the French professor says, women have everything to write about their sexuality, about their femininity and about their becoming erotic. Now, using the language of rock music, that is exactly what women are doing" (xii). Moments like this in popular rock criticism are more evidence that significant changes have been taking place in rock culture, and as a result it has become a major site of postmodern identifications that could pose interesting challenges to the old ontological categories.

After examining the popular culture of U.S. feminisms in the 1970s and 1980s, in the form of literary texts and songs that came out of and were addressed to women in feminist movements, Katie King concludes that "the apparatus for the production of feminist culture profoundly reconfigures so-called academic feminism" (122). I agree, but would also urge scholars to recognize that this process continues. There seems no reason to doubt that Holly Near, whose work receives extensive discussion in King's study, influenced the development of feminism in academe, but obviously so did Madonna, who is never mentioned. And the dialogue between gender theorists and rock 'n' roll continues, although sometimes sounding as if only one side is really listening to the other.

Cultural theorists, including bell hooks, Stuart Hall, Simon Frith, Angela McRobbie, and Greil Marcus, have persuasively demonstrated the centrality of rock 'n' roll to youth cultural formations that determine subject positions and sites of identification, if not a sense of core or foundational identity, for their members. Up until very recently this has been seen as by no means a promising cultural development for feminism. Paula Kamen, describing the pop music scene of the late 1980s, deems it an area where "backlash" is particularly virulent not only against ideas popularly associated with feminism but against any recognition of women's humanity. She remarks, "In popular culture, hateful music once consigned to the fringe has entered the mainstream" (116). Yet it may be that the very mainstreaming of reaction against women stimulated the emergence of clearly articulated responses to misogyny in the form of female-identified rock groups and rock criticism. A recent explosion of popular publications on and by women in rock lays the groundwork for analysis of how gender now plays into this field of identity formation.

Perhaps the most initially discouraging impression conveyed by these texts is that there frequently seems to be less difference than one wanted to think between female performers, critics, and groupies. Amy Raphael seems right in saying, "The pervading picture of women's role in rock is as groupie and muse" (xxxi). Writers from Marianne Faithful to Sonic Youth's Kim Gordon confess that what attracted them to "the scene" were fantasies about closeness to their idols, the boys who make the music. As Gordon puts it, they wanted to be "right under the pinnacle of energy, beneath two guys crossing their guitars." But this continuation of the Cinderella-like move to empowerment through association with masculine privilege is qualified by her assertion that this was how she felt "*before* picking up a bass" (66; emphasis mine). Gillian Gaar shows that the history of women in rock 'n' roll as performers, from the earliest Rhythm and Blues singers to riot grrls, is a record of occupation, often under attack, of a subject position that has been culturally reserved for masculinity.

Still, we are left with the problematic figure of the female audience member, as an other excluded from the female performer's construction of herself as guitar hero(ine). Joanne Gottlieb and Gayle Wald write that, prior to the Riot Grrl movement, women usually participated in rock culture "as consumers and fans—their public roles limited to groupie, girlfriend, or backup singer, their primary function to bolster male performance" (256). Ann Powers takes an even bleaker view, noting that "the girl . . . standing rapt in front of the stage [is one] of the most enduring manifestations of the feminine in pop, surfacing in songs, commentary, and common lore as both essence and enemy" ("Who's That Girl" 460). In the female rocker binary, this weak, passive figure defines, through the contrast she offers, power, presence, and subjectivity in the rock culture.

Some troubling questions are raised by this opposition. Must the female performer's heroic move against gender hierarchy always be undercut, even deconstructed, by the existence of her traditionally feminized double? And must the female audience, as would-be groupies, always receive the performances of female rockers in a way analogous to male audience reception of pseudo-lesbian sequences in pornography: as a warm-up for the real action, the drama in which one can imagine oneself taking a central part? In other words, if the relation between rock performers and audiences can only replicate the Cinderella plot that still seems to define gender relations in mainstream culture, if, under the guise of rebellion against bourgeois roles, it simply provides a space for regeneration of the retro-dream of rescue by the prince, then how much cultural significance does the female performer's defiant occupation of the place of rock power have?

In answering that question, I want to begin by agreeing with Lori Twersky that "an inordinate amount of drivel has been written about" the female rock audience (177). The academic attitude toward this audience is similar to that toward the consumers of pornography. As Laura Kipnis observes, "Pornography isn't viewed as having complexity, because its *audience* isn't viewed as having complexity" (177; emphasis Kipnis's). Girls squirming in pleasure as they listen to a band are generally read as simplistically as boys squirming with pleasure as they view a pinup.

Patrocinio Schweickart's modification of Judith Fetterley's famous theory of immasculation, with its attention to the mechanisms by which male-centered literary texts can interpellate female readers other than as objectified victims, suggests another way to understand what rock culture has consistently provided the female spectator. Schweickart argues that primarily masculinist cultural products can elicit a dual hermeneutic from the female audience member, including both her recognition of the text's sexism and her "recuperat[ion of] the utopian moment" in which art offers identification with a universalized, transcendent subjectivity (35). If in the past female audience members have been able to identify with the singer or central figure presented in the rock 'n' roll culture spectacle of rebellious self-assertion, no matter what the boy embodying that fantasy thought about the girls watching him, then a basis for powerful resignification of the rock rebel was already available when female performers appropriated his place.

Reading the first-person accounts of the fans collected in currently popular writings on rock suggests some of what inhabits audience imaginations beyond the narrow boundaries of Cinderella, and other, dependency fantasies. As Cheryl Cline puts it, "The question is: does a macho stance always elicit a submissive reaction? . . . The tough, cool sexual outlaw is one of rock's most romantic images. It's supposed to be for boys to imitate, but there's no reason to suppose that girls don't want to be 'bad boys' too" (374). I would modify that to read that there is "no reason to suppose that girls don't want to be *rebels* too." As Gaar shows throughout *She's a Rebel,* the women who make the music are rebels, and frequently the female audience members are also. As is made clear in Emily White's groundbreaking overview of the Riot Grrl movement, having a woman on center stage can make a profound difference in the substance of audience identification: "getting lost in a song or a show is fundamentally different when you're getting lost in the sound of a woman's voice. And if rock has built itself on the foundation of screaming girl fans, suddenly that fandom isn't based in pent-up worshipful sexuality" or in willful misreading of the universalized male other as self, but "in recognition of woman" as legitimated subject (403).

Lucy O'Brien quotes the all-women band L7 as saying (presumably collectively), "Our fans couldn't give a shit if we're women" (162). But one may tend to doubt that who sees them, as I have several times, in front of a hall of predominantly female adoring fans, performing "Fast and Frightening," a song expressing passionate admiration for a wild girl. The band's aggressive style brought shrieks of joy from tattooed leather girls in the style of the song's heroine, and so did their expressions of approval for the antics of the girl whose "glance hits me like lightning." At stage shows like this where audience, performers, and the figures evoked by the songs all attempt to embody heroic femaleness, the successful communication of proud pro-female identification seems to be flowing both ways. Kathleen Hannah of Bikini Kill sums up the feeling of playing to girl fans: "every time I looked into their eyes I knew that feminism was alive" (Juno 101). The collectivist identifications of contemporary female rockers are also suggested in The Donnas' teen independence anthem, "Get Outta My Room," in which the singer may have "Cinderella on my TV," but she also plays her music loud enough to enrage the neighborhood because doing so helps her imagine "a crowd" and thus escape "doin' time" in girlhood, through fantasies of clubbing with other transgressive girls. As the motto of the third-wave feminist magazine *Bust,* "The New Girl Order," suggests, the collective vision of Girl/grrl culture resignifies icons of femininities past.

A large number of female performers and female-centered groups appear to be consciously playing with this new dynamic. Probably the most striking evidence of this is the propensity of women band members to interact with dancers in the mosh pit to enforce respect for female audience members. One of the most common sights in the small alternative music clubs is women guitarists or singers pouring beer on or kicking at the heads of male audience members who are shoving females too roughly in front of the stage. Band members' shouts to "leave that girl alone" and threats to "kick ass" if the bullying does not stop are so common as to be conventional parts of performance not only of riot grrls and neo-punks but of otherwise much "softer" entertainers.

This specific way of demonstrating toughness seems significant because of the meanings that have surrounded dancing, and especially dancing in front of the stage. Angela McRobbie's description of dance both as the main "popular leisure activity where the female body has been allowed to break free of the constraints of modesty" and as "a way of speaking through the body" help explain the way that the girl dancing in front of the stage became, even more than the half-naked groupie lounging backstage, a symbolic representative of audience as sexual conquest (193, 195). Whatever a girl may mean to express through her dance, it has had cultural readability primarily as an expression of sexual availability. No wonder, then, that, as McRobbie says, it is "male youth stylists [who] take to the floor with the direct ambiance of the subculture" and whose dances have heretofore dominated the scene (197), nor is it any wonder that some young males seem to feel entitled to elbow or trample women whom they see as offering themselves unreservedly by joining the dance. Protecting female audience members' right to dance free of sexual harassment may be women rockers' strongest assertion of their possession of the physical and symbolic space of the scene. Kathleen Hannah says, "At a show, as the person with the microphone I feel like I have a certain responsibility because I can communicate with everyone in the room. So if I see a woman being fucked with, I might say, 'You—outta here now!' and make the community responsible for removing that person" (Juno 90). The young women who dance in interpretive response to such performers' music, under their protection, work with the female bands to redefine the experience of gender identity within rock culture.

To focus on some more subtle points in audience/performer interaction, I will look at three of the most widely popular 1990s groups in the subgenres of Rap, alternative/ Grunge, and Neo-Blues: Salt-N-Pepa, Veruca Salt, and the later, more accessible PJ Harvey.[9] Each of these groups represents a style of pop performance that blurs the distinction between entertainer and entertained. As Rap artists, Salt-N-Pepa participate in a regional art form that was originally available to any inner-city person interested in music, because performance depended on vocal and mental dexterity, not instruments or training, and performances were available without cover charge at parties and on street corners. PJ Harvey's bluesy rock style also connects with African American traditions in which vocal abilities are valued above expensive technical equipment. Veruca Salt came out of the Grunge movement, an "alternative" form of rock that, like Punk, valorized the raw energy of garage bands without pretensions. All three groups received attention from critics because of what was seen as their aggressive intrusion into male-dominated genres, and their music has most often been discussed in relation to the work of males who are seen as setting the standard in their areas. However, I will argue that all three groups disrupt conventional gender binarity to open up the process of identification and thus enable us to imagine subjectivity without reference to psychoanalytically grounded phallic economies in which women must understand themselves as feminine in relation to a privileged masculine signifier.

Probably the most explicitly feminist of the three groups is Salt-N-Pepa, whose debut *Hot, Cool & Vicious* was the first Rap album by women to reach the Top 40. It made gold in 1987. The band's founding members Cheryl James (Salt) and Sandy Denton (Pepa) publicly identify their music as feminist. As Gaar explains, "Because rap was perceived as a highly sexist genre, female rappers were expected to retaliate with progressive messages while presenting a positive female image, which, of course translated to being feminist," and Salt-N-Pepa met that expectation eagerly (423). From the beginning they "spoke up for women, slamming men who behaved like 'dogs'" (O'Brien 321). While they emphasize their femaleness, showcasing for example their use of a female DJ in "Spinderella's Not a Fella," Salt-N-Pepa aggressively combat the essentialist views of female sexuality that dominate most popular versions of cultural feminism and result in the dissemination of theories about eroticism based on the assumption that women are not sexually stimulated by visual media.

Salt-N-Pepa's confident rejection of such ideas goes beyond challenging the 1980s' popular reconstruction of woman as essentially chaste and nonsexual, so lamented by radicals like Echols, hooks, Segal, and myself. Their enormously popular song and video *Shoop* could have been commissioned by feminist theorists who opposed the reductive theory of gender identification articulated in Laura Mulvey's classic reading of the function of the Lacanian gaze in film, "Visual Pleasure and Narrative Cinema." An attitudinal descendant of the blues classic "Mama Goes Where Papa Goes," *Shoop* does display the athletic and beautiful bodies of Salt, Pepa, and Spinderella as spectacle. But most frequently their bodies are the loci of point-of-view shots establishing them as desirous subjects, with the camera following their sightlines to zero in on the male bodies the song names as the objects of their desire. The video invites female audience identification, saying through its semiotics that women are the possessors of the gaze. It invites us to come share Salt-N-Pepa's undisguised enjoyment of male physicality, as they travel through the city openly staring at beautiful guys of all different types, attracted to many, permanently choosing none, their eyes always moving on.

A less sexualized depiction of urban space as the background for female self-assertion and realization of power is offered in Queen Latifah's poignantly lovely *Just Another Day* . . . . These videos, and a number of others in the Rap genre, calmly assert that women can occupy the streets without fear and engage in unthreatened pursuit of pleasure. Such visions of the city as a playground for women could justly be called unrealistic, but their utopianism opens political possibilities. Fredric Jameson's assessment of the revolutionary potential of women's science fiction is also applicable here: "In our own time, feminism has been virtually alone in attempting to envision the Utopian languages spoken in societies in which gender domination and inequality have ceased to exist: the result was more than just a glorious moment in recent science fiction, and should continue to set the example for the political value of the Utopian imagination as a form of praxis" (107). Jameson argues that music television "spatializes" the audio to create a new sort of narrative without a story, one that can "mediate between sight and sound" (299–300) to map out new areas in which the imagination can play. The space into which videos like *Shoop* bring the female audience involves a dream of control that is at the same time relaxation, a dream of power without stress. Noting that "daily life in the physical city" is only made possible through "a situational representation on the part of the individual subject of that vaster and properly unrepresentable totality which is the ensemble of society's structures as a whole" (51), Jameson says that "the political form of postmodernism, if there ever is any, will have as its vocation the invention and projection of a global and cognitive mapping, on a social as well as a spatial scale" (54). As one follows the sightlines in *Shoop* and gives in to the pull of shot/reverse-shot sequences in which the lascivious gazes of the women are returned by friendly, welcoming male smiles, one might begin to see how such a mapping could take place and thus could locate female subjectivity differently than it has previously been placed in relation to what we still too often experience as the "City of Dreadful Delight," with the female viewer's emphasis falling on "dread." Salt-N-Pepa define themselves visually as perspective characters in their own drama, perhaps less identifiable as women because they look lustily at men (since male homosexuals have traditionally taken this role when male bodies are sexually objectified) than because they actively share their fantasy with other feminists. Their voyeurism is coded female in that it is collectively experienced among women.[10]

Polly Jean Harvey, less optimistically visionary and quite critical of the inclusion of overt feminism in rock performance (O'Brien 168–169), invites audience identification in far less idealized settings. For the playful beach of "Shoop," her video substitutes the murderous river's edge of *Down by the Water.* The song echoes, perhaps deliberately, the 1987 cult film *River's Edge,* in which the display of a murdered girl's dead body by her murderer forces either misogynist or pro-female identifications among her high school classmates. In Harvey's video the female body, represented visually only by her own, dancing underwater in a tight red dress, remains defiantly alive and the locus of subjectivity. It gives form to eroticism, placing it within female experience, leaving masculinity to occupy at best a position of exchangeable supplementarity. One could imagine the singer to be fantasizing herself as a male who kills the unseen other female, but all we can actually see is a woman in a near masturbatory communion with her own lithe physicality, her hands hovering over her erogenous zones as if to speak in sign language, as if to stroke in love.

For Polly Jean Harvey and her audience this spectacle of female self-sufficient satisfaction represents a definite change. Ann Powers describes the earlier work of PJ Harvey as "envision[ing] a subject between sexes, empowered by the possibilities and entrapped by the limits of both masculine and feminine" ("Houses of the Holy" 328). As Powers explains, the early PJ Harvey song "Dry" "encapsulates the circular movement of male toward female toward male that conventional pop music allows," showing how within the music itself, as well as within the dynamic of performance and reception, "women's expression, linked . . . to an elusive, longed-for, central male figure, falls back into wistfulness or frustration" ("Who's That Girl" 462). No matter that he "put it all on the stage," she can only repeat as chorus "You leave me dry."

The shift in her far more popular 1995 album *To Bring You My Love,* for which *Down by the Water* was a promotional video, is from exterior interactions between women and men in the rock world to the interiority of the female performer (Kalmar 19). The interior Harvey chooses to occupy is not the nineteenth-century domesticated interior as woman's sphere. That interior is only comprehensible in relation to the masculinized exterior sphere, whereas understanding of the fluid interiority of Harvey's later work does not rely on reference to the earlier work's dry space, a combat zone between oppositional masculinity and femininity. Just as Harvey's male band members became interchangeable supporting players as she moved from one style to another, her evocations of masculine figures and the attributes associated with masculinity are pushed to the periphery in her later style, as she invites the audience to enter into her and experience female embodiment of unrestrained emotion. Possibly the most remarkable thing about *Down by the Water,* which has so far mystified critics, is that its entire suggested cast of innocents, whores, parents, daughters, and killers and its entire suggested plot of incest, betrayal, murder, and redemption are compressed into a body marked as feminine without reference to actual men in an exterior world, as the video's tight close-ups of her tranced, undulating body and inwardly smiling face emphasize.

Jameson provides a way to begin to understand Harvey's transmutation of the stuff of many young women's nightmares into a dream of female empowerment. The video fits his description of postmodernist pastiche as "blank parody, a statue with blind eyeballs," in that it seems without the normalizing impulse of parody. Her performance is definitely not overtly comic; it lacks "parody's ulterior motives, [is] amputated of the satiric impulse, devoid of laughter and of any conviction that alongside the abnormal tongue you have momentarily borrowed, some healthy linguistic normality still exists" (17). However, the song's recreation of standard blues and folk-song accounts of the murder of a woman as an act of passion is not the reduction of history to image or commodity that Jameson decries, and decidedly not part of a movement "in which the history of aesthetic styles displaces 'real' history" (18, 20). Instead, the song defamiliarizes the recreation of history through Harvey's deliberate (mis)representation of the eroticization of female death through her own spectacularized body. She dances the weirdness of a sexuality built upon women's dead bodies, even as she references that sexuality as our musical heritage. If any "healthy linguistic normalcy" exists here, it is in her body as it speaks to the audience, as her small, knowing smile and beckoning gestures invite the girls in.

The technology of video works to bind singer to audience because Harvey appears to be herself the victim of the tradition she evokes, a drowned woman underwater, her hair streaming like that of the pathetic mother (Shelley Winters) in what is possibly the most famous scene in that classic depiction of predatory masculinity, *Night of the Hunter*. Like the murderer's hands in the film, on which "love" and "hate" are alternately spelled out, the underwater movements of Harvey's body "tell the story of death and life." She appears to be both moving on the current and moving the water with her hands. The video format allows her to embody two modes of female subjectivity simultaneously, as both song and singer, and in so doing to give her audience two simultaneous identificatory objects. She becomes, in herself, both the cautionary sight of woman destroyed by sexuality, her death transformed into art, and the site of woman's eternal presence as creative artist, making art out of her own sex/death.

This sort of rock performance is central to young women's current efforts to transform a threateningly violent and sexist dominant culture into a pro-woman subculture. The video suggests what Deleuze and Guattari call "the dream of multiplicity," through which we experience the body in its function as a medium of connectivity to society, history, and "the full body of the earth" (*A Thousand Plateaus* 30–31). Although PJ Harvey, especially in her present softer and more "pop" form, does not fit the description of the hard-edged Riot Grrl style, nonetheless one can see in this video how girls become grrls. Watching the video recaptured for me the experience of being in PJ Harvey's audience, close to the stage, swaying along with her and all the other half-hypnotized fans, lost in our dream of the music. "We each go through so many bodies in each other" (*A Thousand Plateaus* 36).

The most unexpectedly wonderful of my experiences of women's rock performances, however, was seeing Veruca Salt at La Luna, a local all-ages club, with hundreds of girls in their early teens. As the band tore into their hit "Seether" the mosh pit suddenly expanded to encompass the entire club floor, and the girls began a version of slam dancing that lifted most of us off our feet. I do not think this wild moment came out of nowhere, or out of mere recognition of a familiar Top 40 song. It seemed to come out of recognition of a representation of self as rocker that had nothing to do with either plaintive articulation of the cultural abjection of femininity or defiant assumption of a space understood to be coded masculine.

The wild acting-out of joy arose from song lyrics that depict female desire as an irrepressible spring of meaning and presence, that posit our sexuality not as something we must summon up from the depths of suppression and denial, but as something that is there, always already prepared to leap right out of us into the world, and finally as something that has more to do with our understanding of ourselves as selves than our relations with men do. The intimacy with the body suggested by the boast about the inner, sexual self, "I know how to conceive her," and the semi-comic laments over the fruitless effort to rein her in, "calm her down," anesthetize, or reinteriorize her and thus gain sexual control, seem to have nothing to do with relating to men and everything to do with relating to oneself as a woman. Hence the intense joy with which the audience joined the band in triumphantly shouting the chorus, "can't fight the seether!" At that moment we knew that "seether is the center of it all."

Louise Post and Nina Gordon, core band members and both guitarists and vocalists, reject the critics' designation of their music as postfeminist, seeing feminism as "an ongoing struggle" in which they are very involved (Raphael 83, 94). While each expresses concern over being seen as a "role model" or "a feminist spokesperson," they enjoy "inspiring" young women to perform rock 'n' roll and especially to play guitar (87). Their love of all-ages venues was evident at La Luna when they leaned together and then leaned out to touch their guitars regally to the tops of the closest fans' heads. At that moment, the crowd reached a level of wildness that I have not experienced since the 1960s. In the ecstatic tear-streaming faces of the screamers closest to the stage I had a vision of a future that actually differs from the past in its constructions of gender. Girls were looking to women for affirmation and to see what they might want to be. Our energy was everything. Femaleness and the female body were things that we possessed individually and in common, and they were good. Our physicality was pleasure. The gaze traveled back and forth between the stage and audience as if in beams of joy. We could look at males, but it was in looking at and with each other that we found a sense of who we were.

That night at La Luna gave me a glimpse into a world in which it just might sound counterintuitive to claim that the feminine is absence in relation to male presence, that the feminine is inevitably culturally constructed as lack, and that desire must always come from men as subjects and can only take us as objects. The phallic economy had never seemed so irrelevant. Desire was losing its reference to any object at all. We were entering a new realm of pleasures, where perhaps, as Foucault speculated, the identities created by institutions and their disciplines could break down to allow a new form of being to emerge.

People around my own age often ask me, how do you feel dancing in a club where everyone else is at least twenty years younger than you? Sometimes the feeling comes to me in a rush of utterly unanalytical joy. Then I enthuse, as the lesbian singer and performance artist Phranc does over a Team Dresch show, also in Portland, "It was so exciting to me. I thought . . . This is where I belong, this is where I fit in. This is rock 'n' roll, and it's *real*" (Juno 163; emphasis Phranc's). At other times it feels like being the sort of feminist intellectual that Foucault seems to be urging us to become. Although "blissed out," I feel that, like the early feminist theorists Foucault admires, I have "actually departed from the discourse conducted within the apparatuses of sexuality." I am not *lost* in the music; rather I am "occupying a specific position," as he says the intellectual today must do (*Power/Knowledge* 220, 132). I am placed in the music, by the performance, in a space that is female because female bodies occupy it and celebrate their particularity within it. A space in which being female and being embodied are the same, not for political reasons, but in ways that do serve feminism's political ends.

Of Foucault's recommendations about sexual life, Leo Bersani writes, "It is not a question of lifting the barriers to seething repressed drives, but of consciously, deliberately playing on the surfaces of our bodies with forms or intensities of pleasure not covered, so to speak, by the disciplinary classifications that have until now taught us what sex is" (81). Dancing to "Seether" with Veruca Salt and the other members of their audience, I could suddenly imagine a time in which the idea that women accede to meaning in culture only as Cinderellas might actually become somewhat obsolete, a time in which it might be more important for us to "find ourselves" in a process of becoming than to reach a determinant meaning, and that we might spin meanings out around ourselves as play, as pleasure, as dance. And so, like Lily Briscoe, I have had my vision.

CONCLUSION

The end of a millennium is bound to make people unusually conscious of cultural and societal changes. Predictably, some deplore the changes while others greet them with joy. The more measured academic response is usually a detached dismissal of the extremes of millennialism, usually with an added observation that what appears to be new does so only because of the hysteria of the cultural moment, and all such apparent change will eventually be reincorporated into the timeless structures from which it emerged. This book has taken a different tack, arguing that our culture is not simply on the brink of what looks like major change. It is already in the process of transforming, often in ways that are invisible to most in the academic world because of the paradigms by which we evaluate the evidence before us and the discourses governing what we can read as significant articulation rather than insane babbling.

Among those who warn us not to expect too much change, some voices are still cautiously hopeful. Particularly relevant to youth cultures at millennium's end is Susan McClary's assertion that while "any given version of the transgressive body" that the pleasures of popular music conjure into being must be understood as ephemeral because it will inevitably be "absorbed" rapidly into the mainstream culture, still, transgression's every ecstatic embodiment should be treated as important because of what each can teach us about the body and pleasure ("Same As It Ever Was" 38). McClary locates the political power of music for "the disenfranchised" in its "ability to articulate different ways of construing the body, ways that bring along in their wake the potential for different experiential worlds" (34). The same might be argued, as I have attempted to do, about the political power of specific ways of loving and having sex. But what are we learning about bodies and pleasures? What experiential worlds are coming into existence?

Many critics looking ahead adopt the crossroads model, seeing us as poised at a moment of crucial choice. The choices most often identified by cultural critics interested in gender are between violent sexuality and gentle egalitarianism. [1] Thus, in *Nightmare on Mainstreet,* Mark Edmundson warns us that "our culture remains in many ways divided between Gothic and visionary impulses" (179). Noting the increasing popularity of "consensual sadomasochistic sex," especially among the young, Edmundson fears we have already taken the wrong turn. Sadomasochism is the premier danger in this study because "in a culture of Gothic—and an S & M encounter may just be a very compressed Gothic culture—there is no love to mitigate the drive to domination, not even a conception of love that can counter the Gothic myth that all is haunted and that death inevitably wins out" (135). Since Edmundson has adopted an analytic system in which S/M can only be read as loveless and deathly, his foray into examination of the sex styles of the young leaves him no option but this sort of gloom.

While more hopeful than Edmundson, and definitely not sharing his condemnation of "feminist tracts" and overly aggressive women (14), Claudia Springer also sees us as facing a choice between entering "an era when pain and pleasure will become indistinguishable" or creating "a new beginning, one in which technology will become part of an egalitarian social configuration and inequalities will be rejected as anachronisms from a bygone age that was merely human" (161). For Springer "male fantasies," which she refers to throughout *Electronic Eros* as if men's fantasies were by definition identical, are fantasies of domination, in which vulnerability is ultimately feminized. Thus the "power relations between the sexes" that she sees as central to our current love affair with cyborg modes of being can only be resolved beneficially for women if we reject the eroticization of violence as masculinist oppression (91).

Springer's and Edmundson's intolerance of the fusion of sex and violence is certainly unobjectionable in terms of the standard American ideology of love. And I must concede that gentle, kindly, nurturing love is certainly a fine thing. It can make relations between parents and children very pleasant; I had ample experience of this while growing up. However, whether love can now be pressed into taking such a form between sexual partners is another matter. As Valerie Steele points out in her book on fetish fashion, the "disappearing boundary between the 'normal' and the 'perverse'" is a feature of late-twentieth-century life about which "we" are seemingly ambivalent, but which stands out all the more strongly for that reason (197). Perfect normalcy is impossible to attain not only because, as Steele says, all "straights" like "us" retain some "polymorphous perverse behavior" after socialization (31). It is also an impossible goal because, lest we forget, "normal" means different things within different, but concurrent, cultural discourses.

Sitting around talking about horror films with my favorite film students, a bunch of "well pierced and tattooed" youths such as Edmundson relentlessly criticizes (119), I often hear that *The Stepfather* (1987) is a perennial favorite. Its appeal, as my young friends are quick to explain to me, is that it exposes the abnormality of the family values the dominant culture tries to foist on the young as a norm.[2] The eponymous villain's dementia lies in his fetishization of stereotypical American normalcy. He is not interested in molesting his stepdaughter or playing weird sex games with his wife; he wants everything to be exactly as it is in 1950s family situation comedies—or he will kill them all. But what if he did not kill when disappointed? Would his inflexible need to act as a traditional husband and father then be unreadable as insanity or fetishistic perversity? My conversations with the young suggest that he would remain insane within some of their frames of reference, as he does to his stepdaughter, who complains long before he begins his rampage that he must be unbalanced because he is "like Ward Cleaver."

From what vantage point is such behavior uncanny? In Judith Butler's most recent development of her theory of melancholia as the foundation of gender identity, she speaks of her desire to "shed light on the predicament of living within a culture which can mourn the loss of homosexual attachment only with great difficulty," in which "homosexual love" cannot be seen "as a 'true' love" (*Psychic Life* 133, 138). This is a laudable goal, but since I do not currently inhabit such a culture, except insofar as it may surround the subcultures in which I do live, the only way I could pursue this sort of study would be by acting as an anthropologist, by going away from my family and friends, departing from my own milieu, and immersing myself in cultural products that I ordinarily take no interest in. In my world, homosexual love is respected and valued. An important moment in my every homecoming to San Francisco occurs when I enter my old neighborhood and pass the Castro Street memorial to those lost to AIDS. I feel then, as I do when surrounded by my counterculture family, that I have returned to the normal, the real world.

For me, nothing was ever more evocative of my early sense of home than standing in a North Beach postcard shop and hearing a fellow San Franciscan exclaim indignantly, as she looked at cards of recent U.S. presidents, "Who votes for these people!" I also think of my mother, in her late seventies, responding in annoyance to another woman's assessment of her life: "I could have had the American Dream? What's that? A big house and a lot of stuff? I never wanted that!" Butler's book, consequently, tells me a great deal about the formation of subjectivity in a mainstream America with which I have had little direct contact, it gives me insight into all those "stepfathers" and "stepmothers" to whom the capitalist discourse of normative sexuality makes sense, but it tells me nothing at all about how I or any of the people whom I have been able to love understand their own subjectivity. Where my world welcomes unrestrained sexual activity as a force for radical social diversity, the mainstream, along with many millennial academics, fears it as destructive chaos.

At the end of her study of *fin de siècle* gender styles, Elaine Showalter optimistically tells us, "What seems today like the apocalyptic warnings of a frightening sexual anarchy may be really the birth throes of a new sexual equality" (208). Yes, I want to answer, but why should sexual anarchy be frightening? What would make it seem to preclude sexual equality? And even, dare I ask, would sexual (rather than gender) equality actually be desirable—in any sense of the word? Certainly, it is desirable to feminists if by this we mean social and legal equality for all people irrespective of their biological sex. But could equality in sexual relationships be attained without getting rid of the passionate extremes of feeling that effect disorienting power imbalances between lovers? And finally, as an unreconstructed Lawrencian, I am not sure I oppose apocalypse, if I can count on it to sweep away the world as I no longer wish to know it.

Commenting on her experience of Women Against Pornography's New York City Porn Tour, Showalter describes "the adult bookstores, film arcades, and sex emporia of Times Square" as "unsettling, sometimes comic . . . and sometimes frightening" and voices her suspicion "that few female viewers who saw [Madonna's *Open Your Heart* video] knew that the [peep show] carousel really exists outside MTV" (165). I scarcely know how I could begin to explain how alienating I find this passage in her book. Suffice it to say that watching an hour of almost any contemporary situation comedy on network TV, complete with commercials, has an effect on me similar to the Porn Tour's on Showalter. The idea that something like the sexless, banal repetition of clichés that passes for communication and the worship of mass-produced objects that governs the characters' lives might actually be played out between living human beings in some suburban theme-park of antiquated gender roles is more than I can bear to contemplate for very long. And no strip show could possibly fill me with the shock and horror that I feel when I watch an obviously liposuctioned model voguing in a commercial for carcinogenic diet soda as a song about freedom plays, or an off-road vehicle is shown needlessly destroying the ecological balance in a section of wilderness, as if such activities were supposed to be liberating fun.

Perhaps what it all comes down to is that groups of Americans value different things and are appalled by different things, and as a result, we understand the world in utterly incommensurate ways. But our work as feminists can hardly end with such an observation. As Robyn Wiegman points out, in reference to feminism's constructions of the gendered and raced subject, "political resistance entails a struggle against reconstituting, among and between us, that which has and continues to systematically destroy us" (174). Irritating as we can sometimes be to each other, feminists must generate theories based on honest, nonpathologizing attempts to understand the ideological and experiential bases of other women's points of view.

The speculations about the reception of pornography that end Laura Kipnis's study, *Bound and Gagged,* provide a model for a feminist interpretation of cultural trends and artifacts that truly takes difference into account. Kipnis first notes that women who feel assaulted by the monogendered world of pornography, where everyone feels compatible desires, understand the one gender represented to be masculine and thus they legitimately "worry that . . . men have the power to force their fantasy of a one-gender world onto unwilling women." However, she also takes the crucial step of recognizing that pornography's vision of absolutely compatible sexual desires is attractive as futuristic fantasy to some women and men who do not see the sexual attitudes and behaviors it depicts as especially masculine and who have no interest in imposing any monolithic reconstruction of gender, love, or sexuality on others (200–201)

In trying to understand why some feminist theorists fail to recognize that differences in perception of the intersections of gender and sexuality are not necessarily indicative of misogyny, Kipnis speculates that the failure is due to the theorists' opposition to psychoanalytic theory (189–190). Her conception of anti-psychoanalytic theorists seems almost identical to my conception of psychoanalytic theorists, as I have outlined it in the previous chapter. In addition to this difference in our views, there is a vast gulf between Kipnis's personal reception of pornography and my own. She sees it as primarily reflecting (some) men's fantasies about "big-breasted porno bimbos [who] want to have sex all the time with any guy no matter how disgusting" (199), while, as I discuss in this book's introduction, I have always experienced it as a collection of narratives and images that affirm my own perception that impractical, unsentimental sexual experiences are often fun. Yet we reach the same conclusions about the relationship between the pornographic texts that so many of our fellow feminists find intolerable expressions of woman-hating and those texts' audience. Kipnis's account of pornography's reception by others besides herself leaves me feeling recognized and understood. How this agreement between us can be possible suggests a direction for feminist theorizing more productive than the current generational clash and related impasse over sexuality.

Like Deleuze, I look forward to a time in which "people are more and more fed up with being told about 'papa, mama, Oedipus, castration, regression,' and with the properly imbecilic image of sexuality in general, and of their own in particular, that they are offered. [Consequently] the psycho-analysts will have to take the 'masses' into account; the small masses" (114). I would also like to believe that adhering to methods recommended by the philosophers I love and attempt to follow, such as Foucault and Deleuze and Guattari, would necessarily result in a revolution in academic feminisms that would produce enlightening dialogue among women with differing world views, but I have seen little evidence in the feminist theories currently prominent in the academy that this is the case. At present, no matter what philosophy one begins with, the most valorized, although unstated and unexamined, methodology for feminism's unending task of personalizing the political and politicizing the personal seems to be as follows: identify a problem shared by a large number of women, assume that women who claim not to have this problem are deluded or insignificant, and then investigate the now universalized problem. I am far from being the first feminist theorist to lament this method.

In *Feminist Theory: From Margin to Center,* bell hooks, writing of her college days, remarks that while sisterhood was a new concept to her white classmates, "I had not known a life where women had not been together, where women had not helped, protected, and loved one another deeply" (11). Her shock increased when she saw that instead of taking this cultural and experiential difference into account and learning from African American women, white bourgeois feminists universalize lack of sisterhood and then set to work creating a body of writings explaining it as the result of women's acceptance of standards imposed by men through the medium of a culture most often described as if it were unitary and omnipotent. Complaints from African American feminists that this approach erases their own experience as irrelevant to feminism mainly go unaddressed. *Feminist Theory* was published in 1984, but most of us know what followed.

The feminist theories that came to dominate academe subsequently worked from Lacan to theorize all culture as structured by gender-biased language, which was in turn seen as predetermined by a process of language acquisition taken to be inevitable for any who achieved access to the Symbolic, that is, for all but the incomprehensibly insane. Back in 1984, with *Feminist Theory,* hooks had suggested that instead of continuing in this already not very encouraging vein, bourgeois feminists striving to establish networks of sisterly solidarity in their lives might ask women who had already achieved that goal for advice. Was anyone listening? The simple and elegant strategy hooks recommended, of looking for groups of women who do not have a problem that is common to others under patriarchy and working with them to find solutions, is the only feminist method I have yet discovered that promises a way out of the trap of feminist reinscription of bourgeois norms.

I think the question of why so many heterosexual women find erotic relations profoundly unsatisfying would generate different and more useful answers in feminist theory if the theorists who are engaged in finding answers always kept in mind the point Kipnis insists on, that some women do practice heterosexuality in ways they find satisfying. It is possible for an anti-psychoanalytic theorist like me to find common ground with a staunch supporter of the psychoanalytic like Kipnis because our theories stem from a foundational belief in and respect for what I call "subjectivity" and what she refers to as "psychic reality."

The ordinary mode of understanding subjectivity through psychoanalytic theory entails looking at a given subject's conscious psychic reality as constructed in response to both unalterable features of the material world and currently powerful cultural and social ideologies. The latter are imagined to be internalized by the subject in fairly predictable ways. Thus a woman under patriarchy would be assumed to feel inferior to males and to crave their approval. Because most of the construction of subjectivity deemed important by psychoanalysis is unconscious, the subject's own concept of her psychic reality is hardly more than a symptom of what is understood to actually be going on in her unconscious. Healing takes place through the therapist's assisting the subject to stop emphasizing the discrepancy between her desires and the world's demands and instead to examine why she wants what others apparently do not. While such a shift does not necessarily mean that psychoanalysis pathologizes difference or promotes conformity, the ways that psychological approaches have been appropriated in America, and everywhere, by official agencies of social control suggests that this approach is quite amenable to serving the interests of those who wish to suppress difference. It would seem that therapy can escape a normative function only through a vision that, like Kipnis's, accords the subject's conscious psychic reality greater importance than the dominant cultural construction of reality. Sex radicals do not seek to know why the subject deviates, because this is an unanswerable question, but rather into what communal patterns of deviation from the norm the subject's reality fits.

Since all academics these days are supposed to see objectivity as belonging to antiquated cultural myth, one would think that feminist academics would easily recognize that others think and feel differently and thus construct different truths and realities. Moreover, one would think that we would all be able to recognize that these partial and subjective truths and realities exist in relation to each other, not to transcendent Truth and Reality. But, as Wiegman notes about feminism in the 1990s:

> while skepticism toward transcendental methodologies has exposed the myth of universal man and articulated ways in which the production of knowledge is linked to women's oppression, feminist theory has nonetheless remained tied to a variety of modernist methodologies. Chief among these has been an assumption of the universal status of "woman." (181)

We continue collectively to construct a world simpler and more schematic in terms of gender than the intersecting and overlapping ones we all inhabit together. It is only through examining the relations among our separate visions and experiences of gender, love, and sexuality from all possible perspectives that we can hope to create a more useful picture of what it can mean to be a woman or a man at the millennium's turn.

Understanding contemporary gender relations entails looking at current sexual practices, not for a few nose-holding moments on some feminist tour, but by venturing into unfamiliar realms and making a good-faith effort to understand them on their own inhabitants' terms. In arguing for more recognition of those sexual practices of contemporary heterosexuals that break down stereotypes of masculine aggression and feminine receptivity, Catherine Waldby says, "Theoretical feminism is, I suspect, rather inhibited about employing an explicitly erotic or pornographic imagination because it is still for the most part caught up in the academic aesthetics and politics of reason and sobriety, and in a liberal distaste for the violence of desire." I can agree so far, but differ with her view that another large part of the problem is the imagistic impoverishment of "the domain of public culture." She observes that "while at the moment, images of phallic woman have quite a presence in this domain, the correlative masculine desire [sexual receptivity] is only implied, never represented" (275, 274). Of what public domain does she speak? Surely not the one in which Bob Flanagan performed until his death and Gerry Witbeck now displays himself as pierced "human sculpture," nor the domain in which the intensely dramatized masochism of Nine Inch Nails filled stadiums, nor the one in which Poppy Z. Brite's lush romances of Goth male submission and "complete deconstruction of gender and gender roles" (Brite 79) have delighted thousands of avid fans, nor the fetish nights at rock clubs across America where male submissives writhe happily to the sound of songs written about their feelings, as well as those of the women who use them.

In sum, Americans already live in different experiential worlds governed by vastly different value systems, even when inside the same general socio-economic group. The problem is not that a world of nonbinary differences detached from patriarchal constructions of gender cannot come into being. Rather, the academic world seems to be having difficulty recognizing this other world's existence because its inhabitants do not fit comfortably into the narratives and discourses of American therapy culture or its counterparts in feminist theory. For some who formerly styled themselves as radicals the big chill has fallen. The ecologist Richard Manning presumably addresses them when he writes, "Freedom is a holy word of our culture and as such has lost its meaning. We no longer mean we want freedom; we want security, and they are very different goals" (281).

Yet, as Manning recognizes, some of us still know the difference. Consequently, we speak within different language systems. Those who see the world of suburban housing developments, malls, and freeways as a plain of freedom may welcome the ways therapy culture seeks to help the young tame their passions enough to fit comfortably into it. But those of us willing to forego security in order to experience what we consider freedom may feel our hearts wrenched with pity for the young people pressured to attain conformity. Thus, as Donna Gaines observes, it is difficult but necessary for us to try "to explain to 'helping professionals,'" including sometimes our own colleagues, why conventional American psychotherapy, with its emphasis on ending "gender identity confusion" and generating personalized programs for economic success, "ends up being so useless to young people." We must keep in mind that, as she observes, "Shrinks have a heavy social-control agenda that is transparent to young people, but which has an air of irreproachable legitimacy to adults" (233). And this is as much the case when the "shrinks" are feminist psychoanalytic theorists discussing something they call *the* male imaginary as when they are high school guidance counselors explaining that there is a difference between girls' and boys' sexuality.

As the world of sexual and gender politics that we thought we knew recedes, it becomes more and more important to listen attentively to those who already find their identities outside mainstream constructions of gender. hooks forecast:

> A shift that will undoubtedly emerge as the struggle to end sexual oppression progresses will be decreased obsession with sexuality. This does not necessarily mean that there will be decreased sexual activity. It means that sexuality will no longer have the importance attributed to it in a society [that uses] sexuality for the express purposes of maintaining gender inequality, male domination, consumerism, and the sexual frustration and unhappiness that deflects attention away from the need to make sexual revolution. (*Feminist Theory* 156)

I would add that, in the subcultures associated with the young, both sexuality and love are now coming to have different meanings than they do in older discourses that assign them value according to their impact on the attainment of individualistic material success. Perhaps we can become "obsessed" with sex and love in different ways when we see them as forces that can work to transform the power dynamics of our world. This book is a call for new approaches for a new age.

Feminism is neither dead nor irrelevant to the concerns of the young. The growing presence of its third wave should delight those of us who became feminists during the second wave. Obviously, it is important for us to retain a sense of history. Second-wave feminists are right to keep alive the memory of a time when being masculine or feminine was the foundation of one's identity, and when failure to perform a gender identity that matched one's perceived biological sex was almost universally seen as a tragedy. It is also important to acknowledge that the experience of passionate erotic love is likely to interfere with the attainment of material success, and that there was a time when few women could live with a reasonable amount of comfort outside the protection society offered in return for complete capitulation to bourgeois standards.

However, it is equally important to historicize these moments in culture, to recognize that it is no longer true that we are compelled to live as if under the surveillance of the Stepfather. In formulating their "schizoanalysis," Deleuze and Guattari suggest that the "revolutionary path" now available goes deeply into what capitalism both makes possible and also most fears as the absolute limit, where it would dissolve: the deterritorialization of desire (*Anti-Oedipus* 239–240). We must follow that path, that line of flight into "the wide open spaces glimpsed for a moment" before the institutionalization and popularization of allied bourgeois psychoanalytic and feminist theories reterritorialized both sexuality and love in the deathly stasis of the familial box (270). Really we have only to stop, for a moment, listening to the discourses of reason, and attend as unreason sings its siren song.

NOTES

INTRODUCTION

1. A good example of the fissures that have appeared in feminist interpretation in recent years, as a result of changes in women's perspectives, is provided by Elayne Rapping's contribution to a symposium on Woody Allen in *Cineaste*. Rapping discusses the rage she and other feminists she knew felt watching his films during the early part of feminism's second wave. "Our rage was rooted in a real sense of vulnerability and powerlessness" (38). Over time, Allen began to "seem less important, less infuriating, less a figure to be reckoned with or taken seriously," until finally his type of misogyny, marked as "more and more passé, less and less hegemonic and powerful," not only began to interest Rapping as a subject of dispassionate criticism but became enjoyable to her as a sign of what she, and her daughter, "would never have to put up with again, thanks to changes wrought by feminism" (38). Rapping carefully and defensively concedes that many women still do have to put up with contempt and abuse from men and may see no alternative to enduring the sort of "mean-spirited" cruelty Allen's protagonists dish out. Her reading of *Deconstructing Harry* is firmly placed in the perspective of the woman who knows that there are alternatives for women besides humiliating submission or loneliness, but it is marked with the unease of one who fears being misunderstood by other feminists.

2. See Alice Echols, especially 217–218, for a history of these debates within feminism. Also see Katie King's *Theory in Its Feminist Travels* for an extensive rebuttal to Echols.

3. See Nan Bauer Maglin and Donna Perry's *"Bad Girls"/"Good Girls": Women, Sex, and Power in the Nineties* for an excellent range of essays covering the tensions over sexuality in

feminism's third wave. The essays all respond to critiques of feminism promulgated by influential self-described feminist writers, including Camille Paglia, Katie Roiphe, and Naomi Wolf.

4. This seems a good place to go on record saying that, despite the revisionist historicizing of the "Castro Clone" period as misogynist, I never experienced any of that. I was made welcome in all the gay bars and discos and treated with unpatronizing protectiveness on the streets. My goddaughter, who is African American, recently told me that when she was a child, in the same era, the Castro was the only part of San Francisco where she didn't have to fear being treated in a racist manner. This seems to me more anecdotal evidence that experiences with men are far from being as universal as theorists of patriarchy would sometimes have us believe, since here we are not talking about the few good men who constitute an exception to the rule, but a whole male (sub)culture.

5. See Lynda Hart's discussion in *Fatal Women* of Chauncey's essay, which places it within a history of representations of lesbianism. Interestingly, as I will discuss in chapter 2, Hart herself seems to find it difficult to imagine that any woman can desire men in the way that a subject desires an erotic object, and consequently she repeatedly implicitly defines female heterosexuality as submission to males or the desire to be desired by them.

6. I wonder if the biggest difference between Gallop's and my experiences as academics is that she is far more successful and thus considered more authoritative than I am. I was astonished to read in Gallop's *Feminist Accused of Sexual Harassment* that a fight in a meeting in the mid-1990s shocked her because "I had imagined that, as feminists, we were 'on the same side'" (65). Gallop has not always made this claim. In "Criticizing Feminist Criticism," published seven years earlier in *Conflicts in Feminism,* she and her coauthors claim that "it's a myth that there was a moment feminists didn't attack feminists" (365). Her observation in *Feminist Accused* that "*most* feminists do not see [pornography] as essentially more sexist than other parts of the culture, such as great literature, advertising, or the bridal industry" (73; emphasis mine), similarly made me wonder, where has she been all these years? But then I realized the answer was that she has been a star whose students consider her to have "power over them" (21)—and rightly so. She has been transformed through the transference processes she so powerfully describes in her writing into "the subject-presumed-to-know," not just by students but by colleagues. In contrast, I remember fondly a student in one of my theory classes who, for a month, addressed his e-mail messages to me teasingly as "Dear One-Presumed-To-Know." Someone in my position is likely to hear about it very directly and insultingly when others disagree with her. Moreover, as Gallop's own autobiographical account of her student days reveals, her introduction to feminism was very different from my own, and she "credits" feminism and feminists with awakening her ability to experience sexual desire and pleasure (3–6).

My differences from Frueh are less extreme, mainly centering in our different valuations of sexuality and love. While I strongly agree with Frueh about the transformative and pedagogical value of erotic love, I think I am closer to some Queer theorists, like Michael Warner, in seeing casual, impersonal, and even anonymous sex as equally important.

7. Diana Fuss points out that "in the history of psychoanalysis, female homosexuality is theorized almost exclusively in terms of the 'pre': the preoedipal, the presymbolic, the prelaw, the premature, even the presexual" (43). One might easily make the same argument about female sexual aggression and dominance in relation to the anthropologically interpreted mythology from which psychoanalytic theory draws not only metaphors but so much of its authority. If lesbianism "occupies the space and time of an origin" (Fuss 43), so does a matriarchy posited as female dominance of men. Thus the sexually aggressive woman, when not denied any actual existence in the world or relegated to fantasy as the phallic mother, is coded as an atavistic freak, primitive, precivilized. For a discussion of Saartjie Baartmann, the real "Hottentot Venus," and her place in feminist theory, see Robyn Wiegman's *American Anatomies,* 56–59.

8. Looking back at texts like Valerie Solanis's *SCUM Manifesto* now, I am a bit stunned that

anti-sexual manifestos had such appeal to me. But when I also reread my journals from these years, it becomes clear that what attracted me was their anger and violence, their affirmation that my fight-rather-than-flight reflex when directly threatened was a good thing.

9. In "'Putting Your Body on the Line': The Question of Violence, Victims, and the Legacies of Second-Wave Feminism," Pamela Haag gives a useful account of how early feminists' valorization of women's violence on behalf of women's rights has been effectively erased from the record of second-wave feminism, and traces the rise to ascendance in feminist ideology of a concept of sisterhood based on the assumption that all women want bourgeois comfort and insulation from danger.

10. I now understand that some of the interest these feminists were beginning to show in local sex industries probably had to do with changes external to feminism, such as the reduced enforcement of San Francisco's vice laws, which resulted in greater visibility of the extensive sexual services provided for local men and in support of the tourist industry. Feminists outside the sex industries were probably also responding to assertions about free choice by sex workers, such as the women organized in C.O.Y.O.T.E., who wanted legalization of pornography and prostitution. Living for three years in the Tenderloin in my girlhood had disabused me of any romantic *Never on Sunday* idea that the average prostitute was in control of her own situation. I had also seen how operating outside the law left prostitutes vulnerable to all sorts of extortion from men who could offer them protection or immunity from the law.

1. NONSENSE TERMINABLE AND INTERMINABLE

1. In *Intimate Matters: A History of Sexuality in America,* John D'Emilio and Estelle B. Freedman discuss the American marital "'sex-as-work' ethic" as becoming bothersomely prominent in the period after World War II (267), but this chapter will demonstrate the earlier origins of this approach to marital sexuality.

2. See Jean Baudrillard's "The Precession of Simulacra" in his *Simulacra and Simulation* for a persuasive argument that the globalization of capitalism inaugurated "the era of simulation," characterized by profound alienation from Nature and a consequent nostalgia for a "natural life" that never was, resulting in Americans increasingly inhabiting isolated spaces (the suburbs, the mall, the theme park) structured to simulate "natural" environments (2).

3. To recall how persuasive conflation of the psychoanalytic (in a reductive, stylized form) and attention to the detail and structure of art works were in the late 1950s and early 1960s, see Susan Sontag's 1964 essay "Against Interpretation" in her book by the same name, in which she writes that contemporary reactions to art are governed by the "elaborate systems of hermeneutics" developed by "Marx and Freud" (7), and gives various depressing examples.

4. In *Civilization and Its Discontents,* Freud worries that in discussing the unhappiness civilization causes, what he is "describing is common knowledge," that he is wasting time "in order to expound things which are, in fact, self-evident" (71). For Freud "the two processes of individual and of cultural development *must* stand in hostile opposition to each other and mutually dispute the ground" (99; emphasis mine).

5. Despite its optimistic tone, D'Emilio and Freedman's *Intimate Matters* provides an extensive history of resistant sexual subcultures in America and their repeated defeats by a dominant culture that continues to treat permanent monogamous marriage as necessary to national health.

6. One of the few areas in which I am in complete agreement with Lacan is in his scathing condemnation of "the concept of psychoanalysis in the United States [because it] has inclined towards the adaptation of the individual to the social environment" so that "its practice in the American sphere has been . . . summarily reduced to a means of obtaining 'success' and to a mode of demanding 'happiness'" (*Écrits* 38, 127). As Lacan shows, because American therapy at almost all levels has concentrated on shoring up "'the American way of life'" (*Écrits* 307), it

cannot address goals or desires other than the achievement of material success and domestic harmony.

7. D'Emilio and Freedman both exemplify this sort of thinking and show how pervasive it has been in the American marital/sexual advice genre. While throughout their book they carefully analyze the factors contributing to differences in men's and women's experiences of sexual intercourse, such as women's fear of pregnancy before the development of reliable birth control, they also frequently present the binary gendering of sexual differences as if it were biologically founded.

8. See Karmen MacKendrick's _Counterpleasures_ for a useful discussion of similarities between Foucault's writings on resistance and the Situationist International position on sexuality articulated in Raoul Veneigem's 1979 "manifesto" _The Book of Pleasure._ As she shows, in both philosophic systems pleasure is valued for being "not inherently productive (however readily it may be reappropriated by production, or by consumption—that is, by modes of exchange), [so that consequently] it has the power, in its polymorphous multiplications, to disrupt a society based on production and consumption, the creation and commodification of the artifact and the construction of the productive and consuming subject" (3). On the other side of the debate on pleasure: "In its construction of the erotic as the handmaiden of the procreative, contemporary Christianity lines up startlingly well with both Freudian biologism and capitalist culture—and even . . . with the traditional feminist demand for equal time in gratification" (66).

9. See bell hooks's _Feminist Theory: From Margin to Center_ for detailed analysis of the sexism and racism inherent in such definitions of feminism "by bourgeois women to support their class interests," which leave "the masses of women as poor as ever, or poorer" (8). hooks's discussion of Caroline Bird's _The Two-Paycheck Marriage_ and Leah Frith's _Dreamers and Dealers_ is particularly good in this respect (58–60).

10. Elizabeth Grosz astutely notes that "what lust has in common with the appeal of illicit drugs [is that] their intensity melts a certain subjective cohesion, the 'high' more or less obliterates key boundaries between the body and its others" ("Animal Sex," 292).

11. Although a believer in the need to cure "sexual addiction" through therapy, David Mura provides a searching and interesting account of this particular postmodern condition. He notes that questioning "the metaphor of addiction when applied to sexual experience" makes sense because "sexuality is a part of our biological nature in a way that drinking alcohol or shooting heroin is not" (218). For this reason, "recovery [from a compulsion to have sex] entails a more radical altering of your essential self" (219). Nonetheless, he explains that giving up the sexual adventuring that he felt defined him for most of his life was fully compensated for by the solid comfort of his life with his physician wife and three children in a "new house . . . built . . . with impeccable craftsmanship" (133). The honest self-analysis in his story makes plain what more naturalizing and moralistic accounts gloss over: that such changes in sexual behavior are best achieved by people who not only want bourgeois comforts but are financially able to attain them.

12. Although the book examines art products from a range of Western nations, Kern's reception of these works seems to me in some ways representative of American attitudes and it is on that reception that I focus here.

2. HORIZON VISIONS AND UNCHAINED MELODIES

1. See Katie King for an overview of Dickinson's "ideological centrality" within feminist criticism and theory (102).

2. See also Sandra Gilbert's discussion of "the sorceress and the hysteric, the witch and the madwoman" in Dickinson's poetry and in feminist theory in her "Introduction" to _The Newly Born Woman_ (xi-xii).

3. In November 1992, Ballot Measure 9 was defeated by a 54-to-46-percent vote, but by March 1994, anti–gay rights measures had been passed in twenty Oregon cities and counties. The struggle has continued in almost every subsequent election.

4. For a discussion of some of the costs to feminism of the erasure of male feminism see Robert Vorlichy, "(In)Visible Alliances: Conflicting 'Chronicles' of Feminism."

5. For a feminist defense of *Basic Instinct* (on other grounds than I will argue here) see "Icepick Envy," a *Village Voice* two-column section consisting of C. Carr, "Reclaiming Our Basic Rights," and Amy Taubin, "The Boys Who Cried Misogyny."

6. See Amelia Jones, "'She Was Bad News': Male Paranoia and the Contemporary New Woman" (301–303), for a discussion of connections between voiceover and male authority in both noir films and the recent films dealing with male paranoia that Jones terms "new women's films."

7. See J. Hoberman's argument that '80s films are characterized by an attitude of "nuclear family *über alles*" (246), as is exemplified by films like *Fatal Attraction* (directed by Adrian Lyne, 1987) and *Cape Fear* (directed by Martin Scorcese, 1991). But also note that such films' staging of the triumph of domestic affection is based both on an anachronistic presentation of sex styles (both films posit traditional suburban domestic arrangements and singles-bar cruising as the only two arenas in which heterosex is available to adults) and on the husband's choice of comfort over passion.

8. See my essay "'This thing I like my sister may not do': Shakespearean Erotics and a Clash of Wills in *Middlemarch*" for a detailed discussion of nineteenth-century realism and its intrinsic heterophobia.

9. For a discussion of the development of the killer lesbian stereotype in fifties films, see Vito Russo (99–105). One's sense of the retrospective aspects of *Basic Instinct* may be heightened by noting that among the films Russo discusses is the 1950 *Young Man With a Horn,* in which Michael Douglas's father, Kirk, stars opposite Lauren Bacall, who plays a "murderous" lesbian.

10. Linda Grant calls Catherine "polymorphously perverse" rather than lesbian, and reads her sadistic play with men as evidence of a yearning for "real power" such as is reserved in her times for conservative politicians and "Wall Street" (222–223). However, she seems far more geographically placed to me than this. Catherine's interactions with San Franciscans other than the police reveal a community in which the choice to have sex with both males and females is deemed neither perverse nor intrinsically interesting. In fact, it seems ordinary.

11. Carby specifies that this is a feature of African American fiction rather than of fiction by whites about African Americans, a move that raises questions about authorial identity and intention similar to those that this chapter attempts to address in relation to gender.

12. The white, bourgeois tendency of academic feminist analysis is nowhere clearer than in the assumption that all women identify most strongly with those culturally marked as belonging to the group "women." Identification across binary gender lines is treated, as in psychoanalytic theory and practice, as a pathology (gender identity confusion) rather than as something that might be determined by politics of race and/or class. Compare the voice of the child-narrator Esperanza in Sandra Cisneros's *The House on Mango Street:* "All brown all around, we are safe. But watch us drive into a neighborhood of another color and our knees go shakity-shake . . . Yeah. That is how it goes and goes" (28). See also bell hooks's "Whiteness in the Black Imagination," in *Killing Rage:* "Oh, that feeling of safety, of arrival when we finally reached the edges of [the grandparents'] yard, when we could see the soot black face of our grandfather, Daddy Gus, sitting in his chair on the porch, smell his cigar, and rest on his lap" (46).

13. In analyzing Slavoj Žižek's belief that representation of the sexual act is radically incompatible with "the diegetic reality of film," Mandy Merck observes that his concept of "the unattainability of the sexual object, insofar as it is identified with the impossible object of desire,"

results in a view that "real sex" in film is not only "unaesthetic" but "downright immoral" (225–226). As Merck goes on to explain, this logic is inherently anti-sexual, or at least predicated on the view that the explicit representation of sexual feeling is antithetical to art.

3. GLASS-SLIPPER BOYS, RUBY-SLIPPER GIRLS

1. My alienation, I recognize, is also a product of my adherence to a set of values inherited from my bohemian parents and mainstreamed briefly in the 1970s that became outdated for many middle-class Americans in the 1980s. As Linda Grant observes: "In the eighties, families found that the sensuousness of sex could be replaced by the hedonism of possessions" (176).

2. I kept notes from discussions with sixty-seven young men and thirty-eight young women. (Many other discussions seemed to me not significant enough to warrant recording, since they simply reiterated what many others had told me.) The majority of the people with whom I spoke were between the ages of seventeen and twenty-four. Of the men, six are African American; of the women, eight. I was able to speak with only one young man who identified himself as Latino, and with two Latinas. Six of my informants are Asian American, one man and five women. One informant described himself simply as "mixed race." Fourteen of the young people I interviewed identified as homosexual and six as lesbian. Four women and two men said they were "somewhat bisexual," but primarily heterosexual. Four women and two men described themselves as virgins, although of these, two women and both men had experienced some form of voluntary sexual activity with a partner (oral sex, anal sex, mutual masturbation, etc.). Fourteen (including one male "virgin") said they were at least occasional practitioners of sadomasochism, with two (one man and one woman) describing this as their "lifestyle" or "real sexuality." Two of the women in this group described themselves as primarily dominant "switches." All the men in this group said they preferred the submissive position. Since twelve discussions were conducted via e-mail, I cannot be as sure about the ages, genders, or racial identities of these informants as if I had seen them, thus I rely on their self-descriptions. And as in all surveys, sexual practices of the participants must be taken on faith.

3. There was no difference at all here between those who described themselves as conservative and those who found the labels "liberal" or "radical" a better fit. Serious dating seemed to include, by definition, some sort of sexual activity to climax, with oral sex being the preferred mode for religious youth. The conservative young people generally practiced a sort of serial monogamy in which they would pair-bond for a period of time with a person they called a "fiancé/fiancée," but with whom no actual wedding plans had been made, and then move on to another. Two or three such "fiancé[e]s" seemed an average number for a conservative male or female to have had by age twenty-one.

4. One reason for this generational difference may be that, while women over thirty usually claim they do not consider a man's physical appearance important and deem such considerations immature or shallow, all the young women with whom I spoke said that the first thing they looked for in a male partner was physical appeal. (Young lesbians seemed similarly unashamed to emphasize that they wanted a woman who fit their definition of beauty.) Young women's standards for males can be very exacting, with most of my informants mentioning as indispensable to their pleasure such things as a muscular belly, an attractive hairdo, and fashionable clothing. A large number said they had a "type," which they then proceeded to describe in primarily physical terms.

5. Throughout *The Morning After* Roiphe refers to "rape crisis feminism," which is her name for a hyperconsciousness of the possibility of being sexually victimized by men.

6. Many of the young women with whom I talked brought away from their participation in the Riot Grrl movement, through reading or writing 'zines and playing in or listening to Grrl bands, a sense of freedom to discover and express their own sexual and gender identification(s).

"Because the feminism of Riot Grrrl is self-determined and grassroots, its greatest power is that it gives girls room to decide for themselves who they are" (Rosenberg and Garofalo 811).

7. In Rosenberg and Garofalo's interview with a group of self-identified riot grrls in New York, a number express frustration with or distrust of males and emphasize the importance of the movement to women ("Ok, Riot Grrrl—it's feminism, it's music, it's making sure we're not alone, it's communicating"), but the inclusion of like-minded males is also frequently discussed, as when one informant says of a riot grrl event, "I've seen a hundred girls and boys sitting in a circle in tears and experiencing total healing" (816).

8. Although "deeply reluctant" to praise horror films, Clover concedes that such films do, "in [a] perverse way and for better and worse, constitute a visible adjustment in the terms of gender representation" (64). It is important to keep in mind that her analysis of these films is structured by her assumption, based on the research available, that young males make up most of the audience for horror films (6–7), which may have been true in 1992, but no longer seems to be the case.

4. *CLOSER* TO GENDER DISSOLUTION

1. Of course, those who continue to follow Butler's work know that she positioned herself further from such optimism and closer to Lacan with her next two books, *Bodies That Matter* and *The Psychic Life of Power.*

2. While it would be naive to credit Trent Reznor with complete artistic control over either his music or his music videos, I think it is fair to take seriously his frequent announcements, such as the one on the jacket of the CD *Pretty Hate Machine,* that "Nine Inch Nails is Trent Reznor." For convenience's sake I will adhere to the auteur-theory practice common in music video criticism of discussing all music products credited to specific groups or singers as if they had sole authorship. I have also chosen to focus my discussion of Nine Inch Nails on the period of Trent Reznor's greatest fame and cultural influence, 1989–1997. I forgo discussion of his 1999 "comeback" CD *The Fragile* because I believe it is too early to analyze whatever impact it may have on youth cultures. Also, while they have much in common with his earlier work, the songs on this CD are less radically de-gendered in the ways I discuss here than the earlier work. It is, perhaps, worth noting that in the second week of October 1999 this CD, which also lacks the direct references to S/M so prevalent in Reznor's other music, set a new Billboard record for the biggest-ever fall in the charts, from number one to number sixteen.

3. Simon Frith addresses this issue extensively in both the collection *Sound Effects* and "Toward an Aesthetic of Popular Music."

4. For a history of textual representation of male masochism as the essence of romantic love, see my *Male Masochism: Modern Revisions of the Story of Love.*

5. For analysis of the complexity of Heavy-Metal's use of "androgynous spectacle" to resist "patriarchal control" and the liberatory potential of this music style for women and gay men, see Walser 170–176.

6. Walter Hughes makes a similar point about disco's cyborgian and liberatory potential in "In the Empire of the Beat," 151–152.

7. While academics generally insist that within S/M culture submission is gendered feminine and dominance masculine, empirical support for these claims is slight. Within contemporary hard-core S/M practice the most frequently recognized genders are "top" (dominant), "bottom" (submissive), and "switch" (willing to play either role). These positions are independent of biological sex and are not usually seen as indicative of an identification with traditional binary genders. (E.g., male-to-female transvestite tops are common.) See my *Male Masochism* for further discussion of the gap between academic representations of gender in S/M and the self-representations generated within S/M cultures. As Laura Kipnis points out, most members of

mainstream culture fail to recognize that S/M "is a distinct subculture, with its own rules and etiquette, its own customs, values, and language," but instead impose upon it anxieties about sexism and exploitation that are irrelevant to its central fantasies (61). See also Karmen Mac-Kendrick's *Counterpleasures* for an overview of work on S/M as one of "the practices of the postmodern, in which the identity of the subjects becomes a performance, sometimes fluid, sometimes an open question" that radically unfixes gender (100).

8. For a useful discussion of the type of "mass media misunderstanding" marketing strategy *Time* appears to be following here, see Sarah Thornton's "Moral Panic, The Media and British Rave Culture."

9. The question that elicited these responses was "What do you see in the video and/or hear in the song that refers to sexual behaviors, feelings, or activities?" Since the songs I asked about are explicitly about sexual passion, there was no reason for my interviewees to assume I was looking for that notorious embarrassing "hidden meaning" English professors are so fond of. As a note of interest, the older (over-thirty) fans with whom I spoke almost never recognized bondage equipment or references to S/M in the songs.

10. And before dismissing the song as, thus, sexist or disrespectful of both animals and the potential human sex partner, one might want to consider Baudrillard's theory that "animals were . . . demoted to the status of inhumanity as reason and humanism progressed," and as psychology established our current "empire of meaning" in which the silent animals stand as emblems of continued resistance (133, 137). If we look from that perspective, the desire to treat the other as if she were an animal may mean to adore her as the very figure of resistance.

11. I feel compelled to add, for those critics of popular youth culture who are always on the alert for signs of misogyny in the young, that the members of W.A.S.P. are middle-aged and that while Nine Inch Nails fans, apparently primarily youthful, currently maintain hundreds of Web sites on the Internet, W.A.S.P. has one solitary Web page, maintained by one fan. By any standard used to measure success in popular culture W.A.S.P. scarcely merits comparison to Nine Inch Nails.

5. ALTERNATIVE WOMEN

1. One might compare this view to Laura Kipnis's much more original observation that "Not all women dislike pornography; some even like it a lot. So obviously there's a spectrum of female identities" (199). To Kipnis a woman whose fantasies do not match those of the majority of women does not necessarily suffer from male colonization of her imagination or sexuality.

2. A few exceptions include Michael Jackson's "Dirty Diana," Prince's "Little Red Corvette," and Rod Stewart's "Maggie May."

3. Joplin's appreciation of African American women's song stylings also no doubt contributed to her assessment of Tina Turner as the most gifted performer of her time.

4. In a later issue, Eve Sedgwick's angry letter to the editor brings up another reason to be depressed by the article: its "exploitive cynicism" about working-class African Americans, whom Ehrenreich recommends as potential partners but then notes are in short supply. The whole experience made me realize that laziness is not the only reason I fail to organize my belongings more frequently.

5. See Segal (233–239) for an interesting personal exploration of the former phenomenon, including some useful placement of it within articulated feminist theories of subjectivity. See Teresa de Lauretis's *The Practice of Love* for discussion of the latter identification (156–167).

6. As many feminist students have told me, the psychoanalytic imperative makes them feel the same way that economically compulsory heterosexuality does: compelled to subordinate themselves and thus create locally the phallic power that is posited as "always already there." I

want to specifically thank Kelly Cutter-Green for pointing out the connection when she read this chapter.

7. Another problem with the Freudian economic model of sexuality is that, as Elizabeth Grosz explains, the "temporality" of sexual experience is not "that of investment (a relation between means and ends)"; rather it is always "unhinging any determination of means and ends and goals" ("Animal Sex" 285–286).

8. See Rosi Braidotti for a much more complete discussion of what "the various feminist figurations of a new female subjectivity gain by intersecting with Deleuze's project of transforming the very image we have of thinking, and with his new vision of subjectivity as an intensive, multiple, and discontinuous process of interrelations" (162).

9. I am avoiding comment here on the exceptionally popular Alanis Morrissette because her popularity was so exceptional, and also because this popularity relegated her performances to arenas in which crowd response is more controlled by outside forces. I am also avoiding detailed commentary on less well known female-fronted favorites of my own, like the notoriously hard-edged and confrontational L7, the influential but never really famous Sonic Youth, the delightful rising all-woman band The Donnas, and more obscure bands like Ovarian Trolley and Babe the Blue Ox, because audiences for these performers tended to be less heterogeneous and more likely to be composed almost exclusively of people who define themselves as counterculture and acted accordingly.

10. That the pleasures offered by these videos are not just visual and aural seems important as well. The rhythms, felt in the bodies of audience members, allow for an experience of pleasure that exceeds the limits of discourses and semiotics. Thus, to say that the videos make possible reimagination of the urban space does not exhaust their revolutionary potential. They also make it possible to *feel* differently about being a woman in the city.

CONCLUSION

1. James Mellard gives an interesting account of similarities in the visions of the future expressed by "a cadre of psychoanalytic critics of culture called the new Lacanians[, which includes] Joan Copjec, Slavoj Žižek, Elizabeth Cowie, and Juliet Flower MacCannell" (395). Because "[p]sychoanalysis identifies desire as oedipal, pacific, passive, and tolerant, drive as narcissistic, violent, aggressive, and preemptive," these critics (including Mellard) see the future as threatened by "the forced choice left by the shift within social life from a traditional oedipal subject founded on an ethics of desire to a posttraditional subject founded on an ethics of *jouissance,* the one on the side of Eros and social life, the other on that of Thanatos and the death drive" (398, 396). Mellard argues that within the Lacanian system the only choices are patriarchy or "worse."

2. For more extensive analysis of the gender politics of this film and of audience response to it, see Isabel Cristina Pinedo's "*The Stepfather* as Feminist Horror Film" (*Recreational Terror* 87–95). Although Pinedo sees the film's central problematic as the battle between patriarchal representatives of the American Dream and their rebellious daughters, it is worth noting that, as she herself points out, the stepdaughter "is bound to upset [the stepfather's] need for a strictly ordered world," not because she is female, but because "as a teenager" she inhabits "a liminal state between childhood and adulthood" (92). As the sequel, in which a teenage boy fights the stepfather, suggests, what is at stake is accession to or refusal of a place within "the cult of domesticity and the idealized white suburban nuclear family" (89), no matter how that place is gendered.

BIBLIOGRAPHY

Acker, Kathy. *Empire of the Senseless.* New York: Grove Weidenfield, 1988.

Adderholdt-Elliott, Miriam. *Perfectionism: What's Bad about Being Too Good.* Minneapolis: Free Spirit, 1987.

Addicted to Love. Directed by Griffin Dunne. Miramax, 1997.

Afghan Whigs. "My Curse." *Gentlemen.* Electra, 1993.

Allan, Blaine. "Musical Cinema, Music Video, Music Television." *Film Quarterly* 43.3 (1990): 2–14.

Altman, Meryl. "Everything They Always Wanted You to Know: The Ideology of Popular Sex Literature." In *Pleasure and Danger: Exploring Female Sexuality,* edited by Carole S. Vance, 115–130. Boston: Routledge, 1984.

Armstrong, Nancy. *Desire and Domestic Fiction: A Political History of the Novel.* New York: Oxford University Press, 1987.

Arnold, Gina. *Route 666: On the Road to Nirvana.* New York: St. Martin's, 1993.

Barker, Clive. "Sympathy for the Devil." Interview by Tim Woodward. In *The Best of Skin Two,* edited by Tim Woodward, 19–30. New York: Masquerade, 1993.

Basic Instinct. Directed by Paul Verhoeven. Guild/Carolco, 1992.

Baudrillard, Jean. *Simulacra and Simulation.* Translated by Sheila Faria Glaser. Ann Arbor: University of Michigan Press, 1994.

Bell, Shannon. "Pictures Don't Lie. Pictures Tell It All." *Journal of the History of Sexuality* 6.2 (1995): 284–321.

Benjamin, Jessica. *The Bonds of Love: Psychoanalysis, Feminism, and the Problem of Domination.* New York: Pantheon, 1988.

Berger, Joshua, and Eric Lengvenis. "NineInchNails." *Plazm* 7 (1994): 48–51.

Bersani, Leo. *Homos.* Cambridge, Mass: Harvard University Press, 1995.

Description of *Bestiary of Love and Response,* by Master Richard de Fournival, translated by Jeanette Beer. *The California Sale Catalog.* Berkeley: University of California Press, 1997: 18.

Bogue, Ronald. *Deleuze and Guattari.* New York: Routledge, 1989.

Bonnie and Clyde. Directed by Arthur Penn. Warner, 1967.

Booty Call. Directed by Jeff Pollack. Columbia, 1997.

Boston Women's Health Book Collective, The. *Our Bodies, Ourselves: A Book by and for Women.* 2nd ed. New York: Simon and Schuster, 1973.

Boyles, Denis. *The Modern Man's Guide to Modern Women.* New York: HarperPerennial, 1993.

Bozza, Anthony. "The Fragile World of Trent Reznor." *Rolling Stone* 823, Oct. 1999: 58–62, 140.

Braidotti, Rosi. "Toward a New Nomadism: Feminist Deleuzian Tracks, or, Metaphysics and Metabolism." In *Gilles Deleuze and the Theater of Philosophy,* edited by Constantin V. Boundas and Dorothea Olkowski, 157–186. New York: Routledge, 1994.

Brite, Poppy Z. *The Crow: The Lazarus Heart.* New York: HarperPrism, 1998.

Broken. Nine Inch Nails. Music video compilation, directed by Peter Christopherson and Trent Reznor. 1992.

Brontë, Emily. *Wuthering Heights.* Edited by William M. Sale Jr. New York: Norton, 1972.

Brooks, Meredith. "Bitch." *Blurring the Edges.* EMD/Capital, 1997.

Brumberg, Joan Jacobs. *The Body Project: An Intimate History of American Girls.* New York: Vintage, 1997.

Burchill, Julie, and Tony Parsons. *The Boy Looked at Johnny: The Obituary of Rock and Roll.* London: Pluto, 1978.

Burns, David. *Feeling Good: The New Mood Therapy.* New York: Signet, 1980.

Butler, Judith. *Bodies That Matter: On the Discursive Limits of "Sex."* New York: Routledge, 1993.

———. *Gender Trouble: Feminism and the Subversion of Identity.* New York: Routledge, 1990.

———. *The Psychic Life of Power: Theories in Subjection.* Stanford: Stanford University Press, 1997.

Butterfly Kiss. Directed by Michael Winterbottom. CFP/Dan Films, 1995.

Cape Fear. Directed by Martin Scorcese. Universal, 1991.

Caputi, Mary. "Identity and Nonidentity in Aesthetic Theory." *differences* 8.3 (1996): 128–147.

Carby, Hazel V. "The Quicksands of Representation." In *Reading Black, Reading Feminist: A Critical Anthology,* edited by Henry Louis Gates Jr., 76–90. New York: Meridian, 1990.

Carr, C. "Reclaiming Our Basic Rights." *The Village Voice,* 28 April 1992: 35–36.

Chapman, Tracy. "For My Lover." *Tracy Chapman.* Electra/Asylum, 1988.

———. "For You." *Tracy Chapman.* Electra/Asylum, 1988.

———. "Talkin' 'bout a Revolution." *Tracy Chapman.* Electra/Asylum, 1988.

Chasing Amy. Directed by Kevin Smith. Miramax, 1997.

Chauncey, George, Jr. "From Sexual Inversion to Homosexuality: Medicine and the Changing Conception of Female Deviance." *Salmagundi* 58–59 (1982–1983): 114–146.

Chemical Brothers, The. *Block Rockin' Beats.* Music video, directed by Dom and Nic. 1998.

Cisneros, Sandra. *The House on Mango Street.* New York: Random, 1989.

Cixous, Hélène. "The Laugh of the Medusa." Translated by Keith Cohen and Paula Cohen. In *Feminisms: An Anthology of Literary Theory and Criticism,* edited by Robyn R. Warhol and Diane Price Herndl, 334–349. New Brunswick, N.J.: Rutgers University Press, 1991. Originally published in 1975.

Cixous, Hélène, and Catherine Clément. *The Newly Born Woman.* Translated by Betsy Wing. Minneapolis: University of Minnesota Press, 1986.

Cline, Cheryl. "Little Songs of Misogyny." In *Rock She Wrote: Women Write about Rock, Pop, and Rap,* edited by Evelyn McDonnell and Ann Powers, 369–375. New York: Delta-Dell, 1995.

Clover, Carol. "Crossing Over." *Film Quarterly* 45.2 (1991–1992): 22.

———. *Men, Women, and Chain Saws: Gender in the Modern Horror Film.* Princeton, N.J.: Princeton University Press, 1992.

Clueless. Directed by Amy Heckerling. Paramount, 1995.

Congreve, William. *The Way of the World. Complete Plays of Congreve.* Edited by Alexander Charles Ewald. New York: Hill and Wang, 1966.

Cooper, Dennis. *Closer.* New York: Grove Weidenfeld, 1989.

Cowan, Connell, and Melvyn Kinder. *Smart Women/Foolish Choices: Finding the Right Men and Avoiding the Wrong Ones.* New York: New American Library, 1985.

Cox, Ida. "Wild Women Don't Get the Blues." *Wild Women Don't Have the Blues.* Rosetta, 1981.

Creed, Barbara. "Dark Desires: Male Masochism in the Horror Film." In *Screening the Male: Exploring Masculinities in Hollywood Cinema,* edited by Steven Cohan and Ina Rae Hark, 118–133. New York: Routledge, 1993.

Crow, The. Directed by Alex Proyas. Miramax, 1994.

Danzig. *It's Coming Down.* Music video, directed by Jonathan Reiss. 1992.

Davis, Angela Y. "I Used to Be Your Sweet Mama: Ideology, Sexuality, and Domesticity in the Blues of Gertrude 'Ma' Rainey and Bessie Smith." In *Sexy Bodies,* edited by Elizabeth Grosz and Elspeth Probyn, 231–265. London and New York: Routledge, 1995.

De Lauretis, Teresa. *The Practice of Love.* Bloomington: Indiana University Press, 1994.

Defoe, Daniel. *Moll Flanders.* Boston: Houghton Mifflin, 1959. Originally published in 1722.

Deleuze, Gilles. "I Have Nothing to Admit." *Semiotext(e)* 11.3 (1977): 110–116.

Deleuze, Gilles, and Félix Guattari. *Anti-Oedipus: Capitalism and Schizophrenia.* Translated by Robert Hurley, Mark Seem, and Helen R. Lane. Minneapolis: University of Minnesota Press, 1983.

———. *A Thousand Plateaus: Capitalism and Schizophrenia.* Translated by Brian Massumi. London: Athlone, 1988.

Dellamora, Richard. *Masculine Desire: The Sexual Politics of Victorian Aestheticism.* Chapel Hill: University of North Carolina Press, 1990.

D'Emilio, John, and Estelle B. Freedman. *Intimate Matters: A History of Sexuality in America.* New York: Harper and Row, 1988.

Des Barres, Pamela. "Rock 'n' Roll Needs Courtney Love." In *Rock She Wrote: Women Write about Rock, Pop, and Rap,* edited by Evelyn McDonnell and Ann Powers, 200–207. New York: Delta-Dell, 1995.

Devil's Advocate, The. Directed by Taylor Hackford. Warner, 1997.

Doane, Mary Ann. "Technology's Body: Cinematic Vision in Modernity." *differences* 5.2 (1993): 1–23.

Dog Day Afternoon. Directed by Sidney Lumet. Artists Entertainment, 1975.

Donnas, The. "Get Outta My Room." *Get Skintight.* Lookout! Records, 1999.

———. "Searchin' the Streets." *Get Skintight.* Lookout! Records, 1999.

Dowd, Maureen. "Feminism Has Deteriorated to Focusing on Male Desires." *Denver Post,* 7 March 1997: 10A.

Dowling, Colette. *The Cinderella Complex: Woman's Hidden Fear of Independence.* New York: Pocket, 1981.

Dunn, Kevin J. "Head Down." *The Village Noize* 6.16 (1994): 26–30.

Durant, Will. "The Breakdown of Marriage." In *The Sex Problem in Modern Society: An Anthology,* edited by John Francis McDermott, 147–169. New York: Modern Library-Bantam, 1931.

Dylan, Bob. "My Back Pages." *Another Side of Bob Dylan.* Columbia, 1964.

Echols, Alice. *Daring to Be Bad: Radical Feminism in America, 1967–1975.* Minneapolis: University of Minnesota Press, 1989.

Edmundson, Mark. *Nightmare on Mainstreet: Angels, Sadomasochism, and the Culture of Gothic.* Cambridge, Mass.: Harvard University Press, 1997.

Ehrenreich, Barbara. "Blue-Collar Lovers and Allies: Can Women Break the Sexual Caste System?" *Ms.* 14.3 (Sept. 1985): 58–59, 117–118.

Eliot, George. *The Mill on the Floss.* New York: Oxford University Press, 1981.

Ellroy, James. *Killer on the Road.* New York: Avon, 1986.

Evans, Liz. *Women, Sex, and Rock 'N' Roll: In Their Words.* Bath, Avon: HarperCollins, 1994.

Fatal Attraction. Directed by Adrian Lyne. Paramount, 1987.

Fein, Ellen, and Sherrie Schneider. *The Rules: Time-Tested Secrets for Capturing the Heart of Mr. Right.* New York: Warner, 1995.

Fetterley, Judith. *The Resisting Reader: A Feminist Approach to American Fiction.* Bloomington: Indiana University Press, 1978.

"Fighting Words." *The New Yorker,* 12 June 1995: 35–36.

Flax, Jane. *Thinking Fragments: Psychoanalysis, Feminism, and Postmodernism in the Contemporary West.* Berkeley: University of California Press, 1990.

Flesh and Blood. Directed by Paul Verhoeven. Orion, 1985.

Foster, Thomas. E-mail to the author. 29 May 1995.

Foucault, Michel. *The History of Sexuality, Volume One: An Introduction.* Translated by Robert Hurley. New York: Vintage-Random, 1980.

———. *Madness and Civilization: A History of Insanity in the Age of Reason.* Translated by Richard Howard. New York: Vintage-Random, 1973.

———. *Power/Knowledge: Selected Interviews and Other Writings, 1972–1977.* Edited by Colin Gordon. Translated by Colin Gordon, Leo Marshall, John Mepham, and Kate Soper. New York: Pantheon, 1980.

Fourth Man, The. Directed by Paul Verhoeven. Cinematheque, 1983.

Freud, Sigmund. *Civilization and Its Discontents.* Translated and edited by James Strachey. New York: Norton, 1961.

Fried Green Tomatoes. Directed by Jon Avret. Universal, 1991.

Frith, Simon. *Sound Effects: Youth, Leisure, and the Politics of Rock 'n' Roll.* New York: Pantheon, 1983.

———. "Toward an Aesthetic of Popular Music." In *Music and Society: The Politics of Composition, Performance, and Reception,* edited by Richard Leppert and Susan McClary, 133–150. Cambridge: Cambridge University Press, 1987.

Frith, Simon, Andrew Goodwin, and Lawrence Grossberg, eds. *Sound and Vision: The Music Video Reader.* New York: Routledge, 1993.

Frueh, Joanna. *Erotic Faculties.* Berkeley: University of California Press, 1996.

Fuentes, Annette. "No Sex Ed: Congress Pushes Abstinence in the Schools." *In These Times,* 28 December 1997: 16–18.

Fuss, Diana. *Essentially Speaking: Feminism, Nature, and Difference.* New York: Routledge, 1989.

Fussell, Paul. *Notes on Class.* New York: Ballantine Books, 1983.

Gaar, Gillian. *She's a Rebel: The History of Women in Rock & Roll.* Seattle: Seal, 1992.

Gaines, Donna. "Border Crossing in the U.S.A." In *Microphone Fiends: Youth Music, Youth Culture,* edited by Andrew Ross and Tricia Rose, 227–234. New York: Routledge, 1994.

Gallop, Jane. *Feminist Accused of Sexual Harassment*. Durham: Duke University Press, 1997.

———. *Thinking through the Body*. New York: Columbia, 1988.

Gallop, Jane, Marianne Hirsch, and Nancy K. Miller. "Criticizing Feminist Criticism." In *Conflicts in Feminism,* edited by Marianne Hirsch and Evelyn Fox Keller, 346–369. New York: Routledge, 1990.

Garbage. "Temptation Waits." *Version 2.0.* Almo Sounds, 1998.

Garber, Marjorie. *Vested Interests: Crossdressing and Cultural Anxiety.* New York: Routledge, 1992.

Geppert, Alexander. "Divine Sex, Happy Marriage, Regenerated Nation: Marie Stopes's Marital Manual *Married Love* and the Making of a Best-Seller, 1918–1955." *Journal of the History of Sexuality* 8.3. (1998): 389–433.

Gilbert, Sandra M. Introduction to *The Newly Born Woman,* by Hélène Cixous and Catherine Clément. Minneapolis: University of Minnesota Press, 1986.

Gilbert, Sandra M., and Susan Gubar. *The Madwoman in the Attic: The Woman Writer and the Nineteenth-Century Literary Imagination.* New Haven: Yale University Press, 1979.

Gitlin, Todd. *The Sixties: Years of Hope, Days of Rage.* New York: Bantam, 1987.

Glengarry Glen Ross. Directed by James Foley. Rank/Zupnik, 1992.

Glyn, Elinor. *The Philosophy of Love.* Auburn, New York: Author's Press, 1923.

Gold, Jonathan. "Love it to Death." *Rolling Stone,* 8 Sept. 1994: 50–54, 88.

Goodwin, Andrew. *Dancing in the Distraction Factory: Music Television and Popular Culture.* Minneapolis: University of Minnesota Press, 1992.

Gordon, Kim. "Boys Are Smelly: The Sonic Youth Tour Diary, '87." In *Rock She Wrote: Women Write about Rock, Pop, and Rap,* edited by Evelyn McDonnell and Ann Powers, 66–73. New York: Delta-Dell, 1995.

Gottlieb, Joanne, and Gayle Wald. "Smells Like Teen Spirit: Riot Grrls, Revolution, and Women in Independent Rock." In *Microphone Fiends: Youth Music, Youth Culture,* edited by Andrew Ross and Tricia Rose, 250–274. New York: Routledge, 1994.

Grant, Linda. *Sexing the Millennium: Women and the Sexual Revolution.* New York: Grove, 1994.

Griffin, Susan. *Woman and Nature: The Roaring inside Her.* New York: Harper, 1978.

Grossberg, Lawrence. "Is Anybody Listening? Does Anybody Care? On the 'State of Rock.'" In *Microphone Fiends: Youth Music, Youth Culture,* edited by Andrew Ross and Tricia Rose, 41–58. New York: Routledge, 1994.

———. "The Media Economy of Rock Culture: Cinema, Post-modernity and Authenticity." In *Sound and Vision: The Music Video Reader,* edited by Simon Frith, Andrew Goodwin, and Lawrence Grossberg, 185–209. New York: Routledge, 1993.

Grosz, Elizabeth. "Animal Sex: Libido as Destruction and Death." In *Sexy Bodies: The Strange Carnalities of Feminism,* edited by Elizabeth Grosz and Elspeth Probyn, 278–299. New York: Routledge, 1995.

———. "The Labors of Love. Analyzing Perverse Desire: An Interrogation of Teresa de Lauretis's *The Practice of Love.*" *differences* 6.2+3 (1994): 274–295.

———. *Space, Time, and Perversion: Essays on the Politics of Bodies.* New York: Routledge, 1995.

Grundmann, Roy. "The Fantasies We Live By: Bad Boys in *Swoon* and *The Living End.*" *Cineaste* 19.4 (1993): 25–29.

Gun Crazy. Directed by Joseph H. Lewis. United Artists, 1950. Rerelease of *Deadly Is the Female* (1949).

Guncrazy. Directed by Tamra Davis. United Artists, 1992.

Haag, Pamela. "'Putting Your Body on the Line': The Question of Violence, Victims, and the Legacies of Second-Wave Feminism." *differences* 8.2 (1996): 23–67.

Halperin, David M. *Saint Foucault: Towards a Gay Hagiography.* New York: Oxford University Press, 1995.

Haraway, Donna. "A Manifesto for Cyborgs: Science, Technology, and Socialist Feminism in the 1980s." In *Feminism/Postmodernism,* edited by Linda J. Nicholson, 190–233. New York: Routledge, 1990.

Harris, Frederick. "The Sexual Relationship in Marriage." In *Getting the Most Out of Life: An Anthology from The Reader's Digest,* 97–100. Pleasantville, N.Y.: Reader's Digest, 1948.

Hart, Lynda. *Fatal Women: Lesbian Sexuality and the Mark of Aggression.* Princeton: Princeton University Press, 1994.

Heath, Chris. "Nine Inch Male." *Details* 13.11 (1995): 138–145, 203.

Hoberman, J. *Vulgar Modernism: Writings on Movies and Other Media.* Philadelphia: Temple University Press, 1991.

Hole. "Violet." *Live through This.* Geffen, 1994.

———. *Hole.* Music video, directed by Seliger-Woodward. 1994.

hooks, bell. *Feminist Theory: From Margin to Center.* Boston: South End Press, 1984.

———. *Killing Rage: Ending Racism.* New York: Holt, 1995.

———. *Outlaw Culture: Resisting Representations.* New York: Routledge, 1994.

Horsley, Katherine, and Lee Horsley. "*Méres Fatales:* Maternal Guilt in the Noir Crime Novel." *Modern Fiction Studies* 45.2 (1999): 369–402.

Hughes, Walter. "In the Empire of the Beat: Discipline and Disco." In *Microphone Fiends: Youth Music, Youth Culture,* edited by Andrew Ross and Tricia Rose, 147–157. New York: Routledge, 1994.

Hunter, Nan D. "Marriage, Law, and Gender: A Feminist Inquiry (1991)." In *Sex Wars: Sexual Dissent and Political Culture,* edited by Lisa Duggan and Nan D. Hunter, 107–122. New York: Routledge, 1995.

Jackson, Michael. "Dirty Diana." *Bad.* Epic, 1987.

Jameson, Fredric. *Postmodernism, or the Cultural Logic of Late Capitalism.* Durham: Duke University Press, 1991.

Jane's Addiction. *Been Caught Stealing.* Music video, directed by Casey Niccoli. 1991.

Jeffords, Susan. "Can Masculinity Be Terminated?" In *Screening the Male: Exploring Masculinities in Hollywood Cinema,* edited by Steven Cohan and Ina Rae Hark, 245–262. New York: Routledge, 1993.

Jerry Maguire. Directed by Cameron Crowe. Columbia-Tristar, 1996.

Johnson, Albert. "Bacchantes at Large." *Film Quarterly* 45.2 (1991–1992): 22–23.

Jones, Amelia. "'She Was Bad News': Male Paranoia and the Contemporary New Woman." *Camera Obscura* 25–26 (1991): 297–320.

Joplin, Janis. "Piece of My Heart." *Cheap Thrills.* Columbia, 1967.

Juno, Andrea, ed. *Angry Women in Rock.* Volume One. New York: Juno, 1996.

Juno, Andrea, and Stacy Wakefield. *Bob Flanagan: Supermasochist.* San Francisco: Re/Search Publications, 1993.

Kafka, Franz. *The Castle.* Translated by Willa and Edwin Muir. New York: Vintage-Random, 1974.

Kalmar, Veronica. "PJ Harvey and the Cycle of Success." *The Rocket,* 17–31 May 1995: 18–19.

Kamen, Paula. *Feminist Fatale: Voices from the "Twentysomething" Generation Explore the Future of the "Women's Movement."* New York: Donald I. Fine, 1991.

Kaplan, E. Ann. "Is the Gaze Male?" In *Powers of Desire: The Politics of Sexuality,* edited by Ann Snitow, Christine Stansell, and Sharon Thompson, 309–327. New York: Monthly Review Press, 1983.

———. *Rocking around the Clock: Music Television, Postmodernism, and Consumer Culture.* New York: Methuen, 1987.

Katie's Passion (Keeje Tipple). Directed by Paul Verhoeven. Rob Houwer Productions, 1975.

Kern, Stephen. *The Culture of Love: Victorians to Moderns*. Cambridge, Mass.: Harvard University Press, 1992.

King, Katie. *Theory in Its Feminist Travels: Conversations in U.S. Women's Movements*. Bloomington: Indiana University Press, 1994.

Kingma, Daphne Rose. *Coming Apart: Why Relationships End and How to Live through the Ending of Yours*. New York: Fawcett Crest, 1987.

Kipnis, Laura. *Bound and Gagged: Pornography and the Politics of Fantasy in America*. New York: Grove, 1996.

Kristeva, Julia. *Tales of Love*. Translated by Leon S. Roudiez. New York: Columbia University Press, 1987.

L7. "Fast and Frightening." *Smell the Magic*. Sub Pop, 1991.

———. "Shitlist." *Natural Born Killers: A Soundtrack*. Nothing/Interscope, 1994.

Lacan, Jacques. *Écrits: A Selection*. Translated by Alan Sheridan. New York: Norton, 1977.

———. *The Four Fundamental Concepts of Psycho-Analysis*. Translated by Alan Sheridan. New York: Norton, 1978.

Law of Desire. Directed by Pedro Almodóvar. Lauren Film, 1987.

LeBoutillier, Megan. *Little Miss Perfect*. Denver: Claudia, 1987.

Lewis, Lisa A. *Gender Politics and MTV: Voicing the Difference*. Philadelphia: Temple University Press, 1990.

Limp Bizkit. "Nookie." *Significant Other*. Flip/Interscope, 1999.

Living End, The. Directed by Gregg Araki. Mainline/Strand/Desperate Pictures, 1992.

Long, H. W. *Sane Sex Life and Sane Sex Living*. New York: Eugenics Publishing, 1919.

Love Jones. Directed by Theodore Witcher. New Line Cinema, 1997.

MacKendrick, Karmen. *Counterpleasures*. Albany, N.Y.: State University of New York Press, 1999.

Madonna. *Open Your Heart*. Music video, directed by Jean-Baptiste Mondino. 1986.

Maglin, Nan Bauer, and Donna Perry, eds. *"Bad Girls"/"Good Girls": Women, Sex, and Power in the Nineties*. New Brunswick, N.J.: Rutgers University Press, 1994.

Malleson, Joan. *Any Wife or Any Husband: Toward a Better Understanding of Sex in Marriage*. New York: Random, 1951.

Manning, Richard. *Grassland: The History, Biology, Politics, and Promise of the American Prairie*. New York: Penguin, 1995.

Marcus, Greil. *Lipstick Traces: A Secret History of the Twentieth Century*. Cambridge, Mass.: Harvard University Press, 1989.

Martin, Judith. *Miss Manners' Guide for the Turn-of-the-Millennium*. New York: Pharos, 1989.

Martin, Ricky. *Livin' La Vida Loca*. Music video, directed by Wayne Isham. 1999.

Massumi, Brian. "Pleasures of Philosophy." Translator's foreword to *A Thousand Plateaus: Capitalism and Schizophrenia*, by Gilles Deleuze and Félix Guattari, ix–xv. Minneapolis: University of Minnesota Press, 1987.

Mayne, Judith. "Paradoxes of Spectatorship." In *Viewing Positions: Ways of Seeing Film,* edited by Linda Williams, 155–183. New Brunswick, N.J.: Rutgers University Press, 1994.

McClary, Susan. *Feminine Endings: Music, Gender, and Sexuality*. Minneapolis: University of Minnesota Press, 1991.

———. "Same As It Ever Was." In *Microphone Fiends: Youth Music, Youth Culture,* edited by Andrew Ross and Tricia Rose, 29–40. New York: Routledge, 1994.

McDonnell, Evelyn, and Ann Powers, eds. *Rock She Wrote: Women Write about Rock, Pop, and Rap*. New York: Delta-Dell, 1995.

McRobbie, Angela. *Feminism and Youth Culture: From "Jackie" to "Just Seventeen."* Boston: Unwin Hyman, 1991.

Mellard, James M. "Lacan and the New Lacanians: Josephine Hart's *Damage,* Lacanian Tragedy, and the Ethics of *Jouissance.*" *PMLA* 113.3 (1998): 395–407.

Merck, Mandy. *Perversions: Deviant Readings.* New York: Routledge, 1993.

Midnight Cowboy. Directed by John Schlesinger. United Artists, 1969.

Miller, Nancy K. "The Text's Heroine: A Feminist Critic and Her Fictions." In *Conflicts in Feminism,* edited by Marianne Hirsch and Evelyn Fox Keller, 112–120. New York: Routledge, 1990.

Modleski, Tania. *The Women Who Knew Too Much: Hitchcock and Feminist Theory.* New York: Methuen, 1988.

Moore, Suzanne. "Getting A Bit of the Other: The Pimps of Postmodernism." In *Looking for Trouble: On Shopping, Gender, and the Cinema.* London: Serpent's Tail, 1991.

Morris, N. and G. Hawkins. *The Honest Politician's Guide to Crime Control.* Chicago: University of Chicago Press, 1970.

Morrison, Toni. *Beloved.* New York: Penguin-Plume, 1987.

Morrissette, Alanis. "You Oughta Know." *Jagged Little Pill.* Maverick/Warner, 1995.

Mulvey, Laura. "Visual Pleasure and Narrative Cinema." *Screen* 16.3 (1975): 6–18.

Mura, David. *Where Body Meets Memory: An Odyssey of Race, Sexuality, and Identity.* New York: Doubleday, 1993.

My Beautiful Laundrette. Directed by Stephen Frears. Working Title Films, 1985.

My Father's Coming. Directed by Monika Treut. Hyane, 1991.

'N Sync. *I Drive Myself Crazy.* Music video, directed by Tim Story. 1999.

Natural Born Killers. Directed by Oliver Stone. Warner, 1994.

Nestle, Joan. "My Mother Liked to Fuck." In *Powers of Desire: The Politics of Sexuality,* edited by Ann Snitow, Christine Stansell, and Sharon Thompson, 468–470. New York: Monthly Review Press, 1983.

Night of the Hunter. Directed by Charles Laughton. Warner, 1955.

Nine Inch Nails. "The Becoming." *The Downward Spiral.* Nothing/TVT/Interscope, 1994.

———. "Big Man with a Gun." *The Downward Spiral.* Nothing/TVT/Interscope, 1994.

———. "Burn." *Natural Born Killers: A Soundtrack.* Nothing/Interscope, 1994.

———. *Burn.* Music video, directed by Hank Corwin and Trent Reznor. 1994.

———. "Closer." *The Downward Spiral.* Nothing/TVT/Interscope, 1994.

———. *Closer.* Music video, directed by Mark Romanek. 1994.

———. *The Downward Spiral.* Nothing/TVT/Interscope, 1994.

———. *The Fragile.* Nothing/Interscope, 1999.

———. "Happiness in Slavery." *Broken.* TVT/Interscope, 1992.

———. *Happiness in Slavery.* Music video, directed by Jonathan Reiss. 1992.

———. "Head Like a Hole." *Pretty Hate Machine.* TVT, 1989.

———. *Head Like a Hole.* Music video, directed by Eric Zimmerman. 1989.

———. "Hurt." *The Downward Spiral.* Nothing/TVT/Interscope, 1994.

———. *Hurt.* Music video, directed by Simon Maxwell. 1994.

———. "Maybe Just Once." *Purest Feeling.* Kaleidoscopic Music, 1994.

———. "The Perfect Drug." *Lost Highway* (soundtrack). Nothing/Interscope, 1996.

———. *The Perfect Drug.* Music video, directed by Mark Romanek. 1996.

———. *Pretty Hate Machine.* TVT, 1989.

———. "Purest Feeling." *Purest Feeling.* Kaleidoscope Music, 1994.

———. *Purest Feeling.* Kaleidoscopic Music, 1994.

———. "Ringfinger." *Purest Feeling.* Kaleidoscopic Music, 1994.

———. "Sanctified." *Pretty Hate Machine.* TVT, 1989.

———. "Sin." *Pretty Hate Machine.* TVT, 1989.

———. "Twist." *Demos and Remixes.* Blue Man Records, 1992.

————. *Wish.* Music video, directed by Peter Christopherson. 1992.

Nirvana. "Heart-Shaped Box." *Heart-Shaped Box.* Geffen, 1993.

Nomads. Directed by John McTiernan. Atlantic, 1986.

O'Brien, Lucy. *She Bop: The Definitive History of Women in Rock, Pop, and Soul.* New York: Penguin, 1995.

O'Connor, Flannery. "A Good Man Is Hard to Find." In *The Complete Stories.* New York: Farrar, Straus, and Giroux, 1979.

Official 1992 General Election Voter's Pamphlet. Portland, Oregon, 1992.

Official 1994 General Election Voter's Pamphlet. Portland, Oregon, 1994.

Opposite of Sex, The. Directed by Don Roos. Tristar, 1998.

Ortner, Sherry B. "Is Female to Male as Nature Is to Culture?" In *Woman, Culture, and Society,* edited by Michelle Zimbalist Rosaldo and Louise Lamphere, 67–88. Stanford, Calif.: Stanford University Press, 1974.

Parrish, Edward. *Sex and Love Problems.* New York: Psychology Institute of America, 1935.

Pater, Walter. *The Renaissance: Studies in Art and Poetry.* New York: Oxford University Press, 1990.

Peale, Norman Vincent. *A Guide to Confident Living.* New York: Prentice-Hall, 1948.

Pearsall, Paul. *Super Marital Sex: Loving for Life.* New York: Doubleday, 1987.

————. *The Ten Laws of Lasting Love.* New York: Avon, 1993.

Phair, Liz. "Flower." *Exile in Guyville.* Matador, 1993.

Pinedo, Isabel Cristina. *Recreational Terror: Women and the Pleasures of Horror Film Viewing.* Albany: State University of New York Press, 1997.

PJ Harvey. *4-Track Demos.* Island, 1993.

————. "50ft Queenie." *Rid of Me.* Island, 1993.

————. *Down by the Water.* Music video, directed by Maria Mochnacz. 1995.

————. "Dry." *Rid of Me.* Island, 1993.

————. "Rub It 'Til It Bleeds." *Rid of Me.* Island, 1993.

Pollitt, Katha. "Women and Children First." *The Nation,* 30 March 1998: 9.

Post, Emily. *Etiquette.* New York: Funk and Wagnalls, 1942.

Powers, Ann. "Houses of the Holy." In *Rock She Wrote: Women Write about Rock, Pop, and Rap,* edited by Evelyn McDonnell and Ann Powers, 326–329. New York: Delta-Dell, 1995.

————. "Who's That Girl?" In *Rock She Wrote: Women Write about Rock, Pop, and Rap,* edited by Evelyn McDonnell and Ann Powers, 459–467. New York: Delta-Dell, 1995.

Prince. "If I Was Your Girlfriend." *Sign O The Times.* Paisley Park Records, 1987.

————. "Little Red Corvette." *1999.* Warner Brothers, 1982.

Queen Latifah. *Just Another Day . . . .* Music video, directed by Mark Gerard. 1993.

Question of Silence, A. Directed by Marleen Gorris. Sigma, 1983.

Rafferty, Terrence. Review of *Basic Instinct. The New Yorker.* 6 April 1992: 80–83.

Ramanathan, Geetha. "Murder as Speech: Narrative Subjectivity in Marleen Gorris' *A Question of Silence." Genders* 15 (1982): 58–71.

"Random Notes." *Rolling Stone,* 16 Sept. 1999: 32.

Raphael, Amy. *Grrrls: Viva Rock Divas.* New York: St. Martin's, 1996.

Rapping, Elayne. "A Feminist's Love/Hate Relationship with Woody." *Cineaste* 23.3 (1998): 37–38.

"Readers Poll." *Spin* 11.11 (1996): 44–46.

Red Hot Chili Peppers. *Scar Tissue.* Music video, directed by Stéphane Sednaoui. 1999.

Reynolds, Simon. *Blissed Out: The Raptures of Rock.* London: Serpent's Tail, 1990.

Reynolds, Simon, and Joy Press. *The Sex Revolts: Gender, Rebellion, and Rock 'n' Roll.* Cambridge, Mass.: Harvard University Press, 1995.

Rich, Adrienne. "Compulsory Heterosexuality and Lesbian Existence." In *Powers of Desire: The*

Politics of Sexuality, edited by Ann Snitow, Christine Stansell, and Sharon Thompson, 177–205. New York: Monthly Review Press, 1983.

River's Edge. Directed by Tim Hunter. Hemdale, 1987.

RoboCop. Directed by Paul Verhoeven. Orion, 1987.

Roiphe, Katie. *The Morning After: Sex, Fear, and Feminism.* Boston: Little, Brown, 1993.

Rolling Stones, The. "Tumbling Dice." *Exile on Mainstreet.* Musidor, 1972.

Ronstadt, Linda. "Tumbling Dice." *Simple Dreams.* Electra, 1977.

Rosenberg, Jessica, and Gitana Garofalo. "Riot Grrrl: Revolutions from Within." *Signs. Special Issue: Feminisms and Youth Culture* 23.3 (1998): 809–841.

Roxy Music. "Love Is the Drug." *Siren.* Reprise/Atlantic, 1975.

Rubenstein, Sura. "OCA Prevails in Marion County, Three Cities." *The Oregonian,* 23 March 1994: A1–A8.

Rubin, Gayle. "Thinking Sex: Notes for a Radical Theory of the Politics of Sexuality." In *Pleasure and Danger: Exploring Female Sexuality,* edited by Carole S. Vance, 267–319. Boston: Routledge, 1984.

Russo, Vito. *The Celluloid Closet: Homosexuality in the Movies.* New York: Harper and Row, 1987.

Salt-N-Pepa. *Shoop.* Music video, directed by Scott Kalvert. 1993.

———. "Spinderella's Not a Fella." *A Salt with a Deadly Pepa.* Polygram, 1988.

Sandell, Jillian. "Adjusting to Oppression: The Rise of Therapeutic Feminism in the United States." In *"Bad Girls"/"Good Girls": Women, Sex, and Power in the Nineties,* edited by Nan Bauer Maglin and Donna Perry, 21–35. New Brunswick, N.J.: Rutgers University Press, 1994.

Santoro, Gene. "50 Foot Queenie." *The Nation,* 24 May 1993: 715–716.

Savage, Jon. *England's Dreaming: A Biography of the Sex Pistols.* London: Faber and Faber, 1991.

Schlossberg, Alan. *Marriage: This Time Will Be Perfect!* Meridian, Idaho: n.p., 1995.

Schweickart, Patrocinio P. "Reading Ourselves: Toward a Feminist Theory of Reading." In *Gender and Reading: Essays on Readers, Texts, and Contexts,* edited by Elizabeth A. Flynn and Patrocinio P. Schweickart, 31–62. Baltimore: Johns Hopkins University Press, 1986.

Scitovsky, Tibor. *The Joyless Economy: The Psychology of Human Satisfaction.* Revised ed. New York: Oxford University Press, 1992.

Scream. Directed by Wes Craven. Miramax, 1996.

Sedgwick, Eve Kosofsky. Letter. *Ms.* 14.6 (Dec. 1985): 6.

———. *Tendencies.* Durham: Duke University Press, 1993.

Seeley, Boudinot. *Christian Social Hygiene: A Guide for Youth.* Portland, Oregon: n.p., 1919.

Segal, Lynne. *Straight Sex: Rethinking the Politics of Pleasure.* Berkeley: University of California Press, 1994.

Shange, Ntozake. *For Colored Girls Who Have Considered Suicide When the Rainbow Is Enuf.* New York: Bantam, 1976.

Shepherd, John. "Music and Male Hegemony." In *Music and Society: The Politics of Composition, Performance, and Reception,* edited by Richard Leppert and Susan McClary, 151–172. Cambridge: Cambridge University Press, 1987.

Showalter, Elaine. *Sexual Anarchy: Gender and Culture at the Fin de Siècle.* New York: Viking, 1990.

Showgirls. Directed by Paul Verhoeven. United Artists, 1995.

Siegel, Carol. *Male Masochism: Modern Revisions of the Story of Love.* Bloomington: Indiana University Press, 1995.

———. "'This thing I like my sister may not do': Shakespearean Erotics and a Clash of Wills in *Middlemarch.*" *Style* 32.1 (1998): 36–59.

Silverchair. "Abuse Me." *Freak Show.* Sony, 1997.

Simonds, Wendy. *Women and Self-Help Culture: Reading between the Lines.* New Brunswick, N.J.: Rutgers University Press, 1992.

Skunk Anansie. "Intellectualize My Blackness." *Paranoid and Sunburnt.* Sony, 1995.

Smith, Bessie. "'Taint Nobody's Bizness If I Do." Columbia, 1923.

Smith, Patti. "Rock N Roll Nigger." *Natural Born Killers: A Soundtrack.* Nothing/Interscope, 1994.

———. "Babelogue." *Easter.* Arista, 1978.

Smith, R. J. "Meet John Doe." *Village Voice,* 6 June 1995: 61, 64.

Smiths, The. "You Just Haven't Earned It Yet, Baby." *Louder than Bombs.* Sire, 1984.

Snitow, Ann. "Mass Market Romance: Pornography for Women Is Different." In *Powers of Desire: The Politics of Sexuality,* edited by Ann Snitow, Christine Stansell, and Sharon Thompson, 245–263. New York: Monthly Review Press, 1983.

Snitow, Ann, Christine Stansell, and Sharon Thompson, eds. *Powers of Desire: The Politics of Sexuality.* New York: Monthly Review Press, 1983.

Soldier of Orange (Soldaat van Oranje). Directed by Paul Verhoeven. Film Holland/Tuschinski, 1977.

Sontag, Susan. *Against Interpretation.* New York: Delta, 1964.

Soundgarden. "My Wave." *Superunknown.* A&M, 1994.

Species II. Directed by Peter Medak. MGM, 1998.

Spetters. Directed by Paul Verhoeven. VSE Film, 1980.

Spiegelman, Art. "Beau and Eros." Cartoon. *The New Yorker,* 25 August and 1 September 1997: cover.

"Spin Top 40, The." *Spin* 13.1 (1997): 69–135.

Springer, Claudia. *Electronic Eros: Bodies and Desire in the Postindustrial Age.* Austin: University of Texas Press, 1996.

Starship Troopers. Directed by Paul Verhoeven. Tristar, 1997.

Steele, Valerie. *Fetish: Fashion, Sex, and Power.* New York: Oxford University Press, 1996.

Stepfather, The. Directed by Joseph Ruben. Miramax, 1987.

Stewart, Rod. "Maggie May." *Every Picture Tells a Story.* Mercury, 1971.

Strangers in Good Company. Directed by Cynthia Scott. National Film Board of Canada, 1991.

Taubin, Amy. "The Boys Who Cried Misogyny." *The Village Voice,* 28 April 1992: 35–36.

Terminator 2: Judgement Day. Directed by James Cameron. Guild/Carolco, 1991.

Thelma and Louise. Directed by Ridley Scott. UIP/Pathé, 1991.

Thomas, Ronald R. *Dreams of Authority: Freud and the Fictions of the Unconscious.* Ithaca: Cornell University Press, 1990.

Thornton, Sarah. "Moral Panic, The Media, and British Rave Culture." In *Microphone Fiends: Youth Music, Youth Culture,* edited by Andrew Ross and Tricia Rose, 176–192. New York: Routledge, 1994.

Titanic. Directed by James Cameron. 20th Century Fox/Paramount, 1997.

TLC. *Unpretty.* Music video, directed by Paul Hunter. 1999.

Tolman, Deborah L., and Tracy E. Higgins. "How Being a Good Girl Can Be Bad for Girls." In *"Bad Girls"/"Good Girls": Women, Sex, and Power in the Nineties,* edited by Nan Bauer Maglin and Donna Perry, 205–225. New Brunswick, N.J.: Rutgers University Press, 1994.

Tompkins, Jane. "Sentimental Power: *Uncle Tom's Cabin* and the Politics of Literary History." In *Feminisms: An Anthology of Literary Theory and Criticism,* edited by Robyn R. Warhol and Diane Price Herndl, 20–39. New Brunswick, N.J.: Rutgers University Press, 1991.

Total Recall. Directed by Paul Verhoeven. Tristar/Carolco, 1990.

Tridon, André. *Psychoanalysis and Love.* New York: Sun Dial, 1922.

Tucker, Nita, with Debra Feinstein. *Beyond Cinderella: How to Find and Marry the Man You Want.* New York: St. Martin's, 1987.

Turkish Delight. Directed by Paul Verhoeven. EDDE Entertainment, 1973.

Twersky, Lori. "Devils or Angels? The Female Teenage Audience Examined." In *Rock She Wrote: Women Write about Rock, Pop, and Rap,* edited by Evelyn McDonnell and Ann Powers, 175–183. New York: Delta-Dell, 1995.

Van de Velde, Theodore H. *Ideal Marriage: Its Physiology and Technique.* New York: Random, 1926.

Vance, Carole S., ed. *Pleasure and Danger: Exploring Female Sexuality.* Boston: Routledge, 1984.

Vertigo. Directed by Alfred Hitchcock. Paramount, 1958.

Veruca Salt. "Seether." *American Thighs.* Geffen, 1994.

Voice of Experience, The. New York: Dodd, Mead, and Co., 1932.

Vorlichy, Robert. "(In)Visible Alliances: Conflicting 'Chronicles' of Feminism." In *Engendering Men: The Question of Male Feminism,* edited by Joseph A. Boone and Michael Cadden, 275–290. New York: Routledge, 1990.

Waldby, Catherine. "Destruction: Boundary Erotics and Refigurations of the Heterosexual Male Body." In *Sexy Bodies: The Strange Carnalities of Feminism,* edited by Elizabeth Grosz and Elspeth Probyn, 266–277. New York: Routledge, 1995.

Walkowitz, Judith. *City of Dreadful Delight: Narratives of Sexual Danger in Late-Victorian London.* Chicago: University of Chicago Press, 1992.

Walser, Robert. "Heavy-Metal Sounds and Images of Gender." In *Sound and Vision: The Music Video Reader,* edited by Simon Frith, Andrew Goodwin, and Lawrence Grossberg, 153–181. New York: Routledge, 1993.

W.A.S.P. "Animal (Fuck Like a Beast)." *Animal (Fuck Like a Beast).* Restless, 1990.

Weisbard, Eric. "Sympathy for the Devil." *Spin* 11.11 (1996): 34–42, 96.

White, Emily. "Revolution Girl Style Now." In *Rock She Wrote: Women Write About Rock, Pop, and Rap,* edited by Evelyn McDonnell and Ann Powers, 396–408. New York: Delta-Dell, 1995.

Wiegman, Robyn. *American Anatomies: Theorizing Race and Gender.* Durham: Duke University Press, 1995.

Williams, Linda. "Film Bodies: Gender, Genre, and Excess." *Film Quarterly* 44.4 (1991): 2–5.

Willis, Ellen. "The Satanic Verses (No, Not *The New Yorker*)." *The Village Voice,* 9 January 1996: 17.

———. "Villains and Victims: 'Sexual Correctness' and the Repression of Feminism." In *"Bad Girls"/"Good Girls": Women, Sex, and Power in the Nineties,* edited by Nan Bauer Maglin and Donna Perry, 44–53. New Brunswick, N.J.: Rutgers University Press, 1994.

Wingo, John, and Julie Wingo. *At Long Last Love: How to Find the Best Relationship of Your Life.* New York: Warner, 1994.

Wolf, Naomi. *Promiscuities: The Secret Struggle for Womanhood.* New York: Random, 1997.

Woolf, Virginia. *Three Guineas.* New York: Harvest/HBJ, 1966. Originally published in 1938.

———. *To The Lighthouse.* New York: Harbrace, 1955.

Wright, Rebecka. "San Francisco v. *Basic Instinct.*" In *The Best of Gauntlet: Exploring the Limits of Free Expression,* edited by Barry Hoffman, 199–127. New York: Masquerade, 1994.

X-ray Spex. "Oh Bondage, Up Yours." *Germfree Adolescents.* Virgin, 1977.

Young Man with a Horn. Directed by Michael Curtiz. Warner, 1950.

Zimmerman, Bonnie. "What Has Never Been: An Overview of Lesbian Feminist Literary Criticism (1981)." In *Feminisms: An Anthology of Literary Theory and Criticism,* edited by Robyn R. Warhol and Diane Price Herndl, 121–122. New Brunswick, N.J.: Rutgers University Press, 1991.

Zoglin, Richard. "A Company under Fire." *Time,* 12 June 1995: 37–39.

INDEX

CAROL SIEGEL

is Professor of English and Cultural Studies at Washington State University, Vancouver. She is author of *Lawrence among the Women: Wavering Boundaries in Women's Literary Traditions; Male Masochism: Modern Revisions of the Story of Love;* as well as various articles on Modernist and Victorian literature, gender theory, film, and rock music. She also co-authors the journals *Genders* and *Rhizomes*.